Leadership Processes
and Follower Self-Identity

LEA'S ORGANIZATION AND MANAGEMENT SERIES

Series Editors
Arthur P. Brief
Tulane University
James P. Walsh
University of Michigan
Associate Series Editors
P. Christopher Early
Indiana University
Sara L. Rynes
University of Iowa

Leadership Processes
and Follower Self-Identity

Robert G. Lord
University of Akron

Douglas J. Brown
University of Waterloo

NEW YORK AND LONDON

First Published by Lawrence Erlbaum Associates, Inc., Publishers
10 Industrial Avenue
Mahwah, New Jersey 07430

Published 2010 by Routledge

Routledge
Taylor and Francis Group
711 Third Avenue,
New York, NY 10017

Routledge
Taylor and Francis Group
2 Park Square,
Milton Park, Abingdon,
Oxfordshire OX14 4RN

First issued in paperback 2014

Routledge is an imprint of the Taylor and Francis Group, an informa business

Copyright © 2004 by Lawrence Erlbaum Associates, Inc.

Lawrence Erlbaum Associates, Inc., Publishers
10 Industrial Avenue
Mahwah, NJ 07430

Cover design by Kathryn Houghtaling Lacey

Library of Congress Cataloging-in-Publication Data

Lord, Robert G. (Robert George), 1946-
  Leadership processes and follower self-identity / Robert G. Lord, Douglas J. Brown.
      p. cm. — (Organization and management series)

  Includes bibliographical references and index.

ISBN 0-8058-3892-9 (alk. Paper)
1. Leadership—Psychological aspects. 2. Self-perception. 3. Identity (Psychology). I. Brown, Douglas J. II. LEA series in organization and management.
HM1261.L67 2003
158'.4—dc21   2003040767
                                                              CIP

ISBN 13: 978-0-8058-3892-3 (hbk)
ISBN 13: 978-0-415-65540-8 (pbk)

*For their inspiration, companionship, love,
and patience, we dedicate this book
to Rosalie Hall, Lisa Keeping,
Jason Lord, and Nicole Lord*

Contents

Contents

Series Foreword

When we began as editors of Lawrence Erlbaum Associates' Organization and Management Series, our lofty aim was to publish works, both theoretical and empirical ones, that would nudge the boundaries of organization studies. Lord and Brown's book admirably achieves this aim. The authors present an innovative theory that, we predict, will drive empirical research. The theory supplies a new way to think about an old topic, leadership. It does so by drawing heavily on ideas about social cognition and self-regulation. Reading Lord and Brown's book is truly eye-opening. Enjoy the adventure.

Arthur P. Brief
Tulane University

James P. Walsh
University of Michigan

Preface

This book presents a follower-centered perspective on leadership. We focus on followers as the direct determinant of leadership effects because it is generally through followers' reactions and behaviors that leadership attempts succeed or fail. Leadership theory, therefore, needs to be articulated with a theory of how followers create meaning from leadership acts and how this meaning helps followers self-regulate in specific contexts. In this book we attempt to develop such a theory. We maintain that the central construct in this process is the self-identity of followers. Many conscious and more automatic self-regulatory processes depend on one's currently active self-identity, and many powerful forms of leadership are thought to influence the identity of followers.

In developing this theoretical perspective, we draw heavily from several areas of research and theory. The most critical constructs do not come directly from the leadership literature, but rather from social and cognitive theory pertaining to followers' self-identity, self-regulatory processes, motivation, values, cognitions, emotions, and perceptions of social justice. Leaders may have profound effects on these aspects of followers, and it is by analyzing such indirect, follower-mediated leadership effects that we develop most of our ideas regarding leadership theory and practice.

Due to its broad theoretical focus, this book is relevant to a number of audiences. Our principal concern is with the development of leadership theory and the practice of leadership. Thus, the book is relevant to audiences in management, applied psychology, and social psychology. We tried to define key constructs clearly and provide practical examples so that the book could be accessible to advanced undergraduate students. However, the diversity of the underlying theoretical literatures and the complexity of the framework we develop also make the book appropriate for graduate courses in management, applied psychology or social psychology, and for readers with a professional interest in leadership theory or leadership practice.

Acknowledgments

We recognize the contributions of many colleagues in helping us develop the ideas and research described in this book. Rosalie Hall and Lisa Keeping served the dual role as professional collaborators in much of our leadership research and patient friends who listened to and shaped many of our thoughts regarding leadership and identities. Chris Selenta collaborated in the development of our ideas on social justice (chap. 7) and in developing the measurement scales we used to assess identity levels. We would like to acknowledge support for Chris Selenta from a Social Sciences and Humanities Research Council of Canada doctoral fellowship (752-2001-0399).

Many other colleagues were instrumental in developing specific research projects or theories that we discuss. They include Steve Freiberg, Loren Naidoo, Alf Illingworth, Russ Johnson, Rebecca Fischbein, Barb Ritter, Christina Norris-Watts, Paul Hanges, Jennifer Harvey, Elaine Engle, Jim Diefendorff, Paul Levy, Mary Kernan, Karen Maher, Carol Oeth, Jerilyn Lewter, Roseanne Foti, George Alliger, Christy De Vader, Steve Cronshaw, Scott Fraser, Mike Campion, Darrin Kass, Wendy Smith, Bruce Avolio, Neil Hauenstein, Ray Gehani, John Binning, Jay Thomas, Jim Phillips, Mike Rush, and Dave Day. Their contributions to our understanding of leadership processes and self-regulation is greatly appreciated. Several other individuals carefully read various sections of the manuscript, providing helpful comments and corrections. For this contribution we thank Rosalie Hall, Lisa Keeping, Daisy Chang, Jennifer Bott, and Nicole Lord. Finally, we thank Art Brief, Jim Walsh, and Anne Duffy and our editors at Lawrence Erlbaum Associates, for their encouragement, support, and patience.

1

Common Sense, Science, and Leadership

"You can dream, create, design and build the most wonderful place in the world ... but it requires people to make the dream a reality."
—Walt Disney (www.quotemeonit.com)

"The great leader is not necessarily the one who does the greatest things; he is the one who gets the people to do the greatest things."
—Ronald Reagan (cited in Strock, 1998, p. 17)

"But I was moved by more than what he stood for or how much he knew. It was how I felt around him...."
—George Stephanopoulis (1999, p. 31)

What is the meaning of *leadership*? The three quotes that begin this book provide some hint to the reader into our thinking on the topic. In combination, these quotes foreshadow two of the key themes that run as undercurrents throughout our book. In the first two quotes, attributed to Walt Disney and Ronald Reagan, a similar sense of leadership has been expressed. Together the Disney and Regan quotes share a common ideal: Leadership cannot simply be reduced to a single great mind or individual. Instead both quotes suggest that the accomplishments of great people are at best indirect, operating through the accomplishments and actions of others.

In the third quote, attributed to George Stephanopoulis, a related idea has been communicated, but this time from a subordinate's perspective. This quote, drawn from Stephanopoulis' recollections of his earliest encounters with Bill Clinton, suggest that in part Clinton's power derived not from his words or actions but rather from his ability to shift how George Stephanopoulis felt about himself.

In combination the messages communicated in these quotes succinctly express the definition of leadership that we develop throughout this book: Leadership is a process through which one individual, the leader, changes the way followers envision themselves. By shifting followers' conceptions of their identity, leaders often generate extraordinary outcomes for their nations, institutions, organizations, and work groups. Such leaders change our perceptions of how we are now and how we may be in the future or whether we see ourselves as autonomous individuals or as members of larger collectives. This has profound implications for how we think, feel, and behave. In psychological terms, such leaders work though changing the composition of followers' self-concepts.

The importance of subordinate self-concepts to leadership processes has been the focus of a limited number of scientific articles (e.g., Lord, Brown, & Freiberg, 1999; Shamir, House, & Arthur, 1993; Shamir, Zakay, Brenin, & Popper, 1998). These articles have laid the groundwork; however, space constraints inherent in the normal journal-length articles preclude a full theoretical integration of the leadership and self-concept literatures. This limitation is not surprising given the extensive scientific treatment of each of these separate topics. A search of the psychological database indicates publication of over 7,000 articles on leadership and more than 12,000 articles on self-concept. Given the expansiveness of each of these literatures, a handful of articles cannot do justice to any integrative efforts. Thus, our overarching goal in writing this book was to present a fully elaborated model of the structure and processes of subordinate self-concepts and to describe the mapping of leadership behaviors and processes onto this structure. For example, we address issues like how a leader's use of pronouns in communications—namely, the use of collective *we* pronouns vs. individualistic "*I*" pronouns—can activate collective or individual self-concepts in subordinates, respectively. This collective or individualistic structure can then frame many other processes, such as a subordinate's responses to organizational events, leadership activities, or other work processes. Ironically, one of the factors that can be influenced by subordinate identities is the schema that subordinates use to evaluate leadership, a topic we discuss in more depth in a later chapter.

Because leaders are often salient and thus provide highly accessible explanations for many types of events (Phillips & Lord, 1981), attempts to understand or influence outcomes of events often focus on the qualities of leaders. Thus, much of the prior leadership literature has taken a relatively one-sided view, emphasizing the leader's traits and behaviors but neglecting aspects of followers that moderate their responses to leadership. Early approaches to leadership focused on traits that distinguished leaders from nonleaders (Mann, 1959; Stogdill, 1948), and this approach has recently regained popularity (Hogan, Curphy, & Hogan, 1994; Lord, De Vader, Alliger, 1986). Overlapping this research, behaviorally oriented scholars focused on leadership styles and their impact on subordinate satisfaction and performance (F. E. Fiedler, 1964; Kerr & Schriesheim, 1974). More recent behaviorally oriented research has emphasized transformational leadership, a quality of leaders that involves both behaviors (Bass, 1985) and traits (Judge & Bono, 2000), that are thought to be critical in changing organizations and individuals. All of these research approaches can be characterized as *leader-focused* research.

These leader-focused studies have advanced our understanding of leaders; they have been less successful, however, in advancing what we know about leadership (Burns, 1978). *Leaders* may indeed be people who can be understood in terms of traits and behavioral styles, but leadership is a social process that involves both a leader and a follower (Graen & Scandura, 1987; Hollander, 1992; Hollander & Offermann, 1990; Lord & Maher, 1991). Although great advances have been made in terms of understanding the leader component of leadership, much less has been done to advance our understanding of followers and the psychological processes and mechanisms that link leaders and followers. Such questions as how or why leaders affect outcomes remain largely uncharted and poorly understood.

In part, we think that the neglect of processes and mechanisms that link leaders and followers stems from the primary focus of prior research. As Bobby J. Calder (1977) noted over 20 years ago, leader-centered research stems from a common sense, implicit understanding of leadership processes that view leaders as origins or causes of important outcomes. Common sense theories focus on what people can see easily, such as a leader's behavior, rather than less observable processes, such as a subordinates's psychological reaction to a leader's behavior or a subordinate's implicit theory of what leaders should be.

Calder (1997) called commonsense theories *first-order constructs*, and he distinguished them from *second-order constructs* that are grounded in scientific theory rather than a perceptually based understanding of events. Even today, leadership scholars often continue to study leadership in terms of easily observable first-order constructs like leader behaviors and their direct impact on easily measured outcomes (this perspective is shown by Path A in Fig. 1.1) rather than in terms of underlying processes and mechanisms that are derived from scientific theory. Unfortunately, easily observed relationships do not necessarily reflect the underlying causal structure of events. More specifically, even though transformational leaders may exhibit certain types of behavior, their effects on people and organizational processes may not be directly produced by these behaviors. Instead, more direct causes may lie in followers who are more proximal to the observed and desired outcomes.

For a specific example of such effects, consider Dvir, Eden, Avolio, and Shamir's (2002) study. Using a longitudinal, randomized field experiment, Dvir et al. applied popular behavioral theories of transformational leadership to train leaders in the Israeli Defense Forces. Potential leaders (cadets in the Israeli Defense Forces officer training program) went through a 3-day workshop that embodied either the major propositions of transformational leadership theory or a blend of eclectic leadership theories. Subsequently 54 of 160 cadets were assigned to lead basic training platoons (34 who had experienced the transformational leadership [experimental] workshop and 22 who had attended the control workshop that covered eclectic leadership theories). The study then assessed the effects of training by comparing the development of noncommissioned officers (NCOs) and recruits in these experimental and control platoons. Results showed significant differ-

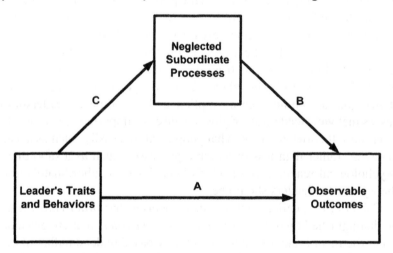

FIG. 1.1.   Leader (A) and follower-centered (B and C) approaches to understanding leadership.

ences in several NCO development variables (self-efficacy, collectivist orientation, extra effort, and critical independent approach) that favored the experimental platoons; in addition, recruits in these platoons showed enhanced performance compared to control groups.

However, in attempting to pin down leadership behavior as the cause of performance, Dvir et al. (2002) were not very successful. They suggested that transformational leaders created "a stronger social bond among their direct and indirect followers, thus improving the indirect followers' performance" (p. 742). Yet, they also acknowledged that several other explanations were possible. What they did not show was that the effects of transformational leadership training were directly mediated by the transformational leadership behavior of the cadets who went through the experimental workshop. Although this is an impressive field experiment, it reveals the weaknesses that a leader-focused theory has in explaining subordinate performance. Without a thorough understanding of the mechanisms linking leader activities to subordinate perceptions and subordinate reactions, we simply cannot translate leadership training programs, even when theoretically grounded, into explanations of subordinate performance.

As shown by this example, Calder's (1977) criticism reflects a very general weakness in typical leader-focused approaches to leadership. When leadership processes are not fully understood, training that focuses on changing aspects of leaders often fails to produce the effects that would be expected based on prior research. To provide another compelling example, consider the case of the leadership research on the Pygmalion effect, which is a type of self-fulfilling prophecy in which managers are led by researchers to believe that their subordinates have higher than normal ability. These experimental manipulations of leader expectations, in turn, lead to greater performance by subordinates.

Pygmalion effects are perhaps the most carefully developed and experimentally tested field intervention in the leadership area (Eden, 1992). Eden and his students have conducted nine field experiments that generally show large effects on subordinates' performance of experimental interventions focused on manager expectations. These interventions may require as little as 5 min to convey high expectations to managers. Nevertheless, Eden et al.'s (2000) seven different subsequent applied interventions that trained managers to convey high expectations to subordinates using workshops that varied from 1 to 3 days have consistently failed to produce higher levels of subordinate performance. As Eden et al. noted, there was little evidence that the workshop influenced follower performance; the mean size of 61 effects from the seven experiments was only .13. Again, this suggests that there is some aspect of the high expectations of leaders who were naive with respect to this manipulation in the original nine field experiments that was not present when leaders were explicitly trained to communicate high expectations to followers in the seven workshops. Perhaps expectations were communicated more genuinely when they were actually believed by managers, and subordinates may have reacted to this nonverbal aspect of leadership.

These examples reflect some of the best field research and field experiments being done in the leadership area. Yet, they still illustrate the weaknesses in leader-focused approaches. Leader-focused training emphasizes processes that are distant or distal to subordinate performance and reactions rather than being tied to processes in followers that were more proximal to the expected change. Consequently, we believe that these distal processes are the wrong place to focus when attempting to understand leadership.

There is an alternative approach to leadership that will produce both more fundamental theoretical insights and more successful leadership intervention. Namely, the typical focus on leadership inquiries can be reversed, emphasizing the follower and factors in followers that produce desired effects like high performance or organizational commitment (e.g., Path B in Fig. 1.1). We can then work backwards and ask how leaders can impact these follower processes (e.g., Path C in Fig. 1.1) Unlike traditional leader-centric perspectives shown by Path A in Fig. 1.1, which begin by documenting leader characteristics or behaviors and then linking these variables to outcomes, we advocate a process-oriented and reverse-engineered approach to leadership that is centered in followers. That is, rather than: (a) describing what leaders do, (b) examining the relationship between these activities and outcomes, and then (c) attempting to understand why leadership effects occur, our approach emphasizes second-order scientific constructs and processes that are localized in followers. After all, subordinates produce the desirable organizational effects that are generally attributed to their leaders. Thus, we maintain that the most defensible strategy for leadership research and practice is to understand factors central to subordinates' motivation, affect, and development and then work backwards to analyze how leaders might influence these processes. That is, we should focus on Paths B and C in Fig. 1.1. Once follower-centered mechanisms and processes are understood theoretically (Path B), sound linkages can be made to associated leader behaviors or qualities (Path C).

In searching for the appropriate subordinate process to examine, we want characteristics and processes that are (a) strongly connected to subordinate motivational, affective, and developmental processes; (b) general enough to explain many different types of behavior; and (c) well-grounded in scientific research. As explained in the following section, based on these criteria, we believe that follower self-concepts should be the focus of leadership theory. We maintain that articulating the connections between leaders and subordinates' self-concepts will provide leadership researchers with a platform to move beyond the study of leader behavior to the study of leadership.

WHY THE FOLLOWER SELF-CONCEPT?

Critical readers will no doubt question why we have selected the follower self-concept as the medium through which to understand leadership. In large part, this choice reflects our conclusion that the self-concept, as conceptualized by social, cognitive, and personality researchers, fits three key requirements for leadership theory: It can account for influence, it is internal to the subordinate, and it is a robust construct. Next, we describe each of these criteria and discuss how the self-concept meets each requirement.

Influence

Ultimately, leadership is a process of influence. In stating this we are not suggesting an idea that is new for leadership researchers. Yukl and Van Fleet's (1992) excellent review of the leadership literature has previously noted that the single thread uniting leadership researchers is their common interest in influence, regardless of whether transformational leadership or leadership perceptions is the focus of study. In particular, how is it that a leader changes the behavior, attitudes, or reactions of a follower? Clearly, the effectiveness of a leader depends on his or her ability to change subordinates—it is fundamental to our scientific and lay understanding of leadership. For example, the firing of Toronto Blue Jays Manager Jim Fregosi following the 2000 baseball campaign was attributed to the fact that he was unable to change the intensity of his players' play at critical times during the regular season. Ultimately, Fregosi was perceived to lack the necessary leadership ability required to raise players' performance in key situations.

Based on this reasoning, our first assumption is that any process that underlies leadership must be dynamic and must allow leaders to originate change. As we articulate later, the dependence of followers' self-concepts on social processes makes subordinates receptive to leader influence; thus, this fits our first criterion.

Internal to Subordinates

To our first criterion we further add that the change must occur within subordinates. That is, leaders must shift cognitive, emotional, and motivational processes within subordinates to exert influence because, as Kanfer and Klimoski (2002) put it, "these components of the human mind form the interactional nexus for ongoing transactions between internal and external forces" (p. 475). Cognitive and social–cognitive researchers have established over the last 20 years that human activity is guided by *accessible* knowledge—the aspects of knowledge that come to mind most quickly (Bargh, Chen, & Burrows, 1996; Fazio, Sanbonmatsu, Powell, & Kardes, 1986; Kunda, 1999). Thus, if a leader is to influence his or her subordinates, he or she must be capable of shifting cognitions like follower attitudes or the schemas, scripts, and other knowledge structures that are most accessible. Emotions are also critical because they are leading systems that alert individuals to danger or potential rewards, and motivational systems translate these emotional or cognitive reactions into environmentally oriented responses.

Our examination of the literature suggests that both the influence and internal criteria are met by what psychologists refer to as the self-concept. The self-concept consists of an individual's knowledge about his or her own self. This knowledge may include knowing which personality traits are self-descriptive, having an image of one's physical appearance, knowing how one has behaved in certain types of situations, knowledge of what type of person one wants to become, and so on. Furthermore, instead of being conceptualized as a single, stable, monolithic structure, the self is believed to be a system or confederation of self-schemas that are derived from past experience (Markus & Wurf, 1987). In essence, the self is a collection of small, relatively independent processing units that are elicited in different contexts and each of which has specific cognitive, emotional, motivational, and behavioral consequences. Because the self-concept is dynamic (i.e., its content is situation dependent), leaders can influence their subordinates by shifting the salience of different aspects of a subordinate's self-concept or by creating new aspects of the self-concept—a topic that is addressed more fully at a later point in this book. Salient aspects of the self, in turn, will guide subordinate's behavior, feelings, and thoughts, ultimately impacting individual, group, and organizational functioning. Thus, the self is an internal aspect of subordinates that can be influenced by leaders and also is critical in regulating subordinate mental and behavioral processes.

Another important aspect of the self concerns its potential to allow mental time travel. People are unique among animals in their capacity for mental time travel (Roberts, 2002; Tulving, 2002). They have the capacity to reinstate a past situation and locate themselves in it; they also have the capacity to project the self into future contexts, anticipating possible actions and their consequences for the self. This capacity develops in 4- to 6-year-old children as they begin to see the self as an abstraction and become conscious of the self, a capacity referred to as *autonoetic consciousness* (Wheeler, Stuss, & Tulving, 1997). People's capacity to escape the boundaries of the present through time travel allows them to conceptualize future selves and to connect future selves with past selves. Issues related to subordinate development would have little motivational or emotional impact without this capacity.

The capacity to represent the self abstractly and to use time travel techniques is also critical to episodic memory (Roberts, 2002; Tulving, 2002). Episodic memory is distinct from the more general semantic memory because it is more context specific and located in a specific time and place. Episodic memory depends on frontal lobe structures central to autonotetic consciousness (S. B. Klein, 2001). Furthermore, the self, episodic memory, and emotions are all part of an integrated self-regulatory system (Allen et al., 2002) that operates automatically as we appraise situations. Without such self-relevant, emotional capacities, human motivation is substantially diminished (Damasio, 1994). Thus, to influence subordinate motivation and behavior, leaders must operate though these self-relevant systems. One powerful way for leaders to do this is to serve as a guide for time travel, articulating for subordinates possible future selves, future contexts, and contingencies that relate these possibilities to the present.

Robust Nature of the Self

In addition to the aforementioned points, we further add that the self-concept has one additional aspect that makes it particularly useful for understanding leadership—it is robust. Any mechanism proposed to underlie leadership must be capable of accounting for a leader's influence on a wide spectrum of follower psychological, social, and cognitive outcomes, including attitudes, schemas, motivation, emotions, external perceptions, and

2

The Working Self-Concept and Behavior

We explained in chapter 1 that our approach to understanding leadership was to work backwards, using well-established psychological theories as a basis for analyzing potential leadership activities and their consequences for followers. We also suggested that the key to understanding effective leadership was to understand follower self-concepts and how a leader influences these cognitive–affective mental structures. In this chapter we address several questions that provide the needed psychological background for this approach to leadership: What is the self-concept and how does it vary as a function of context? What aspects of a follower's self-concept are most critical to understanding leadership effectiveness? What processes and principles explain the linkage of self-structures to cognitions, affect, and behavior? These questions can be answered by understanding what self-theorists mean by the term *working self-concept* (WSC) and its role in self-regulation. We discuss these issues now.

WHAT IS THE SELF-CONCEPT?

Definition and Function

In summarizing William James' seminal perspective on the self, Kihlstrom and S. B. Klein (1994) stated, "the self is the unquestionable, elementary, universal fact of mental life, and the fundamental unit of analysis for a science of mental life. It is the problem about which everything else revolves" (p. 155). Because the mind can both represent the person who embodies it and objects or events in the external world, Kihlstron and S. B. Klein noted that the *self* is the point at which cognitive, personality, and social psychology meet. Thus, understanding the self requires an integration of several areas of psychology. We touch on these streams of thought in this section, and then we clarify our definition of the *self-concept*.

A grasp of cognitive psychology is needed to understand the self-concept because the self is fundamentally a knowledge structure that helps organize and gives meaning to memory. Indeed, it has been argued with merit that attaching an object or event to the self imbues it with a special meaning: For example, *my* car or *my* birthday is much more meaningful than *a* car or *a* birthday. This self-relevance can then serve as a retrieval cue that makes information more easily accessible and more richly connected to other information. Much of the well-established memory advantage of self-relevant information stems from organizational and elaborative processes that, although typical of other types of memory, are much greater for self-relevant memories (Kihlstrom & S. B. Klein, 1994). The self is also central in a particular type of memory—episodic memory—which provides temporal organization to events. Indeed, several researchers (Roberts, 2002; Tulving, 2002; Wheeler et al., 1997) stressed that the ability to locate the self in time, both remembering one's past and projecting oneself into the future, is a uniquely human cognitive skill that develops between the ages of 4 and 6. Wheeler et al. maintained that this capacity for self-relevant time travel is necessary to exercise supervisory control over systems involved with motivation, motor control, attention, and language.

Knowledge of personality psychology is also necessary to understand the self-concept. Just as traits and social categories (e.g., athletes, women, and leaders) are used to understand others, they are also applied to describing oneself. Like other categories, self-relevant categories may begin with exemplars or instances held largely intact in memory—my first dance or my first hockey game. With repeated experience, more abstract, prototype-based representations for such categories develop: The self is seen as a dancer or a hockey player. When these categories are applied to the self, self-description in terms of abstract prototypical qualities can occur: The self is seen as graceful and coordinated or tough and aggressive. Applying such processes to the leadership domain, with repeated leadership experience, one may come to describe oneself in terms prototypical of leaders in general—a category that we have already noted is seen much like a personality trait by many individuals. Hazel Markus (1977) explained that when people see a personality term as being both self-descriptive and important, they are *self-schematic* on this trait. By *self-schematic* she meant that a particular trait category—independent, extroverted, intelligent and so on—operated as a cognitive schema that organized both perceptual and behavioral information for an individual.

A grasp of social psychology is needed to understand self-concept because our self-concept develops from and serves to regulate social interactions. From infancy, babies respond to and mimic facial expressions and voice quality, developing an emotionally based set of communication skills and a sense of who they are in a social space or network. Through social interactions, personality is developed, and social reactions to our behaviors and qualities help to define who we are. The ability to gauge social environments and present appropriate facial expressions then becomes a critical aspect of intelligence (i.e., social intelligence). For leaders who must operate in social environments, traits like self-monitoring, which pertains to the ability to gauge appropriately and respond flexibly to social events, are critical. In fact, research shows that individuals high on self-monitoring ability tend to emerge as leaders in informal groups (Day, Schleicher, Unckless, & Hiller, 2002; Hall, Workman, & Marchioro, 1998; Zaccaro, Foti, & Kenny, 1991).

In short, our understanding of the self-concept is enriched by work in many areas of psychology. Following Kihlstrom and S. B. Klein (1994), we define the *self* as an overarching knowledge structure that organizes memory and behavior. This structure includes many trait-like schemas that organize social and self-perceptions in specific situations. It also includes script-like structures that help translate contextual cues into self-consistent goals and behaviors. The self shares many qualities with other knowledge structures, but it is also multidimensional, overlaying a specific content domain (e.g., self-descriptive skills or personality categories that are self-relevant) with temporal and social dimensions. Localization of the self in time provides a dynamic continuity to who we are and who we are becoming; whereas social reactions often provide feedback that guides these dynamic processes and grounds trends in an emotional context. Because of these dynamic properties, the self can also function effectively as an executive unit, directing attention, language, and other mental or motor processes. The multidimensional nature of the self promotes easy elaboration of self-relevant information, making such information more memorable and more useful for executive control of thoughts and actions.

Contextual Nature of Knowledge

Commonsense views of personality conceptualize individuals as having relatively general traits that are stable across situations. Applied to leadership, this view suggests that individual leaders have relatively fixed styles that will fit in some situations but will be unsuited to others. F. E. Fielder's (1964) contingency theory and most other contingency theories of leadership provide good examples of this perspective in that they assume that there are stable individual differences among leaders that are reflected in behavioral tendencies or styles. F. E. Fiedler, Chemers, and Mahar (1976) took this notion to the extreme by suggesting that situations should be engineered to fit the leader's particular style.

Similar commonsense views guide other social perceptions as well. For example, the widely replicated phenomenon called the *fundamental attribution error* describes an overreliance by perceivers on person-based explanations for behavior and the corresponding underuse of situational explanations: For example, crimes are explained in terms of qualities of criminals rather than poverty and lack of education. Although these commonsense theories have an intuitive appeal and may serve an important cognitive function by simplifying our understanding of social events, they are based on social perception processes that we know are biased.

In contrast to such commonsense theories, more recent views of personality suggest that people behave quite flexibly, with personality being stable only within contexts (Mischel & Shoda, 1995). Mischel and Shoda suggested that personality is actually composed of many context-specific rules (or productions in their terms) that are accessed only in specific situations. More recent thinking in the leadership literature also suggests that considerable situational flexibility exists, with appropriate scripts being accessed in different situations (Wofford & Goodwin, 1994) or perhaps even being automatically modified to fit specific situations (Lord, Brown, & Harvey, 2001). Both of these examples reflect the more general tendency of individuals to rely on situations to cue or construct appropriate knowledge structures, providing a functionally effective means of tuning knowledge and behavior to situational requirements. For example, Wofford, Joplin, and Comforth (1996) found that leaders who were generally participative shifted to more directive scripts when they thought group members were low in ability and when motivation and performance problems occurred.

It is well accepted among cognitive scientists that human knowledge structures are organized contextually. This perspective is captured both empirically and theoretically by cognitive and social psychological research. Empirically, Barsalou's (1987) groundbreaking work provides one of the earliest and clearest indications of the contextual dependency of human knowledge. Barsalou found that the exemplars produced for the category bird were influenced by the context within which the question was framed. When a story context was a barnyard, subjects more readily retrieved the exemplar of a chicken as an example of a bird; but when the context was shifted to a suburban backyard, subjects more readily retrieved a robin as an exemplar of a bird. As this research highlights, humans do not retrieve fixed concepts from memory, instead they construct concepts in a contextually sensitive fashion.

Lest the reader think that contextual sensitivity is limited to abstract constructs, such as birds, we also note that social psychologists and industrial psychologists also have found knowledge activation and use to be contextually guided (stereotypes and questionnaire responses: Feldman & Lynch, 1988; leadership prototypes: Lord, Foti, & De Vader, 1984; attitudes: Wilson & Hodges, 1992). Within the leadership field, the work of Lord and his colleagues (discussed next) best demonstrates the context-driven nature of knowledge.

Using Rosch's (1978) categorization theory as a conceptual basis, a series of studies (Baumgardner, Lord, & Forti, 1990; Lord et al., 1984; Lord & Maher, 1991) suggested that leadership prototypes can be arranged hierarchically into three levels. At the highest level are the most abstract or superordinate categories (e.g., leader vs. nonleader). At the middle, basic level, contextual information is taken into account and different, contextually defined leadership prototypes are created (e.g., military, religious, or sports leaders). For example, business leaders are thought to be honest, insightful, likable, organized, motivators, good communicators, people oriented, and goal oriented; military leaders are thought to be courageous, strong, intelligent, role models, people oriented, and moral; religious leaders are thought to be understanding, caring, intelligent, honest, moral, and humorous (Baumgardner et al., 1990). At the lowest subordinate level in this leadership hierarchy, different types of leaders within a context are differentiated (e.g., distinguishing executive from middle or lower level leaders within a particular context such as business). Most recently, this line of thinking has been expanded to understand cultural differences that may underlie the content of leadership prototypes (Den Hartog et al., 1999).

An interesting issue is how people are able to access automatically the right knowledge in a specific situation, given their vast stores of knowledge and the potentially limitless situations that they might encounter. One recent scientific development provides a model of how this may occur. Connectionist models of cognitive processes, which have gained increasing acceptance among cognitive (McClelland & Rumelhart, 1986; Rumelhart & McClelland, 1986), social (Kunda & Thagard, 1998; E. R. Smith, 1996), and industrial–organizational psychologists (Hanges, Lord, & Dickson, 2000; Lord, Brown, & Harvey, 2001; Lord, Brown, Harvey, & Hall, 2001), emphasize that meaningful units in environments can automatically activate connected knowledge while inhibiting competing knowledge. For example, recognizing the gender of a potential leader automatically activates knowledge relevant to both leadership and gender, leading both male and female observers to expect different types of leadership behaviors from male and female leaders. That is, male leaders might be expected to be more socially influential and decisive; whereas, female leaders may be expected to be more participative or dedicated.

In short, empirical and theoretical work converge on the viewpoint that human knowledge is contextually driven. The relevance of this finding in the present context lies in the fact that the self is like many other conceptual structures that exist in memory (Kihlstrom & S. B. Klein, 1994). Although the precise content of self-knowledge may differ from that of other knowledge structures, the processes and organizational principles are generalizable. Not surprisingly then, like other knowledge structures, the self too is bound by the constraints of the situation (Markus & Wurf, 1987). In fact, Turner, Oakes, Haslam, and McGarty (1994) suggested that all knowledge is recruited, used, and deployed to create a situationally defined self-representation (p. 459). Just as we retrieve very different conceptualizations of what the construct bird means when we move from the backyard to an arctic ice floe, we also retrieve different portions of our self-concepts when we shift between different contexts.

THE WSC

Definition and Function

The WSC is the highly activated, contextually sensitive portion of the self-concept that guides action and information processing on a moment-to-moment basis (Kihlstrom & S. B. Klein, 1994; Lord et al., 1999). This term was introduced to the psychological literature by Markus and Wurf (1987), who emphasized that the self-concept was not a unitary whole but rather a confederation of selves that varied in their activation across times and contexts. All possible selves are not simultaneously active because humans have relatively limited attentional capacity. We cannot simultaneously attend to the memories and behavioral information associated with the many alternative self-concepts that we possess. To simplify processing and avoid potential conflict, one self-concept—the WSC—tends to predominate at any point in time, thereby cueing a much more restricted set of cognitions, fewer potential affective reactions, and a small set of self- (and context-) appropriate behaviors. As described in the next chapter, self-identities can occur at individual, interpersonal, or collective levels, but only one of these levels tends to be active at any one time. We discuss only the individual level WSC in this chapter, expanding our perspective to include the interpersonal- and collective-level WSCs in chapter 3.

The activation of the specific content of the WSC varies depending on the cues in one's current context and immediate past history. For example, one's self-concept may include various role-related selves such as being a parent, a child, a spouse, an employee, a university professor, a church member, a Little League baseball coach, and so on. These alternative self-concepts are associated with different social and physical contexts, and they become active or relevant primarily when the right social and physical cues are present. That is, one's role as a parent is salient at home when caring for one's children, but one's role as spouse may be more salient at home when the children are asleep or not around. Similarly, one's role as a university professor is most salient in the university classroom or when working with students in one's office. Some self-concepts such as parent or spouse may be closely linked, whereas other self-concepts such as parent and employee may be relatively separate or even conflicting.

Self-theorists also distinguish between *peripheral* and *core self-schemas*. Peripheral self-schema like Little League coach tend to be active only in very specific contexts, whereas more central core self-schemas such as parent tend to be active across many more contexts. Core self-schemas also tend to be connected to central values, a topic that will be addressed in chapter 5.

Thus, as noted previously (Lord et al., 1999), "The WSC is a continually shifting combination of core self-schemas and peripheral aspects of the self made salient (i.e., activated) by context" (p. 176). We conceptualized the WSC as mainly involving three types of components: *self-views*, which are one's perceived standing on salient attributes, and two types of comparative standards—*current goals*, which have a short-run duration and are narrowly focused, and *possible selves*, which have a long-term, future focus and provide much broader comparative standards. Current goals and possible selves have very different motivational and affective consequences, although both can impact motivational and affective processes through their comparison to self-views.

Markus and Wurf (1987) theorized that both intrapersonal and interpersonal activities are regulated by cybernetic processes involving the comparison of self-views to either current goals or possible selves. Intrapersonally, self-relevant cybernetic processes are engaged when we choose goals that are consistent with current self-views. These goals then can activate goal-relevant scripts that are the immediate guides for action (Lord & Kernan, 1987; Wofford & Goodwin, 1994), and they provide the fine-grained standards that are needed to evaluate outcomes by comparing self-views to standards (Carver & Scheier, 1981; 1998; Karoly, 1993; Lord & Levy, 1994). Regulation of who we are and who we are becoming occurs through the linkage of possible selves and self-views in more complex, long-term hierarchies that integrate multiple self-identities and task goals (Cropanzano, James, & Citera, 1993). For example, the long-term goal of becoming a competent, practicing psychologist may involve a variety of self-views for graduate students that may include being a teacher, a student, a researcher, or a writer. Each domain, in turn, may have many subidentities and complex sets of associated skills—teaching in large lectures, small groups, or one-on-one may require very different self-views, scripts, and behavioral repertoires.

Interpersonally, the self can have multiple effects on social perceptions. The self may guide choice of partners and situations (Markus & Wurf, 1987). It may also activate dimensions used in social evaluations (Markus, J. Smith, & Moreland, 1985). For example, Markus (1977) found that the dimensions that characterized one's own self-definition (e.g., independence vs. dependence) tended to also be used in evaluating others. The specific level chosen as a referent in such social evaluations may depend on one's self-views. As Dunning and Hayes (1996) showed, individuals who saw themselves as being high in mathematical ability were harsher judges of mathematical ability in others because they had more stringent definitions of what constituted good mathematical ability. Thus, their self-views affected their evaluations of others.

Alternative Motivational Processes and the WSC

So far we explained that the WSC engages a variety of self-regulatory processes by the context-specific activation of three components—self-views, current goals, and possible selves. These three WSC components interact to create *control systems* that regulate motivation and affect (Carver & Scheier, 1981; Cropanzano et al., 1993; Lord & Levy, 1994). Control systems operate by comparing sensed feedback to relevant standards and then responding in a manner that affects discrepancies. Thus, a control system could involve any two of the three WSC components just discussed, with one component providing the standard and the other the source of feedback. Note that, when different comparisons are made, different motivational processes are engaged.

Such possibilities are represented in Fig. 2.1, which identifies three aspects of motivation. The bottom part of this triangle corresponds to the activation of self-views and current goals. When these components are compared, proximal motivational concerns are activated, and responses to discrepancies are often affectively based. In contrast, when current goals are compared to activated possible selves, more distal motivational processes are created because the possible self is projected into the future. This comparison is shown on the right side of Fig. 2.1. The left side of Fig. 2.1 reflects a self-development focus created by comparing self-views and possible selves. Self-views can be mapped onto future selves by creating trajectories over time that are important in self-improvement motives (Banaji & Prentice, 1994) and decision-making theories such as image theory (Mitchell & Beach, 1990). As noted previously, future selves are linked to the current context by the unique capacity of humans to time-travel (Roberts, 2002; Tulving, 2002). In Fig. 2.1, the double-headed arrows in the unlabeled center triangle symbolize possible linkages among constructs

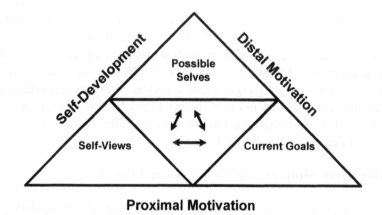

Proximal Motivation

FIG. 2.1.   Model of the WSC.

such as when possible selves activate (or inhibit) goals and vice versa. In the following sections, we define these components in more detail and provide specific propositions that link them to self-regulation. We also elaborate on the three motivational processes represented by the sides of the triangle in Fig. 2.1 and their relation to leadership processes.

WSC and the Regulation of Cognitions, Affect, and Behavior

Self-Views. We already defined self-views as an individual's perceived standing on attributes made salient by a particular context. They may pertain to attributes such as intellect, academic or athletic ability, social skills, or physical attractiveness (McNulty & Swann, 1994; Pelham & Swann, 1989). Many potential self-views can exist in long-term memory, but only a few will be activated by situational cues at any particular moment. These self-views, along with current goals and possible selves, constitute the WSC.

Once activated, self-views are an important basis for self-evaluation (Higgins, 1989; 1998) as well as for evaluating others. As already mentioned, when self-views are used to evaluate others, perceivers may be overly stringent. This effect occurs because of two processes. First, self-views are likely to be positive, leading us to use them as anchors for social judgments. Because these self-relevant comparison points are higher than average, others must be exceptionally good to be evaluated positively (Dunning & Hayes, 1996). Second, self-views are complex, highly organized structures with many features, so it is unlikely that another individual will match all of the attributes contained in self-views. A less-than-perfect fit to a category definition produces lower evaluations (Catrambone, Beike, & Niedenthal, 1996). For example, one may see oneself as being athletic because he or she participates in many sports. Consequently, when evaluating others who are playing well in a particular sport, they will not be seen as being as athletic as their performance might warrant because they match the perceiver's self-views on only one aspect of athleticism. The same type of process can apply to leadership perceptions, with leadership evaluations being especially stringent when the perceivers also see themselves as leaders.

Orienting social relations along self-relevant dimensions can have unintended and unrecognized consequences. In a study of dyadic leadership, we found that supervisors who were self-schematic in terms of leadership (i.e., had chronic self-structures that pertained to leadership) had less favorable relations with their subordinates (Engle & Lord, 1997). One reason for this effect may be that self-schemas provided stringent standards for evaluating others, as we just explained, leading supervisors to form less favorable evaluations of subordinates when those evaluations pertained to activated self-views. In other words, it appeared that individuals who saw themselves as being very high in leadership ability looked down on others whom they saw as less so. Context—specifically, the supervisor–subordinate role—is the key situational factor that could activate leadership self-schemas. Consequently, we would expect this stringency effect to hold for supervisors who were particularly conscious of their differential status and their supervisory role. Although not tested by Engle and Lord, this possible moderator could be examined in future research.

Possible Selves.   Self-views define who the individual currently is, whereas possible selves define who the individual could be (Markus & Nurius, 1986). Hopes as well as fears for the future are contained in possible selves (Markus & Wurf, 1987). Although future-oriented and hypothetical, possible selves have important consequences for understanding current motivation, activities, and affective outcomes. Indeed, we argued earlier (Lord et al., 1999) that the comparison of self-views and possible selves underlies self-development activities. Typically, development involves a projection of the self into the future along a hypothetical time-based trajectory. Beach (1990) and Mitchell and Beach (1990) investigated such self-based trajectories, which are key organizational and evaluation mechanisms in image theory. For example, an individual may have time markers for important life events—graduate from college at age 22, be married by age 30, and have a family by age 35. These future goals are a source of motivation for current activities, but they can also be a source of distress when time markers are passed without goal attainment.

Discrepancies of self-views from possible selves can be a source of effort and motivation, but when salient trajectories exist, the rate of progress toward a possible self may also be a critical variable. Taking a more dynamic view of motivation, Carver and Scheier (1990; 1998) maintained that the rate of progress in discrepancy reduction is more important than the absolute size of discrepancies in explaining affective reactions. Several studies support this assertion (Brunstein, 1993; Hsee & Abelson, 1991; Lawrence, Carver, & Scheier, 1997). For example, using a clever experi-

mental design that altered velocity (i.e., rate of progress) for different experimental groups but created the same final performance level, Lawrence
et al. (1997) found that positive velocity was actually more important than
level of past performance in predicting changes in mood along a negative–positive dimension. Thus, a sense of perceived progress was more important than subjects' current performance or what they had accomplished
in the recent past.

Harvey and Lord (1999) also found support for the importance of velocity, finding that perceived changes over time in social and job factors—that
is, perceived velocity—significantly predicted satisfaction with a wide variety of social processes and job outcomes. The size of discrepancies from
standards did not have effects that were as large or widespread, indicating
that time-based developmental evaluations were more important.
Brunstein (1993) conducted a study of students' attainment of self-generated goals over the course of a semester, finding that perceived progress
bore a strong relation with rated well-being. Perceived progress also fully
mediated the effects of goal commitment and goal attainability on subjective well-being.

Possible selves normally reflect ideals toward which an individual
strives, but they can also represent feared selves that individuals attempt to
avoid. Carver, Lawrence, and Scheier's (1999) work on self-discrepancy
theory shows that feared selves were powerful sources of motivation, particularly for individuals who saw themselves as being relatively close to
feared selves. Thus, the push from avoiding undesired selves at times may
be stronger than the pull toward ideal selves. Effective leaders need to understand that both the feared and the desired selves of employees can be potential sources of motivation or affective reactions. The contribution of
these two motivational components changes with one's perceived proxim-
ity to each, with the more proximal source generally having greater impact.
Consequently, for individuals who are close to feared selves, articulating a
vision of an ideal may not have much motivational impact, but framing
work tasks in terms of feared selves may serve as a powerful motivator.
Conversely, for individuals close to ideal and far from feared selves, explaining how they can avoid feared selves may have minimal effects, but
linking work activities to ideal selves may be very motivating. Thus, leaders must not only understand both ideal and feared selves, they must have
some sense of where subordinates see themselves with respect to these two
possibilities, and leaders must be able to incorporate such information into
leadership processes.

Leaders can have a critical role in articulating possible selves (including feared selves). Although many leadership researchers have focused on issues such as a leader's vision and charisma, a critical element may be the joining of a leader's vision with possible selves in the minds of followers, particularly when followers' collective identities are salient. Thus, a critical task for leaders may be to construct group identities for followers that are both appealing and consistent with a leader's goals. Indeed, this is a critical aspect of political leadership. Effective political leaders do not simply take context and identity as given, but they actively construct both in a way that reconfigures the social world (Reicher, 2002). Reicher noted that, by doing this, political leaders make themselves prototypical of group identities and make their projects normative for group members. In addition, by articulating future collective states, leaders can justify continued striving when current situations may be unacceptable to followers, and they can inspire hope for improvement.

These processes are illustrated by Martin Luther King, Jr.'s, activities in the 1950s and 1960s in which he linked his antisegregation activities with moral values that had broad appeal, arguing that individuals had a moral right and responsibility to disobey unjust laws. Adopting a nonviolent approach to African-American civil rights activities, being arrested for peaceful demonstrations in Birmingham, AL, and risking police brutality enhanced both his moral position and that of the African-American civil rights movement. Such activities not only gained national attention, but they made salient an ideal set of values—justice, nonviolence, and equal rights in public accommodation and employment—that had broad appeal to followers. His "I have a dream" speech, delivered on August 28, 1963, to an audience of more than 200,000 civil rights supporters, articulated a future state for the nation in which people would be treated as equals regardless of their color and be judged by their character, not the color of their skin (Norrell, 1998). Thus, Martin Luther King, Jr., was successful in actively constructing a new identity for African Americans and a new social order for the nation by appealing to core values expressed in the Constitution, "that all men are created equal," and by describing a more appealing future identity for followers. Importantly, King's vision focused on a future ideal, not the current situation, thus inspiring continued striving by civil rights advocates in spite of their discouraging current situation. His message also focused on progress or velocity in Carver and Scheier's (1990, 1998) terms, not current discrepancies. Indeed, the overarching label—civil rights movement—itself focused on velocity and progress, not just the current status of African Americans. Furthermore, part of the motivational basis that galvanized so many individuals was the change in velocity associated with the movement and the activities of Martin Luther King, Jr.

Goals and Standards. Goals are contextualized schemas that often direct current information processing (Chartrand & Bargh, 1996; Markus & Nurius, 1986). Because of their close relation to context, goals often pertain to specific tasks, and they have a well-documented relation to motivation (Locke & Latham, 1990). We include them in the WSC because they have linkages to possible selves and self-views. They are needed to help explain the self-regulatory aspects of the self-concept (Carver & Scheier, 1998; Cropanzano et al., 1993; Markus & Wurf, 1987). Because they are contextually defined, goals have a strong impact on proximal motivational processes, and they are crucial in activating the scripts (Lord & Kernan, 1987; Wofford & Goodwin, 1994) that actually produce behavior.

Another important function of goals is that by providing a standard, they help make feedback meaningful (Carver & Scheier, 1998; Hyland, 1988). Social feedback from peers or leaders can gain meaning, in part, through comparisons to goals. To illustrate this process, consider the fact that performance feedback and performance levels typically show low relationships with satisfaction (Iaffaldano & Muchinsky, 1985; Petty, McGee, & Cavender, 1984). Yet, when such constructs are connected to goals and feedback is interpreted in terms of how discrepant it is from current goals, there may be very strong relations to satisfaction. Kernan and Lord's (1991) experimental study nicely illustrates this process. They found that feedback on task performance had almost no relation with satisfaction, but when both feedback and task goals were jointly used to predict satisfaction, both components showed strong relationships with satisfaction. Leaders need to be aware of such goal-based interpretations to manage feedback processes effectively in organizations.

However, leaders also need to be aware that, although goals by themselves can have powerful effects on motivation and behavior, the full impact of goals may depend on their connection to self-structures. For example, the volitional functions of goals are enhanced through connections to the self (Kuhl, 1994, chap. 1). Kuhl stressed that the self-relevance of goals helps one focus mental activities on current intentions and thereby enhance volitional control, but self-relevance also provides flexibility to change intentions when appropriate.

Self-relevance can also engage different characteristic motivational orientations that are important in guiding affective reactions to goal attainment. For example, Rusting and Larsen (1998) noted that some individuals (extraverts) tend to be oriented toward cues signaling rewards; tend to elaborate positive, reward-relevant information cognitively in memory; and, consequently, can activate positive information faster. Contrasting personality types (neurotics) tend to be more sensitive to punishment, tend to elaborate negative information in memory, and can activate negative information faster. Extraverts tend to experience positive moods and inhibit negative moods, whereas individuals high on neuroticism show the opposite pattern. Such broad personality differences should produce self-structures with different emotional organizations for extraverts and neurotics and goal orientations that emphasize attaining rewards and avoiding punishment, respectively.

Within this context, it is useful to consider how leadership theories have approached the topic of goals. Some leadership theories such as path-goal theory (House, 1971, 1996) focus directly on goals but ignore self-related linkages. We might expect such leadership to produce volitional deficiencies in subordinates or task activity that is not very satisfying to followers. Alternative leadership perspectives (Shamir et al., 1993) build on understanding the motivational consequences of self-relevance, arguing that leaders have much more powerful effects when they engage self-relevant motivational processes. Much of this literature has focused on understanding what leaders need to do to be seen as charismatic, but our emphasis is on how self-structures can serve as mediational processes, linking leadership activities to subordinate motivational dynamics. For this reason, we return to the issue of goals and self-relevant motivational processes, before extensively considering how leadership fits into this process.

As shown in Fig. 2.1, goals engage different types of motivational processes when combined with self-views than when combined with possible selves. When goals are tied primarily to self views, proximal motivational processes are engaged. Proximal motivation increases the need to see oneself in a favorable light because one's current standing is fully determined in the short run. For this reason, self-enhancement motivation should predominate when self-regulatory activities are centered on maintaining a favorable self-view. Interestingly, Banaji and Prentice (1994) maintained that self-enhancing motives are rooted primarily in the basic tendency to seek pleasure and to avoid pain. Thus, focusing on the connection between goals and self-views should make the affective relevance of tasks particularly salient. Goal achievement can produce elation and failure creates dejection when performance goals are relevant to self-views. The former emotions should be particularly strong for extraverts, with the latter emotions being accentuated in neurotics.

In contrast, as shown in Fig. 2.1, when goals are connected to possible selves rather than self-views, more distal motivational processes predominate. Because the path from goals to possible selves is an internal, hypothetical construction, there is both uncertainty and considerable flexibility in this linkage. Accurate information is needed to gauge progress; therefore, self-verification processes should predominate. Self-enhancement is less critical because future outcomes are not yet determined. According to Banaji and Prentice (1994), self-verification motivation is rooted primarily in the needs for uncertainty reduction, consistency, and the ability to predict and control the environment. Thus, distal motivational processes should make cognitions especially salient. This reasoning is encapsulated in the following proposition:

Proposition 2.1. Linking goals to self-views will accentuate self-enhancement motivations and affective reactions to task feedback, whereas linking goals to possible selves will promote self-verification motivation and cognitive reactions to task feedback.

We already mentioned that goals and feedback can be combined to produce affective reactions to task performance. Yet, this process can be quite different when proximal and distal motivational processes are involved. Consider again Kernan and Lord's (1991) study that involved a short-term experimental task. Here the primary feedback one can get from performance pertained to self-views, and the discrepancy of feedback from goals strongly predicted satisfaction. In contrast, in their examination of job satisfaction, Harvey and Lord (1999) found that discrepancies between job characteristics and worker's goals were unrelated to job satisfaction. However, velocity or rate of progress in approaching standards bore a strong relation to satisfaction. This result suggests that a more future orientation was involved in actual jobs, and possible selves may have been more relevant. These differences in proximal and distal motivational processes are summarized in the following two propositions:

Proposition 2.2. The relation of current goal–performance discrepancies to task satisfaction will be highest when task goals are strongly linked to self-views and proximal motivational processes are salient.

Proposition 2.3. The relation of rate of change in goal–performance discrepancies (i.e., velocity) to task satisfaction will be highest when task goals are strongly linked to possible selves and distal motivational processes are salient.

There may be additional consequences of linking goals to important self-views, such as the dimension on which one is self-schematic. One consequence is that the enhanced affective orientation may produce strong negative reactions and self-doubt when goals are not met, particularly when one's predominant orientation emphasizes negative emotions as with individuals who are high on neuroticism. Such affective reactions can interfere with instrumental attempts to respond to discrepancies, especially for individuals who have difficulty suppressing negative emotions (Fabes & Eisenberg, 1997).

Although linking self-views to goals may make goal-discrepant feedback debilitating, linkages to future possible selves can help protect the self from the effects of unfavorable comparisons. For example, Lockwood and Kunda (1997, Study 2) found that having accounting graduate students read about a star fourth year accounting student created self-evaluative standards that had a demoralizing effect on fourth year graduate students, who defined their self-views through comparison to this star pupil. As a consequence, half of these senior graduate students denigrated the comparison process, distancing themselves from this comparison to protect their self-views. Just the opposite effect occurred for first year graduate students, because their comparison involved a future possible self—how they might be when they were fourth year students. They saw the comparison to a star student as inspiring, and they viewed this comparison other as being very similar to themselves. Thus, when interpreted in terms of self-views, poor relative performance can undercut achievement activities through both motivational and cognitive mechanisms; but when interpreted in terms of possible selves, similar experiences do not have such detrimental effects. Such effects are illustrated in the following proposition:

Proposition 2.4. The resiliency of task motivation when discrepancies are encountered will be higher when task goals are strongly linked to possible selves and lower when task goals are linked to self-views.

In this section we considered the effect of goals as an important standard in regulatory structures. We also stressed that this process operates differently when goals are linked to self-views in proximal motivational systems, compared to distal motivational systems in which goals are linked to future possible selves. We also suggested that both of these self-relevant linkages produced more powerful effects on motivation than externally justified goals. This is because self-relevance engages a number of affective, cognitive, and behavioral processes that are not triggered by externally imposed goals.

These deficiencies in externally based motivation create problems for leaders who are responsible to organizations or other constituencies for goal accomplishment because leaders may marshal only impoverished motivational mechanisms if they directly impose goals on subordinates. An alternative leadership approach, which we describe in chapter 5, is for leaders to view self-structures as a key mediational process. Leadership activities then can focus on activating the appropriate self, rather than directly stressing specific goals.

Time, Motivation, and Leadership

Figure 2.1 highlights the fact that leaders need to consider the present and future time distinction, which corresponds to the top-to-bottom dimension in this figure. WSC components sometimes can involve proximal motivational processes that focus on current concerns and yet at other times will emphasize future-oriented, distal processes. Research indicates that there are individual differences in the characteristic time perspective typically adopted (Holman & Silver, 1998), but leaders and the environments they create can also be important influences on time orientation. Leaders can help subordinates develop a more integrated self-identity in which current goals and more aggregate structures such as life tasks (Cantor & Kihlstrom, 1986) or personal projects (Cropanzano et al., 1993) create a cognitive bridge from self-views to possible selves (the self-development [left] side of Fig. 2.1). Because self-structures link the past and future, time travel across this bridge can have profound consequences that have been neglected by motivational and leadership researchers (see Karniol & Ross, 1996).

Leaders can facilitate such time travel by helping subordinates link current self-relevant issues to long-term development. For example, as previously described, Martin Luther King, Jr., linked specific, present-focused, civil rights activities such as marches to long-term issues associated with future ideals. Such linkages can enhance subordinates' motivation and help them surmount temporary setbacks while promoting more positive affective responses. Adopting a future orientation may be particularly important in helping subordinates cope with crisis situations. Despite these potential benefits, there is relatively little research on the time orientations of leaders and how these orientations may influence subordinates. One idea that deserves investigation is the possible effects of leader–subordinate congruence in time orientations. We would expect leader–follower dynamics to be facilitated when they share the same time orientation.

Time, Emotions, and Leadership

Karniol and Ross (1996) maintained that different emotions are generated when the self is focused on the present compared to the future. Happiness, anger and sadness tend to be associated with an immediate temporal perspective (the bottom of Fig. 2.1), whereas fear and hope are related to future states (the left and right sides of the Fig. 2.1). Research suggests that self-structures interact with these two different time orientations in fairly subtle ways when producing emotional reactions.

Considering first the immediate temporal perspective, the favorableness of organizational outcomes creates a sharp divide between positive and negative emotions, with favorable outcomes being strongly associated with happiness. Fairness of organizational processes is also important, with people paying particularly close attention to procedural justice issues when outcomes are negative (Brockner & Wiesenfeld, 1996; Cropanzano, Weiss, Suckow, & Grandey, 2000). When organizational justice processes are seen as unfairly favoring the self, Cropanzano et al. found that favorable outcomes (e.g., a promotion) are associated with guilt. In contrast, when procedures unfairly favor others, favorable outcomes often produce emotions related to pride, whereas unfavorable outcomes tend to result in anger. Because leaders often can influence the favorability of outcomes that subordinates receive, they can have substantial effects on self-relevant emotional processes. Yet, even when leaders cannot ensure favorable outcomes for subordinates, they can often influence the fairness and, perhaps more important, the perceived fairness of organizational processes. Such leadership activities may be critical in differentiating among emotions such as guilt, pride, and anger. We discuss the relation of self-structures, leadership, and procedural justice in more detail in chapter 7 where we suggest that the standards used to evaluate fairness depend on the level (individual, relational, or collective) at which the self is defined.

Turning to the future-oriented time perspective, key constructs appear to be fear and hope. In discussing possible selves, Markus and Nurius (1986) noted that there are both desired selves that we hope to approach and feared selves that we attempt to avoid. Building on Markus and Narius' work, Carver et al. (1999) examined the relative effects of discrepancies between self-views and qualities individuals either desired to attain or feared to become. Discrepancies from feared selves showed the strongest relations to all emotions that were examined (anxiety, guilt, contentment, depression, and happiness). Carver et al.'s results are important in illustrating that we need to know more about feared selves and their role in motivational and emotional processes. Leaders can motivate subordinates by articulating hoped-for possible selves, but in some instances it may be more effective to emphasize avoiding feared selves. This is an area in which there is so little research that no clear recommendations are possible. However, in a laboratory setting, Kass and Lord (2002) found that activating feared selves produced the lowest performance. One area worth investigating is the interaction of hoped-for versus feared selves and other self-relevant individual differences, such as the tendencies of extraverts to be more sensitive to positive emotions and of neurotics to be more sensitive to negative emotions. It seems plausible that, given their negative emotional tone, feared selves may be more critical for individuals high on neuroticism, whereas hoped-for selves may be more motivating for individuals high on extroversion. In short, which aspects of possible selves leaders should emphasize may depend partly, on the emotional orientation of followers.

SUMMARY

In this chapter we developed part of the conceptual framework that will be used throughout this book. We defined the self as an overarching knowledge structure that guides self- and social perceptions, memory, and behavior. We noted that not all elements of the self are salient at any one time, and we defined the currently active components as the WSC. Three WSC components—self-views, current goals, and possible selves—were seen as critical constructs in regulating both intra- and interpersonal behavior. Much of this self-regulatory capacity of the WSC comes from comparisons of self-views to the other two components, with proximal and distal self-relevant motivations having many different consequences.

This theory of the self and self-relevant dynamics is the type of broadly relevant, scientifically based theory that should be used to develop a second-order theory of leadership. Rather than being leader focused, as were most of the commonsense leadership theories mentioned in chapter 1, the perspective developed in this chapter is clearly subordinate focused.

Leaders can be most effective when operating through these subordinate-based constructs.

In the following chapter, we continue to elaborate on this theoretical framework, introducing the distinction among three different levels of self-identities (individual, interpersonal, and collective). As this conceptual framework develops, it becomes increasingly clear how leadership activities should change when different types of self-concepts are emphasized. Nevertheless, our focus is on the scientifically based, conceptual framework in the early chapters in this book. Later chapters are centered on the implications of this framework for understanding applied leadership.

3

Level and Self-Concept

In chapter 2 we defined the self-concept as an extensive knowledge structure containing many pieces of information relevant to the self. An important idea is that not all information about the self is activated at any one time. Different aspects of the self are activated in part by context, producing a working self-concept (WSC) that varied across situations. In addition, we also defined the WSC as including three main components, self-views, possible selves, and current goals. In addition, we suggested that any two of these components created a control system when used together. Pairing self-views and current goals emphasizes proximal motivation and creates an overriding performance orientation that may accentuate self-enhancement motivation; pairing current goals and possible selves, in contrast, creates a distal, learning orientation that accentuates self-verification motivation; finally, pairing self-views and possible selves creates a self-development orientation that grounds the self in standards for progress that may be either external (e.g., social comparison groups) or internal (e.g., personal values). This framework was depicted graphically in Fig. 2.1.

In this chapter we extend these ideas by noting that the self-concept can be defined at alternative focal levels. Many individuals have noted that the self-concept comprises both personal and social identities (Banaji & Prentice, 1994; Turner et al., 1994). However, these identities are active at different times, creating an individual or a personal WSC or, alternatively, a social WSC. The personal or individual self is a categorization based on comparisons to others that emphasize one's own uniqueness. Social selves, in contrast, are based on self-definition through relations with others or through group membership (Banaji & Prentice, 1994; Brewer & Gardner,

1996) and thus emphasize one's similarities and connectedness. Therefore, social identities anchor one's self-concept in the broader social world (D. T. Miller & Prentice, 1994), whereas personal identities anchor the self in one's own set of attitudes and personal values.

When we map the idea of level of self-concept onto the three components of the WSC (self-views, possible selves, and current goals) discussed in chapter 2, we create a rich framework for thinking about the resulting variety of motivational control systems that may direct employee behavior. Figure 3.1 presents a generic, hierarchical control system model patterned after the work of Carver and Scheier (1998) and Cropanzano et al. (1993). In Fig. 3.1 time and information flow from left to right, and the triangles depict *comparators* that compare sensed feedback from relevant environments to standards from higher level systems. Sensed feedback is always an input on the lower, left side of the comparator triangles, and standards are shown on the upper, left side of each comparator. Output from comparators is shown on the right of each triangle as a standard for a lower level system or for determining perceptions, affect, or behavioral reactions. Each comparator, along with input and output connections, thus provides a negative feedback loop that senses discrepancies of perceived inputs from standards and responds in a cognitive, affective, and/or behavioral sense. Discrep-

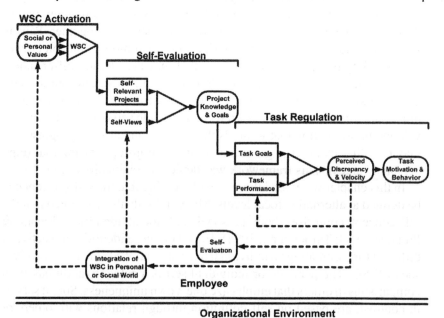

FIG. 3.1.   A hierarchical self-regulatory model lining the WSC to task performance.

ancies are a key motivational construct in motivational and cognitive self-regulatory theories (Carver & Scheier, 1998; Lord & Levy, 1994).

The hierarchical control system shown in Fig. 3.1 indicates how a series of feedback loops can be used to connect self-relevant constructs that vary in abstractness. This connection is accomplished by two types of mechanisms. First, higher level systems (e.g., personal or social values such as hedonism and beneficence, respectively) specify the goals for lower level self-regulatory loops that more directly determine task performance (e.g., allocating resources using equity vs. equality norms). Thus, lower level systems provide the means by which higher level systems achieve their ends. Second, feedback from lower level systems flows back up to higher level systems, grounding them in an appropriate task or project or social–personal reality. As shown in Fig. 3.1, control loops self-regulate by comparing sensed input and standards in the triangular comparators, allowing them to respond to sensed discrepancies with both cognitive and behavioral changes. To simplify this figure, we depict only the behavioral feedback, which is shown by dashed lines. This behavioral feedback operates through the external environment at the task level, but the feedback processes are primarily internal to an individual at higher levels.

One type of feedback that is not shown in Fig. 3.1 but is often strategically important, is the modification of goals based on discrepancies. For example, when task performance is substantially below one's goals (e.g., a student trying for an A in a course receives a C on the midterm), our research (Campion & Lord, 1982; Kernan & Lord, 1991) has found that people often lower goals to reduce the size of resulting discrepancies (e.g., the student decides to try for a B). Campion and Lord (1982) called these types of responses cognitive changes and differentiated them from behavioral responses, which are focused on the external environment. A cognitive adjustment of standards could be shown explicitly with a dashed line from perceived discrepancies to task goals or from the project goals and knowledge oval to the self-relevant projects standard, but we omitted these lines to simplify Fig. 3.1.

Typically, both behavioral and cognitive task activities are focused at lower levels when one is doing a task, but periodically progress is assessed in more abstract, self-relevant terms. When this occurs, self-views are compared to project requirements, and evaluations of self-efficacy or competence in a particular domain are made, as shown in the middle self-evaluation triangle of Fig. 3.1. It is here that the level of the WSC—that is, whether it is personal or social—may result in substantially divergent results, because it determines whether self-views will be compared to personal or socially based project standards. In other words, we occasionally use feedback, particularly negative feedback, from task performance to evaluate the appropriateness of self-relevant projects and self-views in terms of higher level systems. When the control system is personally and internally focused, the issue becomes the consistency of projects and WSCs with the underlying values that organize and solidify one's unique personality. When the control system is socially focused, the issue becomes the consistency of projects and WSCs with social values and higher level social systems such as organizations, family, religious, or social groups. Although such higher level evaluations occur infrequently, they are critical in terms of maintaining task and project engagement. They may also be painful when consistent negative feedback indicates that relevant goals and projects are not being achieved, and a new means of integrating one's activities in personal or social worlds is required.

Figure 3.1 shows that motivation and self-assessments are grounded in a complex, dynamic feedback system involving at least three levels. It aligns both the accomplishment of one's task activities with the relevant WSC and the WSC with higher level personal or social systems in a manner that allows self-integration across projects and over a lifetime. Although motivation can be externally maintained without considering these higher level systems by focusing only on task goals and feedback, such a basis for motivation is often perceived as being coercive, and it undercuts personal autonomy and growth. In the long run, such purely external motivation may rob the individual of intrinsic motivation and joy from task accomplishment (Ryan & Deci, 2000), and it robs the organization of an individual's full creative capacity and development as a member of an organization. Thus, to understand how to motivate and lead individuals in ways that foster autonomy, self-regulation, creativity, and self-development, it is necessary for leaders to adopt an integrated view that links task motivation and the self, as shown in Fig. 3.1. In other words, a leadership style that is exclusively task focused runs the long-term risk of undermining employee creativity, growth, and self-motivation.

We indicated that Fig. 3.1 was generic in the sense that it could be used to depict a variety of systems. Thinking back to our triangular model of the WSC developed in chapter 2, one can see that we have only used two of the three components in this figure, because we link self-views and current goals and ignore possible selves. In the terminology of chapter 2, we showed a proximal motivational system. If we replaced self-views in Fig.

3.1 with possible selves, we would then have a distal motivational system. Similarly, if we used self-views as the standard in the task regulation loop and possible selves as the standard for self-evaluation, we would have the developmental system discussed in chapter 2. It is in this sense that our flow diagram is generic, because it may be easily modified to depict the dynamic relations of proximal, distal, or developmental motivational systems. Figure 3.1 is also generic in the sense that the WSC can be grounded either internally in one's personal values or externally in social values and norms.

We believe that such a generic model can have many practical benefits in guiding a leader's behavior. Consider the issue of giving negative feedback. Such feedback can be accepted by employees and lead to learning and improved future performance or it can be rejected and produce anger and lowered job involvement. What differentiates these two responses? We propose that it is simply the specific content of the flow diagram shown in Fig. 3.1. Specifically, we believe that the demotivating effects of negative feedback can be minimized by emphasizing distal rather than proximal motivational processes. In terms of Fig. 3.1, this shift from proximal to distal motivation simply requires a substitution of possible selves for self-views in the self-evaluation loop. Such a change also transforms the self-evaluation loop to a learning rather than a performance orientation. Again, our point is simply that a clearly articulated dynamic model of motivation provides a means of integrating many dynamic aspects of performance.

The distinction between an internally focused, personal self and an externally focused, social self is the primary topic of this chapter. However, we now want to add one final distinction to this system by indicating that there are two qualitatively different social selves that are grounded in intimate, personal relations or less personal, collective systems. This distinction comes from work indicating that the social self can be partitioned into a *relational identity* that is based on relations with specific others and a more aggregate *collective identity* that is defined in terms of group membership (Brewer & Gardner, 1996; Sedikides & Brewer, 2001). Gabriel and Gardner (1999) reported that relational selves tend to be more important for women, who are socialized to emphasize close social relations and tend to base self-worth on related roles (e.g., being a good mother or wife). Men, however, tend to emphasize collective identities and base self-worth on their contributions to these collectives (e.g., contributing to a team or group objective). Thus, we believe that the partitioning of social selves into relational and collective levels is critical to understanding gender-related differences in leadership.

For these reasons, we believe Brewer and Gardner's (1996) three-level depiction of self-identities—individual, relational, and collective—is a very useful framework for understanding how the self-concept relates to leadership and motivation. As shown in Fig. 3.2, we can use this framework to extend our triangular model of the WSC into a triangular column with three distinct levels. This expanded model of the WSC is described in this chapter. We begin by describing each of these identity levels in more detail and then focus on their implications for understanding how leaders can influence subordinates through these alternative WSCs.

Keep in mind that underlying this discussion of the WSC at each level are complex, dynamic systems of the sort shown in Fig. 3.1 that comprise proximal, distal, and developmental motivational systems that operate at each of these identity levels. To illustrate, consider that distal motivational systems that link task goals and future possible selves could be based on developing one's own competence (personal-level identity), building stronger relations with specific others (relational-level identity), or enhancing the status and functioning of a specific group (collec-

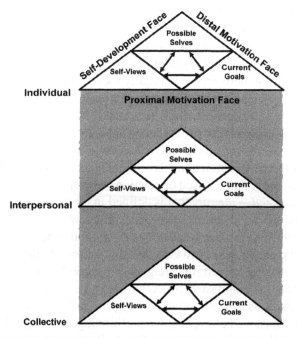

FIG. 3.2.   A model of the WSC at alternative identity levels. Note: From *Organizational Behavior and Human Decision Processes*, by R. Lord, D. Brown, and Freiberg, 1999, New York: Elsevier. Copyright © 1999 by Elsevier Science. Adapted with permission.

tive-level identity). To make this point more concrete, consider the following three examples of distal motivational systems that link task goals and future possible selves—one each for the individual, relational, and collective identity levels:

John's boss is seriously ill, and John must take over some of the boss's committee leadership. Although he must put in some extra hours of work and learn to read and interpret reports from the new management information system, John sees this as an opportunity to demonstrate his skills at public speaking and managing others. He believes that his own chances for promotion may be helped as others also come to realize his competence (individual level).

Vicki's boss is also absent, and she must fill in for the boss. She sees this as an important chance to show her loyalty to the boss and repay the occasions when the boss has gone out on a limb by trusting Vicki's judgment. Vicki hopes this experience will deepen her already good relationship with the boss (relational level).

Although Rafael's boss was in an auto accident and is in critical condition, the software development team he works for is maintaining its reputation for meeting tight deadlines with quality solutions. Each member has picked up one of the boss's functions and is working hard to ensure that the team's high standards are not violated on their watch. They hope that this commitment to the software group will help establish their reputation as a team that can deliver products even under trying circumstances (collective level).

LEVELS OF SELF-IDENTITY

Individual-Level Identity

Self-views arising from these three alternative levels reflect different social processes. Self-views arising from the *individual level* emphasize dimensions or attributes that are personally important and differentiate oneself from others. Consequently, they should closely match salient or chronically available self-schema. The personal meaning constructed from self-views may involve comparisons to future selves when a developmental focus is adopted; however, as Brewer and Gardner (1996) argued, at this level of identity self-views generally gain meaning by comparisons to others.

If, as Brewer and Gardner (1996) suggested, worth at this level stems from favorable comparisons to others, we would expect self-enhancing biases to be common. Yet, when translated into social perception processes, the more favorable self-views arising from self-enhancement processes may, in turn, produce harsher evaluations of others when the self is used as a standard. Thus, leaders who adopt individual-level identities for themselves may self-enhance their own self-views, seeing themselves as possessing more leadership qualitites than their peers. Furthermore, because they use this enhanced self-view as a standard in evaluating others, they may also be overly critical in evaluating the leadership abilities of subordinates, thus fostering a more directive and limiting leadership style with respect to subordinates. Engle and Lord (1997) provided empirical support for this reasoning in a study of 76 subordinates and their supervisors in the marketing area. Specifically, they found that the extent to which supervisors reported normative leadership or performance characteristics as being self-descriptive was negatively correlated with both their subordinate's reported liking of the leader and their subordinate's perceptions of the quality of the leader–member relationship. Thus, supervisors who saw themselves very favorably in terms of leadership and performance characteristics had more negative relations with their subordinates.

We stress that Engle and Lord's (1997) study was correlational and causality must always be interpreted carefully, but it is interesting to speculate on situations when this type of problem may be particularly acute. One such situation is on jobs involving professionals or autonomous groups where high degrees of self-management and self-leadership are required. In such situations, the high standards of bosses who see themselves as leaders may foster overly critical supervisory behavior that limits the leadership development and leadership activities of their group members.

In addition, self-views at the individual level focus on independent selves and may, therefore, be associated more with concerns pertaining to the distribution of resources and instrumental social justice issues. In other words, an individual-level focus may exacerbate worry about "Whether I'm getting my fair share," whether the resource is pay, perks, or praise. Here again, we might expect biases related to self-enhancing self-views. That is, because individuals are motivated to see their skills or abilities as higher than others, they may also expect to receive a disproportionately high level of outcomes. We discuss problems this may create for subordinates' justice perceptions in chapter 7, but here we briefly mention one problem this can create for leaders themselves.

When leaders see themselves as warranting greater rewards, and in fact are successful at attaining substantial rewards for themselves, it limits their ability to develop collective identities in followers. Yorges, Weiss, and Strickland (1999) showed experimentally that leaders who are thought to benefit personally from their actions are perceived by others as being less charismatic than leaders who are seen as being self-sacrificing. Consistent with this finding, David De Cremer (2002) showned that, compared to leaders who benefitted from their activities, self-sacrificing leaders were not only perceived as being higher on charisma, but they were able to motivate others to cooperate more. These effects, in turn, were mediated by the perceived legitimacy of leaders. Thus, it appears that subordinates will grant influence to leaders and cooperate with others when leaders are not perceived as being self-motivated, but subordinates are less willing to do this when leaders themselves benefit. As De Cremer noted, only self-sacrificing leaders were able to transform subordinates' motives from a personal, proself orientation to a collective, prosocial orientation.

Although our focus has been on self-views and problems associated with both subordinate and leader self-enhancement biases, individual-level identities can also involve possible selves and task goals. For both possible selves and task goals, we expect the following three effects to occur: an emphasis on self-relevant dimensions as defined by self-schemas, striving for worth through favorable social comparisons, and a tendency for self-enhancing biases. Thus, one may envision a future self with higher levels of achievement than peers when achievement is defined along personally relevant dimensions (e.g., wealth, physical attractiveness, achievement, and friends) and greater achievement than would be expected based on past performance or abilities. These long-run objectives may be translated into more specific, self-relevant goals through a nesting of feedback loops patterned after Fig. 3.1 (e.g., completing a work project, getting promoted, and saving a given amount of money), which may also be evaluated in self-enhancing ways.

In short, when individual-level identities define the WSC, one's comparative abilities and outcomes are likely to be the critical factor regulating intra- and interpersonal regulation. This may lead to biased perceptions of both the self and others on self-relevant dimensions. Such biases may produce a number of practical problems for leaders pertaining to defining fair rewards both for themselves (overreward problems) and for their subordinates (underreward problems), giving appropriate performance feedback to subordinates, encouraging organizational citizenship behaviors, or eliciting appropriate work behavior (as we discuss in later chapters). To be balanced, we should note that there may also be many benefits from an individual-level focus such as when a leader has a unique insight or goal and the individual-level focus is instrumental in achieving that vision. Such potential benefits need to be balanced against the risk of lowered charisma and overevaluation of one's own self-worth or effectiveness when leaders adopt an individual-level focus.

Relational-Level Identity

At the relational level, our perceptions of how others perceive us, which have been termed *reflected appraisals* (Mead, 1934; Shrauger & Schoneman, 1979), serve as a primary determinant of self-views. In organizational settings where leaders have high status and power, the feedback they provide to others is likely to be a very important reflected appraisal that helps others form self-views. Consistent with this argument, Higgins and May (2001) noted that effective regulation requires that we have both knowledge of our self from our own view point and knowledge from the viewpoint of significant others or social groups with which we identify. Tice and Baumeister (2001) placed even more emphasis on the interpersonal self proposing that, "The self is constructed, used, altered, and maintained as a way of connecting the individual organism to other members of its species" (p. 71). Taking an evolutionary perspective, they argued that the need to be connected with others is powerfully adaptive because it affords access to resources required for both survival and reproduction. They viewed the reflected self as an indicator ("sociometer" in their terms) of belongingness and a proxy for access to social resources. Consequently, when the reflected self is negative, it is likely to produce emotional reactions because it conveys a threat to the resources needed for survival and reproduction. Given the power and resources controlled by organizational leaders, the self-views they communicate to subordinates are likely to feed into this already existing basis for subordinate self-regulation. Thus, the self-appraisal reflected by leaders is likely to be an important organizational sociometer for subordinates. The leader's appraisal signals subordinate's likely access to organizational resources and engages fundamental self-regulatory mechanisms. In addition, this leader-related sociometer is likely to produce both positive and negative emotional reactions in subordinates, depending on the valence of the leader's reflected appraisal.

Because emotions are important social cues, subordinates are likely to be especially sensitive to affective feedback from leaders, using it as a basis for constructing a reflected self-identity. Indeed, one function of communicated emotions is that they allow individuals to discover and maintain social exchanges that are optimal to both parties (Keltner & Kring, 1998). For example, consider what may happen if I inadvertently criticize a group of which a coworker is a member. Upon learning of this unintended insult, I may be acutely embarrassed. My embarrassment communicates that I did not intend to harm my coworker, who is then likely to respond with sympathy and forgiveness. Thus, the emotions of embarrassment and sympathy maintain an effective social linkage that has been inadvertently threatened. Without these mitigating emotions, the likely response from the coworker is anger because the self has been threatened and the effect was to undercut an important work relationship.

For such reasons, communicating their affective reactions may, therefore, be particularly important for leaders. Affective reactions may include feelings of liking or disliking, enthusiasm, boredom, sympathy, trust, and so on. Subordinates are likely to be sensitive to explicit expressions of affect and the communication of affect through more implicit means such as nonverbal behavior. Consequently, behavioral styles that emphasize interactional justice and consideration (Bies, 2001; Tyler & Lind, 1992) may have implications that extend beyond the simple assessment of fairness. For example, Van den Bos and Lind (2002) argued that fairness serves as a heuristic process that creates feelings of trust and a willingness to follow authorities because subordinates who receive fair treatment believe that authorities will not exploit them. These authors also noted that the fairness heuristic is particularly important during times of uncertainty such as when employee's experience transitions or organizations change dramatically. Thus, as noted by the several aforementioned justice researchers, interpersonal treatment conveys a sense of an individual's value or worth to others and the likely future support by others. Good interpersonal treatment could conceivably add to a subordinate's sense of security, willingness to admit and deal with mistakes, and allegiance to the leader and organization.

We add that interpersonal treatment is also likely to be encoded by subordinates in terms of an affective reaction. In other words, positive interpersonal treatment is likely to be interpreted and reciprocated by subordinates not only in terms of fair treatment but also in feelings of liking. Consistent with this argument, affective evaluations tend to form early in superior–subordinate interactions, and the degree to which dyadic partners like each other is a good predictor of the eventual closeness of leader–member relations and the value of leader–member exchanges (LMXs) to both parties (Liden, Wayne, & Stilwell, 1993). The importance of such processes is summarized in the following propositions.

Proposition 3.1. A leader's reflected appraisal will have a powerful impact on a subordinate's self-view. The appraisal will be communicated through both cognitive and affective channels and by both explicit and implicit processes.

Proposition 3.2. Reflected appraisals will be an important medium for signaling the potential benefits of a social exchange to both leaders and subordinates. These signals will be assimilated into affective evaluations of the other party and into evaluations of the value of the dyadic exchange.

It is important to recognize that reflected appraisals occur continuously as a normal part of social interactions; consequently, the processes on which they rely are likely to be highly automated. For this reason, the implications of everyday contact for self-views may be less obvious to leaders than are more formal, yet less frequent feedback processes such as performance appraisals. Yet, the day-to-day treatment of subordinates may have powerful effects on both leaders and followers because of its high frequency and also because of its direct association with affective dimensions. For example, numerous field experiments by Eden (1992) showed that leaders with high expectations of subordinates actually had subordinates who performed better. In addition, over time repeated high performance will increase the subordinate's own view of the self as competent and produce higher expectations for future performance.

Proposition 3.3. The relationship between a leader's self-fulfilling prophecies and a subordinate's expectancies is mediated by changes in subordinates' self-views, a subordinate's affective evaluations of the leader, and the subordinate's satisfaction with the dyadic exchange.

Eden's (1992) work is interesting for another aspect that pertains to reflected appraisals. He conducted numerous studies of self-fulfilling prophecies (SFPs) in field settings and found extensive support for this phenomenon. Being true experiments, all of these studies shared the property that the leaders were unaware of the research hypotheses and of the fact that information provided to leaders regarding their subordinate's ability was part of an experimental manipulation. More recently, as discussed in chapter 1, Eden et al.'s (2000) work has focused on training leaders to manage SFPs. Presumably leaders who are aware of the positive effects of SFPs could deliberately communicate high expectations to all subordinates and thereby use this technique to raise their self-efficacy and performance.

However, results from several of these training studies have produced only small effects, suggesting that SFPs work better when they occur without actual awareness on the part of superiors. There are two plausible reasons for this difference between the effects of deliberate and unaware use of SFPs, and they both warrant future research. One reason may be that when leaders are unaware of SFPs, they respond to subordinates more affectively than cognitively, and affective information may be better at communicating reflected appraisals to subordinates. A second reason may be that social appraisals that are genuine are communicated through nonverbal behaviors that are more affective than cognitive and are believed more readily by subordinates, whereas behaviors that are intentionally produced by leaders in order to elevate subordinate self-efficacy may use less effective cognitive channels. These alternative explanations for the failure of training interventions could be resolved through future research.

Eden's (1992) work illustrates the importance of interpersonal processes to subordinate motivation. We would expect such effects to be accentuated when the self is defined at a relational level. At this level, future possible selves may also have strong ties to social processes. For example, Ibarra (1999) examined the development of new identities for management consultants and investment bankers who were in transitions to higher level roles. She found that both groups adopted a provisional self, which lead to experimentation with new behaviors and adjustment based on feedback.

In Ibarra's (1999) study, three processes were critical to the development of provisional selves, but they occurred with different individuals. We suggest that these three processes may vary with individual, relational, and col-

TABLE 3.1

Development and Evaluation of Provisional Selves as a Function of Identity Level

Identity Level	Development	Evaluation
Individual	True-to-self strategy based on internal values	Based on provisional self inhibiting true character or competence
Relational	Holistic imitation of role model (mentor) with whom strong affective bonds existed	Informal guidance from role models with whom they identified
Collective	Selective imitation from many others to customize provisional self	Implicit and explicit reactions from broader role set

lective self-orientations as shown in Table 3.1. Some people developed a provisional self that was based on their own individual values, which we believe would be most likely when individual-level identities were salient. Others imitated the qualities of a mentor, which should be most likely with salient relational-level identities. Interestingly, wholesale imitation of another's style occurred when there were very strong affective bonds with a mentor, which is consistent with our argument that affect would be particularly strong at the relational level. It is also consistent with Aron and McLaughlin-Volpe's (2001) proposition that in close relationships, one tends to include one's partner in one's self-definition. The third type of person developed a provisional self that was an amalgam of many individuals' styles, perhaps reflecting the development of a group prototype which has proved to be critical to collective-level identities (e.g., Hains, Hogg, & Duck, 1997). Though Ibarra did not frame her research in terms of identity levels, we think the potential synthesis with Brewer and Gardner's (1996) framework for identity levels is very promising. It would be a good area for future research on the transition of employees to new possible selves.

Such research might also examine how feedback processes varied with identity level, as we have done in Table 3.1. Ibarra (1999) stressed that identity construction involves not only developing possible selves but also selecting or discarding possibilities that have been considered. Ibarra reported that participants using a true-to-self strategy discarded provisional selves when behaviors consistent with provisional selves prevented them from discovering their true character and competence. We suspect that such concerns would be particularly troubling for individuals who tended to focus on individual-level identities. Other participants relied on implicit, affectively based guidance from role models. As Ibarra noted, this feedback was particularly meaningful due to identification with the role models, which suggests a relational-level identity. This process illustrates the power of reflected appraisals from leaders to not only convey evaluations of subordinates but to help shape the development of their organizational identity. A more collective use of social feedback described by Ibarra was based on both implicit and explicit feedback from a broader role set. Evaluation and adjustment for these individuals involved the gradual development of a collective-level identity that was consistent with a collective definition of a good management consultant or investment banker.

In sum, both Eden's (1992) research and Ibarra's (1999) discussion of provisional selves illustrates that at relational levels, a leader can have an important impact on subordinates's self-views or future possible selves.

Moreover, such effects tend to be greater when strong affective bonds are present between superiors and subordinates. These identities in turn may give rise to unique task goals and reliance on social feedback sources as ways to evaluate task accomplishment.

It is also likely that leaders differ in their comfort with and tendency to develop close relations with subordinates. Complementing our perspective, Brower, Schoorman, and Tan (2000) analyzed relational leadership from the perspective of leaders. A key factor in their model is the degree of trust that leaders have in subordinates. They argued that the propensity to trust is a trait-like quality that is influenced by experience, personality, and culture. Translated into our terms, we would expect that leaders who emphasized relational identities would be high on the propensity to trust subordinates, and they would also tend to elicit relational identities from subordinates. Brower et al. predicted that leaders high on the propensity to trust subordinates are likely to develop more high-quality exchanges with subordinates than are leaders who are low on this propensity. We would extend this prediction to leaders who are high on relational identities.

Collective-Level Identity

Collective level self-views involve social dynamics that are quite different from the other two identity levels as they are based on the organizational culture or on collective norms. When group identities (e.g., a work group, department or branch, or whole organization) are salient, group members view themselves in terms of the group prototype, and they generally evaluate themselves positively on aspects of the self that are similar to the group prototype. This is a substantial departure from the positive emphasis on differences from others, which is the tendency when individual-level identities predominate, and it even stands apart from the relational identity's positive evaluation of complementary aspects of the self and the relevant other. Hogg and his colleagues (Hains et al., 1997; Hogg, 2001; Hogg & Terry, 2000) investigated this group prototype matching process in terms of leadership definitions. They found that when group identities are salient, leaders tend to be evaluated in terms of their fit with a specific group prototype rather than with a general leadership stereotype.

Collective-level identities have been a concern of leadership researchers for other reasons as well. It is widely thought that charismatic leaders have powerful effects on subordinates because they shift subordinates' identities from an individual to a collective level (Bass, 1985). Such shifts predispose followers to accept and work toward the collective identity defined by a leader's vision. Although such legitimacy of leaders can come from a personally based identification consistent with relational identities, it can also reflect the inclusion of both leaders and followers in ethnic or gender-based groups (Tyler, 1997), which suggests that a more collective identity is critical.

Identities at the collective level also have different dynamic properties. For example, future possible selves may be closely connected to the progress of the group with which one identifies. One's goals may center on contributing to or advancing one's group, and self-evaluation may involve comparison to group-level norms rather than to individual values. Thus, the social dynamics related to both self-development and more immediate motivational issues change as one moves from relational to collective levels, becoming more abstract and independent of relations with a specific individual. Such a difference has already been illustrated in our discussion of Ibarra's (1999) work (see Table 3.1). We interpreted that work as showing that collective-level evaluations of provisional selves used feedback from a much broader role set than did relational-level evaluations (which emphasized feedback from a single, close individual).

IDENTITY LEVELS AND WSCs

Inhibitory Relations Among Levels

There is good reason to believe that organizational members will have difficulty activating more than one self-identity level at a time; when one level is activated by a context, the other two levels tend to be inhibited or deactivated. Martindale (1980) explicitly suggested that activating one identity will inhibit the activation of other self-identities. Also, research on interpreting ambiguous stimuli (Malt, Ross, & Murphy, 1995) shows that people use only a single cognitive schema when forming opinions and making judgments. For example, subjects could not simultaneously encode information about a home from the perspective of a home buyer and a burglar, even though these contrasting schemas were equally available and equally well-known. Thus, we believe that alternative levels of self-identity are unlikely to be accessed simultaneously and incorporated into the WSC, although it should be recognized that dyadic and group-level processes are important to all levels of identity.

When such findings are generalized to an organizational context, they imply that only one schema at a time can be used to understand people, events, or oneself. In terms of Fig. 3.1, this suggests that hierarchical control loops will be formed at the individual, relational, or collective levels, but that they will not involve composites that cross levels. Thus, organizational members may not simultaneously be able to define themselves in terms of a prototype associated with their work groups (e.g., a collective-level identity) and in terms of individual qualities that differentiate themselves from coworkers (e.g., an individual-level identity). Similarly, feedback from task performance will not simultaneously be interpreted in terms of identities at different levels. Consequently, the importance of one identity level should be highest when the other two identity levels are low. This fact also means that subordinate behavior may appear inconsistent over time as different WSCs become active—the same subordinates may be self-centered when individual level WSCs are active yet cooperative and group-oriented when collective level WSCs are active.

Individual Differences in Identity Levels

Chronic Self.   Although we expect that most individuals will have developed identities at all three levels, which identity typically guides the WSC may reflect individual differences in chronic identities, responses to social cues from coworkers and leaders, or constraints from situational factors such as organizational or national cultures. Focusing on better defining and assessing the individual difference component, Selenta and Lord (2002) developed new measures of individual, relational, and collective identities using factor analysis on a sample of 309 undergraduate students. They identified seven dimensions that describe chronic differences in identities at these three levels—three aspects of individual identity and two aspects each of relational and collective identity. These dimensions are described further in Table 3.2. Selenta and Lord also carefully assessed the construct validity of these dimensions by examining their relation to other psychological constructs.

Four aspects of Selenta and Lord's (2002) measurement development and construct validation work are particularly noteworthy. First, there were very clear relations of self-identities with two frequently studied constructs that describe broad differences in where one characteristically focuses attention: *private self-consciousness* (Fenigstein, Scheier, & Buss, 1975), which reflects a focus on one's inner world, and *public self-consciousness*, which reflects a tendency to focus on the external, social world. Specifically, multiple regression analyses showed that private self-consciousness was signifi-

TABLE 3.2

Identity-Level Dimensions Developed by Selenta and Lord (2002)

Subscale	Definition
Individual	
Comparative identity	Individual characteristics or achievements are compared to others
Internal identity	Self is defined through comparison to internal reference points
Independence	Preference for independent rather than social activities
Relational	
Concern for others	Helping, nurturing, and caring relationships with others define the self
Relational identity	Self is defined in terms of close relationships and reflected self
Collective	
Group achievement focus	Group achievement and contribution to group define the self
Group identity	Self defined in terms of group and others' reactions to it

cantly predicted by each of the three individual-level dimensions such that greater private self-consciousness was associated with higher scores on all three individual-level dimensions. In contrast, nonsignificant regression weights were found for all the relational and collective dimensions in predicting private self-consciousness. In contrast, when public self-consciousness was regressed on these same seven measures of identity levels, none of the individual-level dimension regression weights was significant, and all four of the relational-level and collective-level dimensions had significant regression weights. Thus, for the most part, higher levels of public self-consciousness were associated with a chronic tendency to identify the self at the relational or collective levels. In sum, the private versus public self-consciousness measure maps very nicely onto the distinction between individual versus relational or collective self-identities.

Second, Selenta and Lord (2002) found that responses on a measure important in cross-cultural research—Schwartz's (1992) Value Survey—also varied with identity levels. Schwartz extensively investigated cross-cultural differences in values, showing that patterns of values can be differentiated on an individual–collective axis (Schwartz & Bilsky, 1987, 1990). Selenta and Lord's results are mostly consistent with expectations from Schwartz's work, showing that when values are regressed on all seven measures of identity levels: (a) individually oriented values such as self-direction and achievement were positively predicted by the individual-level dimension of internal identity and were generally unrelated to the four relational and collective dimensions, (b) benevolent values received positive regression weights for relational identity dimensions (concern for others) and negative regression weights for the individual-level dimension of comparison to others (CTO), and (c) the collectively oriented values of tradition and conformity had negative weights for the individual-level CTO dimension and positive weights on the collective-level dimensions of group identity. Thus, these results show a clear pattern of individual-level values being predicted by individual-level identity dimensions, relational-level values (e.g., benevolence) being predicted by relational-level dimensions, and collective-level values being predicted by collective-level identity dimensions as well as being negatively related to individual-level identity dimensions. In short, Selenta and Lord's study clearly shows that identity dimensions have sensible relations with self-consciousness and values.

Third, Selenta and Lord (2002) found that when all the items from the seven measures of identity levels were jointly factor analyzed, the resulting factor structure approximated the Individual–Relational–Collective identity-level distinctions of Brewer and Gardner (1996). More specifically, when a four-dimensional factor solution was forced, most individual items tended to load most highly on an Individual factor, relational items tended to load most highly on the Relational factor, and most collective items tended to load most highly on a Collective factor. However, in addition to these three factors, they also found a fourth achievement-related factor composed of the remaining items that cut across all three levels.

Fourth, Selenta and Lord (2002) found that mean scores on the identity-level dimensions varied with both gender and gender orientation. We first discuss the general issue of gender and identities before summarizing Selenta and Lord's findings on this topic.

Gender.   Gabriel and Gardner (1999) provided an important extension of the Brewer and Gardner (1996) framework by noting that there are gender differences in identity level. Building on Eagly's (1987) social role theory, they argued that women are socialized to adopt a more communal, nurturing role that tends to be oriented toward one-on-one relationships. Thus, Gabriel and Gardner maintained that when women adopt an interdependent identity, it tends to be at the relational rather than the collective level. In contrast, men are socialized to adopt a more agentic, competitive, group-level interpersonal identity. Consequently, when men adopt an interdependent identity level, it tends to be at the collective rather than the relational level.

Gabriel and Gardner (1999) found support for these assertions in five different studies. All found no gender-related difference in individual-level identities (which they called independent identities). However, consistent with expectations, all five studies showed that within interdependent levels, women tended to emphasize concerns associated with relational self-identities, whereas men tended to emphasize the more group-oriented concerns associated with collective identities. Gabriel and Gardner's research is noteworthy for the range of variables examined, which included self-descriptions, selective encoding and memory for social information, recollection of emotional experiences, and helping behavior that involved self-sacrifice.

Consistent with expectations based on Gabriel and Gardner's (1999) work, Selenta and Lord (2002) also found gender-related differences in reported identity level. They regressed Spence and Helmreich's (1978) measures of masculinity and femininity on the seven identity dimensions identified in Table 3.2, finding that masculinity received substantial negative regression weight for the concern for others relational dimension (−.40), whereas when they regressed femininity on the same variables, the concern for others relational dimension received a strong positive (.36) weight. Both results show that women place more emphasis on relational identities, which is consistent with Gabriel and Gardner's findings. Based on the previously mentioned Brower et al. (2000) theory of relational leadership, one would also expect more feminine leaders to be more trusting of subordinates and to develop higher level leader–member exchanges.

IDENTITY LEVELS AND LEADERSHIP

Having laid out our conceptual system for understanding the integration of motivational processes with self-identities and understanding how the nature of identities can change with levels, we can now directly address issues related to leaders and leadership. An overriding principle with respect to leadership is that self-identity operates as a boundary variable for leadership theories. Because very different psychological processes are likely involved at individual, relational, and collective levels, the appropriateness of specific leadership theories and the effectiveness of specific types of leadership behaviors will change with identity levels. Because gender also covaries with identity level, this framework subsumes many gender-related leadership effects as well. Before discussing how leadership activities may vary with each identity level, we offer the following general principle suggesting that self-identity is a boundary variable for leadership theory.

Proposition 3.4. Leadership activities will be more effective when they are matched to appropriate identity levels of subordinates.

Individual-Level Leadership

When individual-level identities are salient, differentiation from others is a critical psychological process and personal esteem is maintained by favorable social comparisons. This process underlies the differentiation of leaders from followers in terms of underlying traits (see Lord et al., 1986), with leadership status being an important source of worth and self-esteem to leaders. One might expect threats or stress to accentuate this processes, leading to greater differentiation and more hierarchically oriented leadership during times of crisis.

Considerable research supports the idea that stress or crisis changes leadership dynamics. Research has repeatedly found an association between crisis, leadership, and charisma. For example, Pillai (1996) experimentally created a crisis vs. noncrisis experimental factor by giving subjects bogus bad or good feedback on a course exam. In a subsequent group exercise, she found that emergent leaders in crisis situations tended to be more charismatic. Hunt, Boal, and Dodge (1999) also used an experimental design to show that crisis expands the type of behaviors that produce charismatic leadership perception to include crisis-responsive charisma as well as the more general vision-based charisma. In addition, using a simulated selection task, Emrich (1999) found greater false recognition of leadership behaviors for an applicant for a managerial job when the applicant was expected to manage a team in crisis versus a team that was performing well even though perceivers in both context conditions received identical information about the applicant. We suggest, however, that such effects would be enhanced when individual-level identities were salient for both leaders and followers, because esteem is maintained through differentiation from others and favorable comparisons. This process, in turn, supports the appropriateness to both leaders and followers of a more hierarchical, person-centered type of leadership (i.e., charisma).

When individual-level identities are salient, a leader's behavior and the organizational practices that leaders administer (e.g., feedback, rewards, task assignments, and performance appraisals) can also differentiate one subordinate from another. Leaders must effectively manage the meaning of such processes to subordinates. Two types of meaning are particularly important. First, rewards and feedback can be seen as reflecting either fixed or malleable subordinate skills and performance. Opportunities for growth and development are much higher when skills are viewed as being malleable. Second, equity-based meanings associated with rewards are also likely to be particularly important to subordinates when individual level identities are salient. Rewards signal differences among individuals, and unequal distributions of rewards are likely to be justified in terms of different skills or unequal contributions.

Leaders should be aware that although they may see feedback processes and reward distribution as objectively based processes, they may not seem that way to subordinates, particularly when interpreted in terms of individual-level identities. All subordinates may tend to see themselves in overly favorable terms when compared to coworkers both in terms of selecting dimensions for comparison that are self-relevant and also in constructing overly flattering self-views on these dimensions. Thus, when feedback indicates lower-than-average performance, it is likely to be rejected by subordinates, particularly if its self-relevance is stressed.

Also based on their own upwardly biased self-views, all subordinates may see higher levels of outcomes as being warranted than would a more objective observer. This tendency may be most extreme for individuals who have the least ability. Kruger and Dunning (1999) found that overestimation of one's own ability was particularly acute for individuals who were lowest on ability. More specifically, across four different studies involving humor, grammar, and logic, the bottom quartile of subjects whose ability was actually at the 12th percentile estimated that their ability was at the 62nd percentile. Thus, even individuals who are lowest in ability see themselves as being a better-than-average individual and, therefore, may expect better-than-average outcomes for reward distributions to be perceived as fair.

Because individual identities are internally focused, emphasizing private rather than public self-consciousness, they facilitate behaviors that have an internal origin in an individual's values or attitudes. Thus, individual attitudes predict behavioral intentions much better when individuals are focused on independent rather than interdependent identities, whereas norms have the opposite effect because they are more potent determinants of behavior when collective identities are salient (Illingworth, 2001; Ybarra & Trafimow, 1998). This distinction has many practical implications associated with eliciting or preventing specific types of behavior. Consider, the many examples of poor corporate ethical behavior associated with accounting practices that were uncovered in 2001 and 2002 (Enron, WorldCom, etc). Such behavior is hard to explain when considered from the perspective of typical ethical norms for corporate accounting behavior, but it seems more understandable in conjunction with individual-level attitudes and values that stressed growth, profits, and high stock prices. In other words, it may reflect the conjunction of individually focused identities among executives and self-centered personal attitudes and values. Hence, limiting such behavior in the future may require interventions focused at both typical executive WSCs and their norms and attitudes. More specifically, changing norms to emphasize more ethical behavior may not be very effective unless coupled with the development of more collective identities; if executive identities remain at the individual level, then their private attitudes and values would have to be changed to alter behavior substantially. This may be much more difficult than changing social norms.

Consider the opposite issue—encouraging behavior that benefits collectives such as organizations or society. This may be much easier to do when collective WSCs predominate. Research shows that leaders play an important role in eliciting prosocial behavior, but it may also reflect norms associated with collective units. For example, when building its new union headquarters in the heart of Silicon Valley, Local 332 of the International Brotherhood of Electrical Workers integrated expensive solar photovoltaics into their building design because, as union organizer Jay James said, "It's the right thing to do, plus it's an area that's growing by leaps and bounds, where our members will find plenty of work in the future" (Kerwin, 2002, p. 33). Thus, both societal benefits and anticipated future organizational rewards justified this additional expense, which was overwhelmingly supported by the union membership according to James.

Another important implication of our model in Fig. 3.2 is that leadership practices that focus on individual-level identities do not operate in isolation but instead involve all three aspects of the WSC. That is, self-views, goals, and possible selves interact; consequently, leadership activities focused on one component are likely to be less effective than a leadership strategy that takes a more integrative approach. For example, motivational processes associated with goal setting and feedback may operate differently when goals are linked with self-views as opposed to possible selves because they will engage proximal as opposed to distal motivational processes. As previously noted, focusing on self-views may make affect and self-enhancement more salient. Leaders who focus on cognitive processes associated with measures such as contingent rewards, feedback, or transactional leadership exchanges may be surprised by subordinates' affective reactions and defensiveness, which only make sense when subordinates self-enhancing biases are considered.

Linking goals to self-views may also make subordinates more vulnerable to lower self-esteem when performance is lower than aspirations. This can be seen by revisiting Fig. 3.1 and noting that task performance feeds back to self-views in the self-evaluation loop. As a consequence of this linkage, people may lower goals when faced with even temporary setbacks as a means to manage dissatisfaction (Kernan & Lord, 1991) and to protect self-esteem (Carver & Scheier, 1998).

Consistent with this reasoning, Kluger and DeNisi (1996) conducted a meta-analysis of the literature on feedback interventions, finding that in over one third of the studies, programs that increased feedback actually reduced performance. In explaining when feedback would have a positive or negative consequence, these authors concluded that when feedback was interpreted at lower, task-oriented levels, it increased performance by facilitating skill development; however, when feedback was interpreted at higher self-relevant terms (e.g., How good am I at this task?), feedback interventions tended to decrease performance. This result also is consistent with our argument that an emphasis on self-views makes subordinates vulnerable to a variety of performance disruptions.

In contrast to a focus on self-views, emphasizing motivational linkages associated with possible selves may protect self-efficacy and motivational processes from these negative effects. When the focus is on future possible selves, performance feedback may be interpreted in more cognitive terms that enhance learning and defensive coping responses may be avoided. Indeed, if the association with possible selves maintains high self-efficacy and high goals in the face of lower performance, substantial increases in subsequent effort and performance may result from low prior performance (Bandura & Cervone, 1986). Thus, if we think in terms of Fig. 3.1, focusing on possible selves and distal motivation minimizes the relevance of task-related discrepancies for self-views, whereas focusing in terms of proximal motivation enhances this feedback path to self-views.

In short, the comparison of feedback to goals—a key motivational process—gains meaning from the association between goals and self-relevant constructs in the WSC, as we have shown in Fig. 3.1. This self-relevant context then may moderate both cognitive and affective reactions to goal–performance discrepancies, allowing some individuals to feel challenged and inspired by the same objective circumstance that would be demoralizing to others. Leadership activities and scientific theories of leadership need to be grounded in such comprehensive perspectives rather than focus on isolated components such as goal level, feedback processes, self-esteem, or self-efficacy. This argument is developed more thoroughly in subsequent chapters; for now, we simply emphasize the value of a more comprehensive perspective based on second-order as compared to commonsense theories of leadership.

Relational-Level Leadership

Dyadic processes between leaders and followers can be expected to become more important when the self is defined at the relational level. As already noted, leaders are important sources of reflected appraisal for subordinates, and self-fulfilling expectancies (Eden, 1992) may have especially powerful effects on individual-level identities because subordinates are highly motivated to construct favorable self-views. We were uncertain as to whether Eden's work fit best with individual- or relational-level identities because, although the effects of favorable self-views are more important with individual-level identities, the role of leaders as sources of feedback may be enhanced by relational identities. Consequently, we mention this line of research in both sections.

Brewer and Gardner (1996) emphasized that relational-level identities are based on role relations. Consistent with this position, leadership research has found that role learning and reliable role performance are key determinants of social interactions at dyadic levels (Graen & Scandura, 1987). However, because affective attachment is a key issue at this identity level, we would expect the key medium for role clarification between leaders and followers to be more affective than cognitive. Affect is also central to relational processes between leaders and followers because it conveys acceptable role performance, implies similarity in terms of attitudes and values, and creates an ego-enhancing basis for subordinates to identify with

male leaders at upper organizational levels—namely, the lack of same-gender, higher level leaders to serve as role models and mentors. This absence is likely to be especially limiting for women, because their relational orientation would make mentors more helpful to them than for employees with individual or collective identities.

It is important to emphasize that many types of self-relevant processes may be influenced by the mentoring relationship. For example, individual skill levels and differences in work outcomes are still important, but their interpretation is guided by the mentoring relationship. Ibarra's (1999) research on provisional selves, which was discussed earlier, provides a nice example of this point. That is, the concerns of managers in role transitions were still with self-development, but the way that they developed provisional selves differed when there was a mentor with whom there were strong affective bonds. We suspect that mentoring and other relational leadership processes can also be used to build a strong group-based identity. Indeed, this is likely to be an important aspect of transformational leadership through which individuals are integrated into larger social units. In contrast, if social relations are used to differentiate individuals from others, then leadership is likely to be perceived as more transactional.

Research on LMXs also illustrates the importance of leader–follower relationships. We already noted that early expectations and affective reactions predicted the quality of subsequent exchange relationships (Liden et al., 1993). The point we make here is simply that 30 years of research on LMXs has conclusively demonstrated the effect of exchange quality on a number of important organizational outcomes. Specifically, in a meta-analysis of this area of leadership research, Gerstner and Day (1997) found that the quality of the LMX was significantly related to job performance, satisfaction with supervision, overall satisfaction, commitment, role conflict (negative relation), role clarity, member competence, and turnover intentions (negative relation). After reviewing the extensive LMX literature, Gerstner and Day's conclusion was "we view the relationship with one's supervisor as a lens through which the entire work experience is viewed" (p. 840). Although not stated in terms of self-identities, this observation is quite consistent with the emphasis we have placed on the reflected self as communicated by leaders to followers. We would stress that many dyadic-level processes—LMX, mentoring, interactional justice, and reflected selves—are likely to be more important when relational identities are salient in employees' WSC.

Collective-Level Leadership

When the subordinate WSC is defined at this level, leadership practices that foster group- or organizational-level identities should be particularly effective. Unit rather than individual-level performance should be an overriding focus. Interestingly, Selenta and Lord (2002) found that at this level, group members may be particularly concerned with the status of their group as well as their own contribution to group performance; whereas at individual levels, performance concerns center on differentiating oneself from others. Rewards that focus on group outcomes are likely to be most important at collective levels, and concerns with procedural rather than distributive justice are likely to predominate. Note that, social norms rather than individual attitudes are likely to be major determinants of behavior (Ybarra & Trafimow, 1998) when collective identities predominate, and group members should be motivated by group welfare rather than individual gain.

This process is nicely illustrated by Illingworth's (2001) work. He manipulated independent- and collective-level identities and examined their moderating effect on the development of intentions to engage in organizational citizenship behavior (OCB). He found that an individual's own attitudes tended to be much better predictors of OCB intentions when independent- (individual-) level identities predominated than when interdependent- (relational- or collective-) level identities were elicited. The importance of situational norms in predicting OCB intentions showed the opposite moderating effect—being higher under interdependent than independent conditions—but this effect varied more with specific OCBs.

Such research suggests that one can expect much higher levels of organizational citizenship behaviors and processes like self-leadership (Neck, Stewart, & Manz, 1996) with collective-level identities. Thus, rather than being dependent on a formal leader, leadership processes may have more of an emergent quality, reflecting the confluence of a variety of system factors that impact an entire organizational unit as suggested elsewhere (Lord & W. G. Smith, 1999). With emergent leadership, any group member may exhibit leadership when their unique skills or experiences fit current demands, making leadership a process that is distributed across a group rather than being localized in a specific individual. Ireland and Hitt (1999) maintained that such distributed leadership processes are required for organizations to be successful in a knowledge economy.

Gehani and Lord (2003) extended this argument even further. They maintained that in industries for which there is rapid, technology-driven change (e.g., computers and polymers), the key knowledge for effectively spanning boundaries is likely to be localized in subordinates rather than leaders. Thus, timely innovation and vision will need to reflect subordinate rather than leader beliefs and perspectives even though leaders will still be accountable for financial performance and resource allocation. To facilitate such innovation, Gehani and Lord (2003) maintained that leaders need to learn to trust subordinates and they need to grant greater power and influence to subordinates. Such processes permit top-line growth or value creation rather than just bottom-line growth through cost cutting. The processes Gehani and Lord described amount to more than just empowering subordinates; they reflect temporary role reversals between leaders and followers. We suggest that such role reversals can work best where there is a clear group identity as well as norms that make true leadership from all group members acceptable. To be clear, we suggest that multiple-leader groups, not leaderless groups, are required in such industries.

Social Justice

Social justice involves many complex organizational processes, but there is an emerging consensus that social justice can be conceptualized in terms of three processes that parallel our three levels of identity: *distributive justice, interactional justice,* and *procedural justice.* Distributive justice pertains to perceptions of the fairness of outcome distributions. It seems most consistent with individual-level identities for a number of reasons. First, when the self is defined at the individual level, one's relative standing compared to others is critical to maintaining a favorable self-evaluation. Distributive justice concerns also emphasize the comparison of self to others on job-relevant dimensions because fairness of outcome distributions depends on the perceived ratio of outcomes to inputs for one's self as compared to others. In addition, outcomes often are important sources of feedback regarding one's relative performance in organizations; thus, outcomes may have an important symbolic value when the self is defined at an individual level. An emphasis on distributive justice also is consistent with a social exchange orientation, which is characteristic of transactional leadership. Thus, one would expect that transactional leadership, an emphasis on distribution of rewards, and an individual-level identity all would be mutually compatible.

When the self is defined at a relational level, a different set of concerns is likely to be salient. Specifically, interactional justice or the treatment of subordinates in a manner that conveys dignity and respect is likely to be crucial. Such treatment symbolically communicates to subordinates that they are valued by the leader and their organization (Tyler, 1997; Tyler, Degoey, & H. Smith, 1996; Tyler & Lind, 1992). Such behavior also communicates caring for another individual, a quality that is likely to be particularly important when the self is defined at a relational level. Because women are especially likely to have salient relational-level identities, relational treatment of female subordinates is likely to be particularly important. High levels of consideration and more participative leadership styles may be especially effective for leaders in such situations.

When collective aspects of self-identities are salient, procedural justice is likely to be particularly important. This is because procedural justice indicates that processes and policies are applied in a consistent manner across individuals, benefitting all members of a group or collective, and the welfare of the group as a whole is the primary concern when collective-level identities are salient. Also, extensive research consistently shows that when procedural justice is high, followers are less likely to base justice perceptions on their own outcomes (Brockner & Wiesenfeld, 1996).

Although this suggested parallel between identity levels and social justice has not received much research attention, there is some supporting empirical evidence. Baker (1998) investigated how social communications can prime different identity levels and also influence the salience of social justice concerns. To do this, she adopted Brewer and Gardner's (1996) technique and experimentally manipulated the identity cues inherent in social communications using *I* and *me* pronouns to prime individual levels and *us* and *we* to prime collective levels. This simple manipulation of pronouns in instructions to an experimental task affected the importance of outcome, treatment, and structural neutrality standards for social justice, with outcomes being more important with individual-level cues and treatment and structural neutrality being more important with collective level cues. Tyler's (1997) work indicates that both a leader's perceived legitimacy and subordinates' affective relations with leaders are likely to be more dependent on procedural justice when subordinates identify with a leader. Identification may be increased by value congruence or membership in a common ethnic group.

Our research on social justice (Johnson et al., 2003) nicely illustrates the effects of identity levels. We predicted questionnaire ratings of satisfaction with one's supervisor from the four measures of justice developed by Colquitt (2001). Colquitt separated interactional justice into two separate scales—Interpersonal Justice and Informational Justice. We found that all four types of justice (distributive, informational, interpersonal, and procedural) significantly predicted satisfaction with one's supervisor (beta weights were .13, .33, .34, and .18, respectively). Equally important, we found a significant interaction between interpersonal justice and both identity and gender. Specifically, the strength of the relationship between interpersonal justice and satisfaction with one's supervisor increased with Selenta and Lord's (2002) concern for others measure of relational identities that was described in Table 3.2. Interpersonal justice was also a stronger predictor for women than for men (the beta weight for women was .21 higher than for men). Thus, interpersonal justice perceptions were more important for women and for individuals with relational identities.

One problem with most justice-related research is insufficient differentiation of interdependent identities. Typically, if identities are addressed at all, only the distinction between independent and interdependent identity levels are made. However, we strongly believe that there are important interdependent-level distinctions (relational vs. collective levels) that have gender relevance and also may moderate the importance of interactional versus procedural justice. For example, in the study just mentioned, we did not find collective-level identity dimensions to moderate the importance of social justice scales.

A study by Lind, Kray, and Thompson (1998) nicely illustrates the consequence of ignoring identity levels, which is a problem with many studies of social justice. Using an exemplary experimental design to investigate the impact of social injustice to others verus personally experienced injustice (denial of voice in both instances), they demonstrated that personally experienced injustice had a much greater impact. However, their subjects were essentially strangers who were participating in part for rewards that were distributed at an individual level (all members of groups were participants in a separate lottery for a $100 prize). One would expect that very different preferences might have resulted if a group-based reward structure had been used or if members of the group had a common identity. Alternatively, one might have expected that injustice to oneself versus others might have varied with individual differences among subjects in the tendency to form individual-, relational-, or collective-level identities.

It is important to realize that social justice is not just of academic interest, but it is important to many applied issues. Furthermore, justice and identity are intertwined, as we just mentioned. Consider, for example, the problems faced when large corporations such as Chrysler and Daimler-Benz merge. A common problem in mergers such as this is creating a common identity from different firms with different cultures. Common identities are required to facilitate cooperation across the many functional areas in a combined organization. Such cooperation is needed to allow technology transfer and joint product development. To create integrated identities, leaders must develop strategies to facilitate integration and symbolize a collective- rather than individual-level identity. Unfortunately, in the case of Chrysler and Daimler-Benz and many other mergers, executives who constructed the merger received huge benefits, whereas many lower level employees lost their jobs. Such results symbolize individual- rather than group-oriented concerns on the part of leadership because they emphasize distributive rather than procedural justice and benefits were given to a few individuals but not to all groups. The consequence is that group identities, cross-firm coordination, and the hoped-for synergy used to justify mergers is then much less likely to occur.

One may ask why individual as opposed to collective identities would affect the behavior of individuals in work contexts. There are several answers. First, as Kuhnen, Hannover, and Schubert (2001) showed, individual identities foster self-focused, context-independent forms of information processing rather than context-oriented ways of processing information that are associated with collective identities. This effect can be understood in terms of Fig. 3.1 and 3.2 because the constraints on the WSC arise from individual rather than social values when individual rather than social identities are salient. Thus, possibilities for synergy suggested by a new context may be more likely to be missed when individual compared to collective identities are salient after mergers. Also, as already noted, research shows that behavior is more dependent on individual attitudes and values than on group norms when individual identities are salient (Illingworth, 2001; Ybarra & Trafimow, 1998). Recent research also shows that collective identities and leader self-sacrificing behavior help transform goals from being proself to prosocial (De Cremer, 2002; De Cremer & van Knippenberg, 2002), with cooperative behavior being more likely when prosocial goals are activated. Thus, several lines of research converge to show that the information-processing, normative, and motivational bases of behavior all change when collective rather than individual identities are created by leaders. We expect that with most mergers such identities are required to help integrate the formerly separate parts into a new, interdependent organization. This cannot be done well when leaders' own outcomes symbolize an orientation toward a "me first" mentality rather than a collective orientation.

CONCLUSIONS

In sum, in this chapter we argued that leadership processes are likely to be quite different when different types of identities predominate. To be effective, leadership processes need to operate differently at each level. Although all people have individual, relational, and collective identities, we explained that qualitatively different cognitive, motivational, and social processes occur when each of these three levels is the focus of the WSC. We also suggested that, due to these powerful differences, these three self-identity levels are likely to operate as boundary conditions for specific leadership theories. We can now more fully elaborate this suggestion in the following proposition:

> Proposition 3.5. Identity level is a critical boundary variable for leadership theory, with the importance of many social and leadership processes varying with identity level.
>
> 3.5a. When the self is defined at the individual level, leader expectancy effects, effects of performance feedback, effects of contingent rewards, and procedures related to distributive justice will have greater effects on subordinate behavior and attitudes.
>
> 3.5b. When the self is defined at the relational level, perceived and actual leader–subordinate congruence in attitudes and values, leader affective behaviors, and interactional justice will have greater effects on subordinate behavior and attitudes.
>
> 3.5c. When the self is defined at the group (or organizational) level, structural aspects of procedural justice, organizational identities, and team-based or collective leadership will have greater effects on the behavior and attitudes of group members.

Practical Implications

The theory we laid out in this chapter implies that leaders face a rather daunting task in terms of understanding differences among subordinates in identity levels and in appropriately adjusting both a leader's own behavior and other organizational practices. We agree. Although we expect that leaders who are higher in terms of social intelligence will tend to be most successful in making such adjustments, it seems that the social perceptiveness requirement exceeds the capabilities of even the most sensitive individuals.

What then might be the value of this approach? We think there are several very practical benefits. First, emerging measurement techniques (e.g., Selenta & Lord, 2002) suggest that subordinates can be systematically assessed in terms of identity levels. Thus, there is certainly the potential to use scientific measurement approaches rather than naive social perceptions as an input to leadership processes. Organizations might benefit from careful assessment of their subordinates' identity levels and a systematic analysis of whether they are compatible with desired human resource management practices, organizational climate and culture, and leadership practices. Of particular importance is the potential to understand some gender-related leadership issues in terms of womens' emphasis on relational identities compared to mens' emphasis on collective identities. Second, following such systematic assessment, leadership training could be developed that assists leaders in developing and practicing a leadership style that complements self-concept related processes. Third, and perhaps most important, such an approach implies a need to integrate leadership activities and other motivational and procedural processes in organizations. Consideration of desired worker identity levels could be an important component of an organization's human resources management strategy. Certainly such an approach is consistent with a more scientific and systems-based approach to leadership than are more naive theories that merely focus on a leader's traits or behaviors.

SUMMARY

In this chapter, we explained how the self can be defined at three alternative levels—individual, relational, and collective—and stressed that both self-regulatory and interpersonal processes may operate differently at each level. We reviewed evidence showing that self-focus and values vary with identity levels, and we also found that social justice processes and identity levels were likely to interact. Gender is also likely to affect identity levels, with women emphasizing relational identities and men emphasizing collective identities. Finally, we suggested that identity level operates as an important boundary level for leadership theories, and we offered a general principle of effective leadership—that it should be matched to a subordinate's identity level.

4

Temporary and Enduring Effects of Leaders

In chapters 2 and 3 we developed a structural model of subordinates' self-concepts with many implications: The self-concept is composed of a variety of schema; only a limited number of schema are activated at one time (e.g., WSC); the WSC involves self-views, current goals, and future selves that vary with individual, relational, and collective levels; hierarchies of control systems link task contexts and the self and personal or social values; and the self has an underlying temporal dimension connecting the past, present, and future. Although the structural foundation of subordinates' self-concepts is important, of equal relevance for leadership scholars is the interplay between leaders and this structure. Once the processes that underlie the connection between leaders and subordinates are understood, scientifically based linkages can be established.

In this chapter we discuss this dyadic process abstractly, and in subsequent chapters we deal explicitly with how processes like affect and social justice interact with structure to create organizationally relevant outcomes from leadership. For organizational purposes, the present chapter is divided into two sections. In the first portion of this chapter we discuss how leaders can have short-term effects on their subordinates. Here, our discussion centers on a leader's capacity to activate different schemas temporarily within subordinates' WSCs. Following this discussion, we examine the potential of leaders to alter a subordinate's self-concept permanently by creating new highly accessible self-schemas.

TEMPORARY EFFECTS

As noted in chapter 2, the self is a dynamic, multifaceted structure that contains many more schemas than can be activated at any given moment in time (Markus & Wurf, 1987; Martindale, 1980). Instead of possessing a single monolithic self, individuals possess an array of compartmentalized selves (Kihlstrom & S. B. Klein, 1994; Markus & Wurf, 1987). Although the notion of a multitude of self-concepts may seem strange to industrial–organizational psychologists and organizational behavior researchers, as noted previously, contextual flexibility is widely accepted in social and cognitive psychology. Multiple, dynamic selves allow people to adjust and adapt to their social worlds. In the language we utilized in prior chapters, the composition of the WSC shifts with circumstance—the Little League coach and corporate CEO reflect different selves even when they are the same person.

The notion of a multidimensional self has important implications for leadership theorists. Logically, if the self is a dynamic, shifting structure, then leaders should be capable of exerting some control over the nature of these shifts. In so doing, leaders can indirectly influence their subordinates' behavior, thoughts, and feelings. We elaborate on this form of leadership in the remainder of this section, discuss supporting research, and provide illustrative examples.

Impact of the Organizational Environment on the Self

Categorization and Behavior.   If the WSC is highly susceptible to context as suggested, then both shifts between (e.g., different CEOs) and within (e.g., different supervisors) organizations may have the potential to impact dramatically the aspects of the self that become activated in the WSC. How these contextual shifts influence a subordinate's self-concept is a function of the basic perceptual mechanisms that underlie human cognition.

In our day-to-day activities, we do not simply react to environmental stimuli, we interpret and transform our environments into meaningful internal symbolic structures (Lord & Maher, 1991). Perception is not passive. People make sense of their environmental surroundings by automatically categorizing these events into meaningful semantic structures. For example, when we see a person, we do not see the features that make up the person (e.g., nose, hair, ears, mouth, and legs), but instead we see some meaningful gestalt or category, which we then attach to the individual stimulus (e.g., man, woman, African American, nurse, doctor, or brother).

Thus, rather than being confined to understanding the world in terms of the surface-level features that are readily available, the world is understood in terms of its deeper meaning, particularly its deeper meaning relative to the self. For example, as discussed in the previous chapter, social justice is often interpreted in terms of what it implies regarding the worth of the self to a group, to a specific role relationship, or in comparison to others.

As with any other environment, organizational settings and their participants can be categorized. And this categorization process is an important aspect of how organizational actors interpret and make sense of their surroundings (Weick, 1995). As members of an organization, we can categorize the environment as a threat or an opportunity (Jackson & Dutton, 1988), something to be approached or avoided (Higgins, 1998), as play or work (Glynn, 1994), or as a collectivistic or individualistic setting. Similarly, organizational actors can be categorized into in-group or out-group members (Tyler, 1997), White or African American, supervisor or subordinate, and leader or nonleader (Lord et al., 1984). Such categorization simplifies both perceptual processes and the generation of appropriate responses (Macrae, Milne, & Bodenhausen, 1994). Regardless of the categories used, the role of categorization in simplifying behavior, thought, and feeling remains. Ultimately, *how* we categorize our current situation influences *who* we are (i.e., coach or CEO).

The ease and effectiveness of categorization processes is highlighted in research conducted by Glynn (1994). Glynn hypothesized that categorization of a task as play or work can affect the manner in which a task is completed. To examine this possibility, Glynn recruited 82 graduate business students and had them perform 12 different word puzzles under one of two instruction sets. Participants in the work condition received instructions that utilized work-related words in reference to the task and materials (e.g., *raw material* and *production standard*), whereas individuals in the play condition received instructions that utilized play-related words (e.g., *clue* and *rules of the game*). Consistent with Glynn's a priori expectation, subjects performing under the work-related conditions were more oriented to quantity of responses, whereas those performing under play conditions were more oriented to the quality of their responses. In addition, Glynn's study also indicated that differences in intrinsic motivation existed between the two conditions. Not surprising, a task categorized as play is more intrinsically appealing than one categorized as work. Overall, Glynn's research, as well as others (e.g., Steele, Spencer, & Aronson, 2002), highlights the importance of perceptual categorization on self-regulatory mechanisms.

In part, categorization processes are necessitated by the limitations of our information-processing capacities. Humans do not possess the cognitive resources or the time to analyze each situation or organizational configuration that they confront. Instead, adaptable behavior requires a quick, effortless, and perhaps even nonconscious interpretation of our environmental surroundings. Categories allow us to move effortlessly beyond the information that is given to activate other relevant information, some of which is self-relevant (Macrae et al., 1994). They also allow us to respond quickly to stimuli using generic, category-based responses, rather than manufacturing a new response on the spot. Such processes, which have been called *recognition-primed decision making* (Durso & Gronlund, 1999), increase efficiency by substituting accumulated knowledge for effortful information processing once it is recognized that the situation is a type that has been encountered in the past. The organization and information inherent in self-structures facilitates such knowledge-based responses because the critical recognition is that the situation is familiar to the self. For example, "I (or we) have been here before."

Consistent with this position, Higgins (1996) metaphorically referred to the self as a digest, with different chapters of our self-concepts being aligned to different environmental contingencies. As Higgins noted, a digest "summarizes a body of information, especially contingency rules and conclusions" (p. 1063). From Higgins' viewpoint, the self-digest captures the idea that self-knowledge summarizes information about oneself as an object, facilitating adaptation to our external environment. Ultimately, Higgins' position on the self suggests that how an individual categorizes his or her environment can have self-relevant implications.

Priming and Schema Accessibility.   Perceptual categories are capable of temporarily *priming* or *inhibiting* related aspects of the self (Higgins & Brendl, 1995), which either increases or decreases the salience of schema within an individual's WSC. Priming simply means that aspects of the immediate information-processing context can temporarily make some schemas more accessible than others and consequently more likely to be used in interpreting or responding to other stimuli, often without any conscious awareness of this schema activation process by perceivers. Inhibition makes schemas less accessible and less likely to be used in interpreting stimuli or generating responses.

This priming process is displayed in Fig. 4.1. As indicated, the categorization of the broader social environment as supportive or unsupportive may

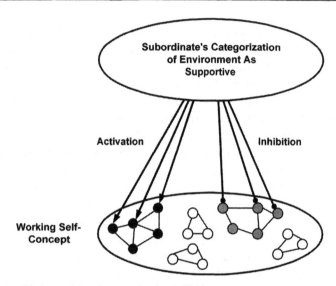

FIG. 4.1.   Priming and the schema-activation–inhibition process.

influence the aspects of the self that are most accessible. In a supportive organizational environment, an individual's WSC may become dominated by
schemas associated with security, self-confidence, and mastery-related
goals; whereas in an unsupportive environment, an individual's WSC may
become dominated by schemas associated with insecurity, low self-confidence, and performance-related goals. Although such relationships are
speculative, the main point is that environmental categorization will increase the activation of some portions of the self while decreasing the activation of other portions of the self. Thus, activation and inhibition are two
means by which the categorization of environments affects self-schemas
and behavior.

A substantial amount of research supports the linkages between the environment and the self (e.g., Baldwin, 1994; Bargh et al., 1996; Chen &
Bargh, 1997; Levy, 1996; Neuberg, 1988; Shoda, Mischel, & Wright,
1994). To provide but one example, Bargh et al. (1996) showed how priming different aspects of the self can influence an individual's thoughts, affect, and behavior. In particular, they examined what would happen if rude
or polite self-views were activated within research participants. To accom-
plish this objective, Bargh et al. randomly assigned subjects to complete
one of three types of scrambled sentence tasks. Some participants unscrambled sentences that contained words associated with rudeness (e.g., *bold*
and *brazen*); other subjects unscrambled sentences that contained words

associated with politeness (e.g., *considerate* and *polite*); and a third, control group unscrambled sentences that contained neutral words (e.g., *exercising* and *send*).

The key dependent variable in Bargh et al.'s study (1996) was how long the research participant would wait before interrupting the experimenter. As part of the instructions for the study, subjects were informed to get the experimenter when they had completed the unscrambled sentence task. However, when subjects found the experimenter, he was engaged in a conversation with a second individual who was a confederate. Not surprising given our previous discussion, participants who had been primed to think of themselves as being polite were less likely to interrupt the experimenter's conversation than participants who had been primed to think of themselves as rude. In fact, although over 60% of those subjects primed to think of themselves as rude interrupted the experimenter within 10 min, less than 20% of those primed to think of themselves as polite did so. Such dramatic results suggest that human categorization of the environment influences action and that the self can be easily and automatically manipulated by seemingly insignificant contextual information. Moreover, this research also suggests that perceivers are not aware of this process.

Although Bargh et al.'s (1996) results may seem impressive, interesting, and perhaps even entertaining to many leadership scholars, some readers may view such examples as tangential for understanding leadership. We, however, believe that the underlying processes investigated by researchers such as Bargh do generalize directly to the leadership field. In fact, they provide the basis for a general proposition that underlies much of the reasoning in this chapter:

> Proposition 4.1. Effective leadership will be directly proportional to the degree to which leaders are able to prime relevant aspects of a subordinate's self-concept.

Given their status and power within most organizational contexts, as well as the fact that they are important sources of feedback and rewards, a leaders' actions, behaviors, and rhetoric are likely to be salient to all subordinates. Consequently, leaders are very potent primes for subordinate knowledge structures. As such, leaders can exert an enormous amount of control over which aspects of the self-concept are most highly activated. In the next two sections, we provide two concrete examples of how leaders can prime different aspects of a subordinate's self-concept.

Communication.   Two subtle priming mechanisms that are available to leaders are the verbal and nonverbal messages that they communicate to subordinates. Language is a social tool that is used to communicate meaning. Coherent themes in a leader's communications provide an interpretive structure for subordinates in their environmental sense-making attempts (Weick, 1979). The extent to which supervisors can influence environmental interpretations through their use of verbal communications is illustrated in many areas of the organizational behavior literature.

In the justice literature, for example, Greenberg (1994) used a field experiment to examine how a company president's delivery style influenced employees' responses to a smoking ban. In this study, participants were presented with one of four taped messages regarding the smoking ban that differed in one of two ways. First, the message presented was either high or low in terms of thoroughness. Second, the message was either delivered in an interpersonally sensitive or insensitive fashion. That is, the message varied in terms of interactional justice. Interestingly, employees' acceptance of the message was dramatically influenced by these two factors. Both thoroughness and sensitivity had the expected effects on reactions to the message. For example, reactions to the sensitive message were more positive than reactions to the insensitive message. Moreover, the effect was stronger for those individuals who smoked than those who were nonsmokers. In effect, Greenberg's study suggests that the communication style exhibited by a leader can influence the meaning of an organizational message. Findings such as Greenberg's are not isolated to smoking bans and have been found across a wide assortment of negative outcomes (e.g., Brockner & Wiesenfeld, 1996).

Not only can the style of communication restructure the interpretive theme that is attached to events by subordinates, it can also influence the aspects of the self that are most highly activated. Supervisory rhetoric conveys meaning to subordinates and, as a result, increases the salience of those aspects of the self-concept that are most appropriate to the meaning attached to current circumstances. Brewer and Gardner's (1996) research suggests that self-relevant shifts may be as easily accomplished as changing pronoun usage. Specifically; they found that dramatic shifts occur when individuals are exposed to the pronouns *we* versus *they*. Brewer and Gardner had subjects complete a word search task that predominantly contained the pronouns *we* or the pronoun *they*. Following the search task, subjects completed an ostensibly separate task, one that required a self-description. Not surprising, subjects exposed to the *we* pronoun had a collective-level identity primed to a greater extent than subjects in the *they* condition. Lest the reader think that such pronoun priming effects are isolated occurrences, it should be noted that similar findings have been reported both in additional studies conducted by Gardner (e.g., Gardner, Gabriel, & Lee, 1999) and by independent researchers (Baker, 1998). Overall, these results suggest that the language used by a leader can activate very different aspects of the self.

Recognizing the power of words, a number of leading leadership scholars have begun to explore the language of leadership (Conger, 1991). For example, Shamir, Arthur, and House (1994; also see C. G. Emrich, Brower, Feldman, & Garland, 2001) persuasively argued that charismatic leaders can be differentiated from their noncharismatic counterparts by their speech patterns. Interestingly, the pattern of communication discussed by these researchers, and which is relevant to our model of self, is the tendency for charismatic leaders to make numerous references to the collective identity of subordinates. According to Shamir et al., relative to noncharismatic leaders, charismatic leaders make more references to the collective history and collective interest of the group while making fewer references to individual self-interest. Consistent with the position advanced by Shamir et al. (1994), Fiol, Harris, and House (1999) found that charismatic leaders used more inclusive language such as *us* and *we* rather than *I* and *you*.

This pattern of language usage among charismatic leaders is particularly interesting to us insofar as it may reflect one of the primary mechanisms through which leaders reorient their subordinates from individual- to collective-level concerns (Bass, 1985). Although much is known about the content of charismatic leadership behavior, little is known about the psychological processes that underlie these effects (Bass, 1999). Based on our previous discussion, we think that it is reasonable to postulate that the language used by charismatic leaders primes collective identities within subordinates. Once activated, these primed collective identities serve to guide subordinate behavior, perceptions, and feelings (e.g., organizational commitment or sacrifice).

Self-Representations Cued by Leaders.   For nearly 100 years, social psychologists have posited that the self-concept adjusts to accommodate our immediate social audiences. Symbolic interactionists (e.g., Mead, 1934), for example, have argued that an individual's self-concept is, to a large degree, based on communications from significant others.

Similarly, W. James (1890, p. 294) noted that an individual has as many selves as persons about whose opinion he or she cares. Cooley (1902) suggested that, in the presence of significant others, individuals tend to adopt the significant other's view of the self. Aron and McLaughlin-Volpe (2001) went even farther, maintaining that we incorporate the identities of significant others into the self.

Anecdotal reports from the business world corroborate the theoretical position of these early social psychologists. For example, Aiko Morita, one of the co-founders of Sony, was once described by a former employee as possessing two distinct personalities, each of which came out in the presence of different audiences (Japanese vs. Western). This employee reported that "Morita was really two personalities: when speaking English—with which he was totally at home—he had a casual, effusive air and an active humorous streak, while in Japanese he was much more the formal corporate leader" (Masters, 2000, p. H2). As this quote illustrates, Morita was profoundly affected by his changing social audience. Similarly, theory and observation suggest that different types of leaders are capable of shifting activation within an individual's self-concept, thereby activating different WSCs.

Other empirical work further bolsters the notion that leaders may be able to influence the aspects of the self-concept that are most salient at any given moment in time (e.g., Baldwin, 1992, 1994, 1997; Baldwin, Carrell, & Lopez, 1990; Baldwin & Holmes, 1987; Baldwin, Keelan, Fehr, Enns, & Koh-Rangarajoo, 1997; Baldwin & Sinclair, 1996). Using a wide variety of techniques, Baldwin and his colleagues showed empirically that self-relevant judgments are changed when the social audience is changed. For instance, Baldwin and Holmes (1987, Study 1) had college women either visualize a college acquaintance or an older family member. Following a 10-min filler task, subjects rated the enjoyability of a sexually permissive piece of fiction, an ostensibly unrelated task. Results indicated a significant difference in the reported enjoyability of the passage for the two visualization groups. Specifically, subjects asked to visualize an older family member reported that the sexually oriented passage was much less enjoyable to read than subjects who had visualized a college acquaintance. Consistent with our position and Baldwin and Holmes' (1987) data, the moment-to-moment construction of the WSC is influenced by our immediate social world.

Although Baldwin's many studies we just referenced (also see McGuire & Padawer-Singer, 1976) have documented links among social audiences, such as grandparents, and attitudes, his research has not explicitly examined whether organizational leaders have a similar impact; nor does it connect leaders to a subordinate's self-concept. Recent data we collected addresses both of these issues (Brown, 2000). In this research, Brown demonstrated that activating the image of an individual's supervisor directly influenced an individual's self-esteem.

Brown (2000) predicted that when leaders were salient, the stored mental representation a subordinate held for his or her immediate supervisor would exert a profound influence over a subordinate's conceptualization of self. He anticipated that supervisors who were perceived to focus on negative outcomes or who were transactional would have a negative impact on the self-concept of followers. In contrast, he speculated that supervisors who were perceived to focus on positive outcomes or who were transformational would have a positive impact on the self-concept of followers. To examine these ideas, a two-session laboratory investigation was conducted in which subjects completed a series of measures regarding their immediate work supervisors and additional significant others (these additional significant others were included to disguise the purpose of the study). Subjects then returned to the lab 2 weeks later to ostensibly complete an experiment dealing with visualization ability. At this session, subjects were randomly assigned to either visualize their immediate work supervisor or an inanimate object (the student center on campus). Importantly, this study used a double-blind procedure in which neither the experimenter nor the subject knew the conditions to which subjects were assigned. The purpose of the leader visualization task was to increase the salience of the leader to participants assigned to this condition. Upon completion of the visualization task, subjects were asked to complete a series of additional tasks that were being piloted for use in future studies. In reality, these tasks were the true dependent variables in our research. A measure of state self-esteem that was embedded among these measures is of primary interest in the context of our discussion.

In keeping with the expectations outlined earlier, a pattern of findings emerged which suggested that leaders do have an enormous influence over the aspects of a subordinate's self-concept that are most salient at any given point in time. After controlling for *trait self-esteem* (a chronic individual difference), we found that *state self-esteem* (which is situationally dependent) was largely determined by the content of a subordinate's mental representation of his or her supervisor. For example, an instrument tapping the degree to which a supervisor focused on mistakes and errors versus positive outcomes was significantly related to self-reported state self-esteem in the supervisory visualization condition but not in the neutral object visualization condition ($r = .37$ and $r = .03$, respectively). Similarly, a significant relationship was found between transformational leadership and state self-esteem in the supervisory visualization condition, but not in the neutral object visualization condition ($r = .28$ and $r = -.18$, respectively). Thus, these aspects of supervisors, which were measured 2 weeks earlier, affected subject's self-esteem only when they were in the supervisor visualization condition.

A recent laboratory study conducted by Paul, Costley, Howell, Dorfman, and Trafimow (2001) provides additional evidence that leaders can prime different aspects of the self-concept of observers. Paul et al. examined whether charismatic leaders increase the accessibility of the collective self-concept. To investigate this possibility, Paul et al. randomly assigned 353 participants to read written vignettes that described a charismatic leader, an individually considerate leader, or a combination of the two. Following exposure to the leader measure, participants completed a measure to assess collective self-concept activation. Interestingly, their results indicated that participants exposed to a charismatic leader had significantly higher activation of the collective self-concept relative to those in the individual consideration condition.

Results such as those reported by Paul et al. (2001) and Brown (2000) are important because they demonstrate that leaders, as members of a subordinate's work environment, can prime different aspects of a subordinate's self-concept. However, these findings may be conservative estimates of the true leader-priming effect that occurs in actual work settings. This is because the Brown (2000) prime was a recalled mental image, not the actual leader, and the experiment was conducted in a context that is entirely different from the work environment (i.e., a university lab). Thus, many of the physical cues that serve to support the leader prime were not available. Similarly Paul et al.'s (2001) study was again an experiment outside of a normal work context, and the leader observed was not the subject's actual leader. We would anticipate that stronger effects would be found in organizational settings with the physical presence of a leader serving as a prime.

In addition to the two priming examples discussed thus far, leaders can influence subordinates' WSC through a myriad of additional ways. The goals, feedback, policies, visions, values, performance evaluation, and compensation patterns implemented by leaders can also serve as powerful environmental constraints on which aspects of a subordinate's WSC is most salient. For example, collectively-oriented goals, feedback, and compensation should all increase the activation of collective aspects of the WSC. Despite our belief that leadership priming is a robust phenomenon, its efficacy may be bounded by at least four factors: the strength of the prime source, the salience of the prime source, subordinate sensitivity to leaders, and the accessibility of the primed self-structure within the subordinate. These moderators are shown in Fig. 4.2, and each of these boundary factors is discussed in the next few sections.

Moderators of Temporary Leadership-Priming Effects

The Strength of the Prime.   The degree to which any event will prime aspects of the WSC is dependent on the strength of the prime source (e.g., the leader). Because priming operates through networks of units, the more strongly activated a construct is, the more activation that will be available to spread to related constructs in these networks. In simple terms, the previous proposition implies that weak primes will have weak effects, whereas strong primes will have strong effects.

Several factors may limit the strength of the leadership-priming effect. One factor that can undermine leadership priming is the consistency of a leader's words, actions, and behaviors. This is because there are inhibitory connections between diametrically different schema (e.g., individual-level self and collective-level self). Thus, leaders who simultaneously activate two incompatible aspects of an individual's self-concept will have a muted effect on the availability of schema in their subordinates. For example, if a leader's verbal communications prime an individual level of identity but the

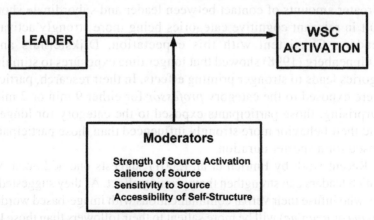

FIG. 4.2.   Moderators of temporary leadership-priming effects.

goals he or she assigns emphasize a collective level of identity, then these two sources of influence will counteract one another (e.g., "*I* want you to cooperate" rather than "*We* need you to cooperate")

As a result of these processes, leaders must take great care to ensure that their actions and words form a coherent symbolic representation to subordinates. Incongruent aspects of the self will either negate one another; produce behavior that is inconsistent over time; or, at a minimum, the less dominant aspect of the self (e.g., the one not activated as highly) will weaken the activation of the more dominant portion of the self. Consequently, not only must a leader's words and actions be consistent to activate desired aspects of a subordinate's WSC effectively, they must also operate in conjunction with other salient primes that may be available in the work setting.

Salience of the Prime Source. In addition to the strength of the prime, the leadership priming effect will also depend on a leader's salience to his or her subordinates. In effect, a leader's actions, words, and policies cannot prime subordinates if they are not perceived. Although this idea has not received direct scrutiny, it is congruent with findings that have been reported in the leadership literature. Howell and Hall-Merenda (1999), for example, found that transformational leaders had a stronger effect on their subordinates when they were physically close as opposed to distant. These findings make sense in terms both of the priming framework developed thus far and recent research findings. Sensibly, physically close leaders will spend greater amounts of time with their subordinates than those who are not as physically close. Greater amounts of contact between leader and subordinate should result in relevant cognitive categories being more strongly activated by leaders. Consistent with this expectation, Dijksterhuis and van Knippenberg (1998) showed that longer time exposures to stimulus categories leads to stronger priming effects. In their research, participants were exposed to the category *professor* for either 9 min or 2 min. Not surprising, those participants exposed to the category for longer time had their behavior more strongly influenced than those participants exposed for a shorter duration.

Recent work by Emrich et al. (2001) suggests one additional way in which leaders can strengthen their priming effect. As they suggested, leaders who infuse their verbal communications with image-based words (e.g., *dream* or *imagine*) will be more salient to their followers than those leaders who infuse their communications with concept-based words (e.g., *produce*, *idea*, or *think*). In part, the strength of image-based communications lies in the fact that this form of communication is more emotionally arousing (e.g., Miller & Marks, 1997) and is more richly connected and easily remembered (e.g., Paivio, 1986) than concept-based communications. As a result of these emotional and memorial differences, we anticipate that image-based communications will generate stronger priming effects than concept-based communications.

Subordinate Sensitivity to Leaders.   It is also likely that subordinates will be more strongly primed when they are sensitive to their leaders. Both personal and environmental factors may play a role in determining a subordinate's sensitivity to the leader. Individual differences among subordinates are not under the control of the leader, but environmental factors that enhance sensitivity to leadership may be controllable by leaders.

Individual differences in subordinates are likely to moderate the strength of the leadership priming effect. All else being equal, we believe that subordinates who are sensitive to their external environments will be more strongly influenced by their leaders than their less environmentally-focused colleagues. For example, individuals high in public self-consciousness (e.g., Fenigstein et al., 1975), high in self-monitoring (Snyder, 1979), or high in collective identities (Kuhnen et al., 2001) may be particularly sensitive to the actions of their leaders; thus, they may be more likely to be primed by a leader's actions and communications. In addition to broad individual differences, individual differences that are more relevant to the leadership field may also influence the ability of leaders to prime aspects of a subordinate's WSC. For example, Meindl and Erlich (1987) proposed that individuals differ in their romantic notions of leaders. In essence, individuals differ in the degree to which they view leaders as focal causes of organizational events. The strength of these romantic notions of leadership should be related to the priming effect discussed thus far.

In addition to individual differences among perceivers increasing the salience of a leader, broader environmental factors can also have a similar effect. Because subordinates look to their leaders to provide direction, leaders become particularly important during times of crisis. By their very definition, crises increase uncertainty and ambiguity which, in turn, increases the likelihood that direction will be sought from one's social groups (Festinger, 1954) in general and a group's leaders in particular. Consistent with this expecta-

under the guidance of either a transformational or transactional leader. Because Asian Americans tend to have more salient collective self-identities and Whites tend to have more salient individual self-identities (Markus & Kitayama, 1991), transformational leaders should have a stronger impact on Asian Americans than Whites. In fact, Jung and Avolio found that Asian Americans working under the guidance of a transformational leader generated a greater number of ideas in an idea generation task than did Whites. In contrast, the reverse pattern was found when the leader adopted a transactional leadership style (which is more individualistic).

On the surface, Jung and Avolio's (1999) findings and other leadership researchers' perspectives (e.g., Shamir et al., 1993) suggest that a leader's behavior must be matched with a subordinate's self-concept. This also was the logic underlying our Proposition 3.5 which stated that leadership is more effective when matched to a subordinate's identity level. Although this is an important principle for understanding leadership, our focus on the WSC and multiple selves implies some flexibility in subordinates. Both collectivists and individualists possess the alternative self-construal. What does differ between these two groups is how easily each aspect of the self can be activated. As a result of this flexibility, given sufficiently strong primes, collectivists can be made to act like individualists and individualists can be made to act like collectivists. Thus, effective leadership when leaders emphasize identity levels not central to subordinates is not impossible, it is just likely to be substantially harder, requiring stronger and more consistent influence attempts, and it may be successful with a smaller proportion of subordinates.

Research supports the idea that the WSC can be influenced by situational information. For instance, Gardner et al. (1999) utilized the pronoun-priming task to prime residents of Hong Kong and the United States with either a matched (e.g., United States with individualistic and Hong Kong with collectivistic) or mismatched identity (e.g., United States with collectivistic and Hong Kong with individualistic). Importantly, the results of this research indicated that participants' self-construals shifted to match the prime. Thus, as a whole, Hong Kong residents responded like residents of the U.S. when primed with the individualistic prime, and United States residents responded like Hong Kong residents when primed with the collective prime. Overall, results such as these demonstrate that the self is a flexible structure, one that adapts to strong, salient environmental contingencies.

Keep in mind, however, that this research shows shifts in group means associated with primes. It is also likely that these distributions overlapped substantially. The Hong Kong subjects with the strongest collective identities and the U.S. subjects with the strongest individual identities may have behaved in ways that were inconsistent with their group's mean. Practicing leaders, in contrast to researchers, are often concerned with the behavior of specific individuals rather than the group mean, and we suspect that there are far fewer individuals who will behave inconsistently with a leader's philosophy when it is matched to the predominant identity levels of subordinates.

Summary of Temporary Leadership Processes

Figure 4.2 provided a simple heuristic diagram of the short-run priming effects that we have discussed to this point. It shows that the degree to which leaders influence followers will be a function of four factors: the strength and coherence of a leader's priming activities, a leader's salience, a subordinate's sensitivity to leadership, and the ease with which different aspects of the self can be activated. Ultimately, effective short-term leadership effects will depend on the full alignment of all these processes, whereas weak or ineffectual short-term leadership effects will be due to a partial alignment of these three factors. These ideas are summarized in the following proposition:

Proposition 4.2. Leaders can prime subordinate identities through multiple means with the effectiveness of priming processes varying with (a) the strength and coherence of primes, (b) the salience of leaders, (c) subordinate sensitivity to leadership, and (d) follower differences in the ease with which different aspects of the self can be activated.

ENDURING LEADERSHIP EFFECTS

Although we believe that temporary priming effects can operate within organizational settings, these effects provide only a limited vista on leadership, reflecting effects that may last a few minutes, a few hours, or at most a few days. Such short-term priming cannot adequately account for how a leader extends his or her influence much beyond an immediate interaction. Most leadership scholars would accept the idea that effective leaders have effects that extend far beyond their immediate interactions with subordinates. An extreme example of an extended effect is the influence that an organization's founder can have on his or her organization when he or she is no longer associated with an organization (Schein, 1992). Any theory of leadership needs to be capable of explaining these enduring effects. Surprisingly, most leadership theories focus narrowly on short-run effects (e.g., contingency views or influence attempts), whereas the theories that are suggestive of long-term effects have not been adequately formalized in terms of the basic psychological mechanisms that could account for these effects (e.g., transformational leadership although currently popular, does not have a clearly specified process as noted in chap. 1). Based on our previous discussion of priming, we think that there are at least two ways for leaders to exert long-term effects on their subordinates. First, a leader can become permanently associated with the work environment and thereby be a permanent but indirect environmental prime. Second, leaders can change the schemas within subordinates, creating new schemas or increasing the chronic accessibility of preexisting schemas.

Permanent Environmental Priming

As noted earlier, the simple presence of a leader in an environment can cue or prime related aspects of a subordinate's self-concept (e.g., Baldwin, 1997; Brown, 2000). Implicitly, many readers probably assumed that such effects are restricted to only those circumstances under which a leader is physically present in a work setting. However, is it not possible for leaders to cue aspects of a subordinate's self-concept indirectly? We believe it is. In fact, classical-conditioning processes that are well-known to psychologists may allow aspects of the broader environment to serve as indirect cues to portions of a subordinate's WSC that were previously primed by leaders.

Probably most readers are already familiar with the general principles of conditioning. Classical conditioning, as illustrated by Pavlov's (1927) demonstration that dogs salivate to a bell repeatedly paired with food, occurs when a neutral stimulus such as the bell is paired with an unconditioned stimulus such as food that already causes a response like salivation. Eventually, through repeated pairings of the neutral and unconditioned stimulus, the neutral stimulus comes to elicit the unconditioned response. Analogously, if subordinates are repeatedly exposed to their leaders in the work setting, those aspects of a subordinate's self-concept that are activated in the presence of a leader should eventually become activated by work-related cues that are not directly associated with the leader. Thus, the color of the walls, smell of the workplace, physical location of work, presence of co-workers, or even the thought of work tasks may activate those aspects of the self that are closely aligned with a leader even when the leader is not present. In other words, the organizational context can serve as an indirect prime of the leader, extending his or her influence.

For several decades organizational scholars have discussed how leaders can influence the broader organizational setting. In his 1960 book, McGregor spent an entire chapter discussing how managers create the organizational climate that is experienced by employees. At one level, leaders influence the overall perceptions of the organization, whereas at another level, the climate of an organization serves as a boundary factor on effective organizational leadership (Kerr & Jerimier, 1978). This intertwining of leaders and organizations has received limited empirical attention, yet the limited research that is available does support this linkage. In one such survey study, Kozlowski and Doherty (1989) found that subordinates' perceptions of their overall relationship quality with a supervisor was positively associated with their work climate perceptions. Although such survey findings and theory are suggestive, experimental work is still required to establish a definitive causal linkage between leaders and environments.

Despite this limited experimental support, anecdotal examples from the business world clearly link the personalities of CEOs, organizational cultures, and organizational performance. Consider the following two examples. Jack Welch, the retired CEO of General Electric Company (GE), has been described as demanding, intense, coarse, sarcastic, volatile, and restless by *Business Week* (2001). They maintained that Welch was able to mold GE's culture to reflect his own in-your-face personality type, rather than conforming to GE's prior culture. Furthermore, through extensive personal reviews of his 3,000 top executives as well as extensive teaching activity in GE's training center, which exposed him to 15,000 GE managers and executives, Welch made his personal approach of micromanagement, punishment of poor performance, and reward of good performance part of the GE corporate culture. During his tenure, GE grew from a market value of $12 billion in 1981 to $284 billion in 1998, but the real test of his effect will be revealed by three factors: (a) whether his corporate style will persist at GE after his retirement, (b) whether it will be carried to other corporations by the many managers who have taken jobs at other organizations, (c) the proportion of GE employees who will be positively influenced by this culture that emphasizes individual identities, competition rather than cooperation among managers, and a perform-or-get-out mentality.

In sharp contrast to Welch, the W. L. Gore company stressed self-management, employee empowerment, and willingness to take risks. Begun literally as a basement operation that fabricated insulated wire in Bill

Gore's home, this innovative company has continued to grow and develop new products. Although Bill Gore died in 1986, the company maintained its original informal, nonbureaucratic, low-overhead style despite growth to $1 billion in sales and 5,000 employees by 1992 (Shipper & Manz, 1992). Emphasizing a team-oriented, "unmanagement" style, based on small plants and a close-knit interpersonal structure of associates (rather than employees), the W. L. Gore company stressed commitment to, and development of, employees and the organization. Compensation is based on salary, profit sharing, and an Associate Stock Ownership Program, and each new associate is required to have a sponsor that serves as coach and advocate. Using four guiding principles (try to be fair, use freedom to grow, make and keep commitments, and consult with others before taking actions that can affect the company's financial stability or reputation), associates are encouraged to make their own decisions as long as the organization's survival is not threatened by the downside risk (Shipper & Manz, 1992). This unstructured environment may require adjustment by new associates, but it encourages people to think, experiment, and generate potentially profitable ideas. The critical feature of this example is that it shows how the values and practices of the W. L. Gore company's founders (Bill Gore, his wife Vieve, and his son Bob) became the core of a common corporate culture and an innovative, informal management style that linked over 44 different plants worldwide.

We think part of the reason the W. L. Gore company's approach was successful is indirect priming. More specifically, the culture and organization as a whole suggest an indirect leadership style (Day & Lord, 1988) that focuses on team members, not leaders. In addition, this approach is very successful in creating collective identities and commitment to collective values (fairness, shared rewards, innovation, and growth) not just individual success. Welch's approach, in contrast, focused on his direct contact with managers and his frequent evaluations of them. Thus, the system he created may be more dependent on his personality than the more group-oriented system at W. L. Gore.

We are not aware of any experimental work in the organizational behavior literature that has shown indirect priming; however, social psychological findings indicate that associations between persons and physical characteristics do occur easily and quickly. In one such study, Lewicki (1985, Study 2) established that the personality traits assigned to one individual generalize to similar others. During the first 30 min of this study, subjects completed a task in which they interacted with a female experimenter who acted in a friendly and warm manner. Following completion of the first part of this study, subjects were then presented with photos of two women and were asked to pick the individual who was kinder and friendlier. Importantly, the two women in the photos differed in their resemblance to the friendly and warm female experimenter (e.g., one of the photographed women had short hair and glasses like the experimenter, whereas the other had long hair and no glasses). Relative to the control group subjects, who were asked to pick the kinder and friendlier woman with no prior contact with the friendly and warm experimenter, experimental group subjects were statistically more likely to choose the photo of the woman who most closely resembled the experimenter.

Findings such as Lewicki's (1985) demonstrate that spontaneous associations are drawn between people and things, yet the issue as to whether specific aspects of the self are linked to physical cues has not been fully explored. Examples such as Welch's effects on GE or the founders' effects on W. L. Gore suggest that not only physical cues, but leaders' values, management practices, and personality can become important associations that link individuals, corporate cultures, and identities. What we need are explicit theories and empirical studies that examine these types of priming.

Despite a dearth of direct empirical evidence linking leaders and organizational cues, research in cognitive and social psychology indicates that the human mind may be biased in favor of finding associative links to abstract qualities of people such as personality, a tendency that is so strong that connections are made even when no actual link exists (e.g., stereotyping and illusory correlations). From an evolutionary standpoint, the human mind has evolved to draw associative links quickly and easily because such a mechanism has substantial survival value for the individual (e.g., eating Plant A leads to illness or death, so people quickly learn disgust emotions in the presence of Plant A). Specifically, there may be a particularly strong tendency to draw contingency links between our external environments and aspects of the self because individuals must regulate themselves in relation to the external world (e.g., Higgins, 1996). Importantly, this external world is both social and physical. Furthermore, the self and context are assimilated in episodic memories (Tulving, 2002) that incorporate the affective basis of such associations.

In a sense, a leader who becomes strongly associated with the work setting will become omnipresent; he or she will permeate the work life of an individual, group, or organization as our two prior examples illustrate. As already noted, this relationship corresponds with prior work that indicates leaders are an important source of subordinate's perceptions of the broader organizational climate and culture of a firm (Schein, 1992). For example, Johnson et al. (2003) found that the social justice perceptions employees held with respect to management as a whole depended on their perceptions of the fairness of their own supervisor. Although the association of a leader's image with the broader work environment should be a powerful influence mechanism, relatively little is known about this process either in terms of the circumstances under which this effect can occur or its pervasiveness in organizational settings. We believe this represents an important avenue of future leadership research, one that has the potential to help explain how leaders' influence organizational outcomes. The possibility for permanent priming effects of the nature described in this section is captured in the following proposition:

> Proposition 4.3. Leaders can become chronic, indirect primes when work environments activate the values and social identities repeatedly emphasized by leaders.

In addition to creating chronic environmental activation of schemas, leaders can also engage in two additional processes that have long-term consequences for the internal structure of the self. First, leaders can increase the chronic accessibility of preexisting components of the WSC. That is, leaders can increase the resting activation potential of a particular knowledge structure. Overall, knowledge structures that possess stronger resting activation will be more likely to be activated in any given context. Second, leaders can create new content within the self. That is, through a developmental process leaders can generate new internal structures within individuals. In the next several sections, we discuss the role of leaders with respect to both of these processes.

Bringing Peripheral Self-Schemas Into the Spotlight

As noted in the previous chapter, schemas differ in their level of chronic activation. Some schemas are central to the self-concept and are chronically available or, at the very least, are easily activated. Other schemas are peripheral and require a strong external push from the environment before they are activated. One implication of this distinction for organizational leaders is that they may need to make organizationally relevant but peripheral aspects of a subordinate's self-concept more central. In part, the frequent activation of particular aspects of the self-concept should increase their chronic accessibility. Such frequency effects can occur either by having leaders repeatedly prime the same aspects of the self or by ensuring that multiple environmental cues activate the same or similar dimensions of the self. Through repeated activation, the resting activation level of a particular knowledge structure should increase, thereby increasing the probability that it will be activated and used again in the future.

To give one brief example of this process, consider the situation faced by an individual upon joining an organization. New employees bring with them many strong individual-level identities, but relational identities linked to organizational members or collective identities based on work groups or the organization as a whole are likely to be peripheral if they exist at all. Thus, a primary task of leadership processes as well as other organizational socialization experiences is to create and strengthen new organizationally based social identities. Although such identities are likely to be peripheral early in an organizational member's tenure, effective leadership will make them more central as a member's organizational tenure increases.

Creating New Content in the Self

In addition to strengthening the accessibility of preexisting schemas, leaders can also generate new schemas within their subordinates' self-concepts. In fact, the creation of appropriate self-concepts may be critical to the success of subsequent leader influence attempts. Nonexistent aspects of the self can no more be activated by a leader or organization than the script to fix a tire will be activated in a mechanically inept individual who has a flat tire. Similarly, enticing subordinates to act in a particular fashion will have little or no effect if the self-relevant knowledge needed to guide and sustain such behavior is not available: Knowledge must exist to be activated in a situation. As a consequence, successful leadership may require leaders not only to prime and strengthen relevant self-structures but also to generate new self-concept dimensions, ones appropriately aligned with the broader organizational system (e.g., collective, interpersonal, or individual). Beliefs that one can do something for low self-esteem subordinates are a good example of this point. Worline, Wrzesniewski, and Rafaeli (2002) gave many examples of this process in their discussion of courage at work. Specifically, they argued that courageous behavior by leaders inspires followers and creates the belief in followers that they too can act in ways they never thought were possible. This work on courage at work is discussed more thoroughly in chapter 6.

To better understand and structure how new schemas can be created, we follow the general model presented by Ibarra (1999) in her qualitative investigation of the provisional selves of investment bankers and consultants. Although not directly linked to organizational leadership, her model does provide a useful heuristic for understanding how new self-knowledge might be created. As such, Ibarra's work provides important clues and insight into the critical points of leverage and the boundary conditions that constrain organizational leaders in their efforts to generate new schemas within subordinates.

Before proceeding to a detailed discussion of the self-development process, we note that in our view (Lord et al., 1999), as well as Ibarra's (1999), future possible selves play a fundamentally important role. In large part, this reflects the fact that the generation of new self-knowledge is developmental and follows a trajectory toward a new view of self at some point in the future. Thus, it involves the time travel capacity afforded by human episodic memory and the autonoetic self (Wheeler et al., 1997). Like most episodic memories, developmental trajectories are likely to have a strong affective component.

As discussed in chapter 3, Ibarra's (1999) work examined how new professional self-identities of investment bankers and management consultants were generated at critical career junctures through a process of experimenting with provisional selves—a construct very similar to possible selves. Generally speaking, these provisional selves represented different possible selves (see chap 2), selves that individuals experimented with at different points in their socialization into new organizational positions. According to her data, new self-concepts were a function of an individual's engagement in the three-stage iterative process of observation, experimentation, and evaluation (see Table 3.1). Although we present this as a sequence, as Ibarra noted, these three processes can occur in parallel.

During the observation stage, individuals observed role models and created a repertoire of possible selves. In large part, this stage involved understanding the relevant behaviors and attitudes displayed by role models (i.e., role prototyping) and comparing the self to these models (i.e., identity matching). The end result of this stage was the generation of a large repertoire of possibilities specifying who the self is and who it can become. During the experimentation stage, the declarative knowledge acquired at the proceeding stage was "perfected experientially" (Ibarra, 1999, p. 776). In other words, the different provisional selves created in the proceeding stage were provisionally adopted and applied in one's organizational context.

The last stage, the feedback stage, incorporated an evaluative component. Here, individuals selected and discarded aspects of provisional selves on the basis of internal and external feedback. Furthermore, we expect this stage was affectively intense because discarding even provisional selves alters one's identity and changes the WSC.

We expect that the process of adapting and discarding selves is dynamic, and it continues over time. However, the end result of this process is the selection of one or a limited set of possible selves that served as self-guides for employees in their new organizational roles (see the self-development face of the model presented in Figure 2.1). In our view, Ibarra's (1999) work can serve as a useful heuristic for understanding the role leaders have in the generation of new schemas, a topic we address in the next three sections using her framework of observation, experimentation, and feedback stages.

Observation Stage. As a first consideration, leaders need to communicate the content of new selves to subordinates during the observational stage. In large part, this can be accomplished by granting subordinates access to a broad array of possible role models. Bandura's (1986) work suggests that those models who are most influential will be those who achieve or continue to achieve important organizational rewards and recognition from key organizational powerholders (e.g., leaders). As a result, leaders can substantially influence who employees will look to in their efforts to create different provisional selves by appropriately distributing organizational rewards and praise. Jack Welch did this extraordinarily well. Furthermore, if organizational leaders themselves hope to serve as a source of provisional selves, they must be proximally available so that vicarious learning processes are facilitated.

In addition, leaders must be discerning in terms of the role models that they choose to make available. A good example of the care that should be taken in selecting available role models is evident from research. For instance, Lockwood and Kunda (1997, Study 2) found that having accounting students read about a star fourth-year accounting graduate student created self-evaluative standards that were deflating for fourth year graduate students. Apparently, having students compare their current selves to such candidates was demotivating given the impossibility of meeting these standards. Indeed, half of these more senior graduate students engaged in self-protective behavior by denigrating the comparison process and distancing themselves from the comparison. In sharp contrast, first year students found the comparison process inspiring apparently because these students still had time to become stars by the end of their graduate career. Furthermore, because this comparison was self-enhancing, first year students saw the star as more similar to themselves. Lockwood and Kunda's work clearly highlights the need for leaders to consider carefully who will serve as the most effective role model when it comes to the generation of provisional selves.

Experimentation Stage. In addition to providing the content of a potential self to subordinates, leaders must also facilitate and nurture the adaptation of appropriate selves. As Ibarra (1999) noted, it is through experimentation that individuals decide whether to adopt or reject a particular self (e.g., should I be a team player or should I look out for my own self-interests?). Here, success and the positive state of "flow" (Csikszentmihalyi, 1990) with a particular provisional self will determine whether it is adopted, whereas failure and frustration with a provisional self may increase the likelihood that it will be abandoned.

At this stage the affect associated with different provisional selves may be particularly crucial in determining which self a subordinate will embrace. The self is not simply a cold cognitive storehouse; instead, it includes both cognitive and affective elements (see chap 6 for a more detailed discussion of affect and the self). These cognitive and affective aspects of the self are intricately woven together through associative connections (e.g., Bower, 1981) that are built up through a lifetime of experiences. The ability of leaders to generate strong internal linkages between provisional selves and positive emotional states should increase both the ease and willingness of an individual to access repeatedly a particular domain of the self. In short, during times of transitions leaders may need to help employees "feel good" about the person they are becoming. Not only is affective information more highly accessible than purely cognitive information (S. T. Murphy & Zajonc, 1993), but individuals should be more motivated to approach pleasant affective states and avoid unpleasant affective states (Chen & Bargh, 1997; Higgins, 1998). As a result of these two interacting processes, we anticipate that the selves that generate the strongest positive affect will be utilized more often; therefore, through use they will increase in strength until they become habitual and unconscious.

A key goal of leaders then is to generate positive emotional linkages to desirable possible selves. To do so, leaders need to be highly supportive and nurturing of desired selves while they are developing. This may have been a critical role of sponsors for new associates in the W. L. Gore organization discussed previously. The nurturing of desired selves may depend on the ability of leaders to create a zone of self-schema development, a notion based on Vygotsky's (1978) developmental psychology. According to Vygotsky, second party assistance in skill acquisition requires the development of a zone of proximal development. In most cases, individuals are unable to engage in behaviors or cognitive operations perfectly the first time around. Vygotsky noted that it was the responsibility of caretakers to create zones of development that remained challenging yet not impossible for the novice. For instance, in teaching a child to eat with a spoon, a parent may begin by feeding a child; once coordination has improved, the parent will then guide a child's hand between bowl and mouth; finally, when the appropriate hand–eye coordination is acquired, the child is freed to feed himself or herself. As this sequence indicates, caretakers must be sensitive to the current capabilities of their charges and dynamically adjust challenges in relation to this moving standard. For example, new associates at W. L. Gore often needed guidance from sponsors to cope with the lack of structure and high autonomy in that organization, but later on they are expected to function more autonomously.

Like skill acquisition and other forms of development, the adoption of selves by subordinates requires leaders to adjust their supportiveness to maximize the likelihood of successful implementation of a particular self and thereby generate positive emotional associations with new schemas. Individuals differ considerably in their resilience when acquiring new selves (e.g., they vary in goal orientation); however, overall supportiveness is essential if leaders are to generate new selves in their subordinates. Not only will such supportive behavior increase the positive emotions experienced when implementing a particular aspect of the self, but it should also increase an individual's self-efficacy for implementing this aspect of the self. Together these two processes should be linked in a self-reinforcing feedback cycle.

Feedback and Evaluation. Finally, individuals require feedback regarding the success with which provisional selves are implemented. Although Ibarra (1999) discussed both internal and external feedback, we restrict our focus to her discussion of external feedback given its clearer linkages with leadership. As noted earlier in this book, the self is molded in part through the reflected appraisals of others (e.g., Mead, 1934). In the current context, how significant others such as leaders react to a subordinate's implementation of a provisional self will reflect back on the subordinate to indicate their degree of success. Reflected approval will result in the replication and strengthening of an aspect of the self, whereas reflected disapproval will increase the likelihood that the individual will abandon this aspect of the self. As a result, a leader's friendly smile, disapproving glare, look of contempt, or words of encouragement will all influence who a subordinate is and who he or she strives to become.

With negative feedback, it may be very critical to distinguish between feedback directed at the particular role behavior and feedback directed at the overall person based on the Kluger and DeNisi (1996) study of feedback discussed in chapter 3. For example, task-focused comments like, "That approach to customers doesn't seem to work in this situation," may be accepted with little discouragement; whereas more person-focused statements like, "That approach wasn't very smart," may have negative consequences for an entire work identity, not just a provisional self.

In view of this research, it is instructive to consider Jack Welch's approach to evaluation. He graded managers as A, B, or C and advocated pushing the C managers out the door to B or C companies, rather than trying to make them into A or B managers (Bernstein, 1997). Clearly such evaluation was person- rather than task-focused, and it upset employees, resulting in the label "Neutron Jack" being applied to their CEO. More important, we suspect that such person-oriented feedback undercuts learning, although it may be a strong source of motivation. It may also unite A and B managers with the A+ GE identity, but alienate the C managers and encourage their turnover. This point is important in another respect because it suggests that powerful leaders can shape organizational cultures through attrition (or selection) processes (Schneider, 1987) as well as through changing the identities of subordinates. Thus, a match between leaders and subordinates identity levels (or goal orientation) can be achieved through human resource management policies, through changed subordinate identities, or flexible leadership.

Critically, the impact of negative reflected appraisals also may depend on the affective bond that is established early between a leader and a subordinate. Negative feelings on the part of a follower toward a leader have detrimental consequences for the ultimate quality of a leader–subordinate relationship (e.g., Liden et al.,1993), which in turn can lead to dysfunctional organizational outcomes (Bauer & Green, 1998). In terms of reflected appraisals, a disapproving glare from a supervisor who is held in contempt may be easily disregarded, ignored, or even viewed positively (although this is unlikely if the manager is also feared). As a result, an imperative skill for organizational leaders, particularly those attempting to change subordinate self-concepts, may be their ability to develop positive interpersonal bonds. Positive bonds operate like an emotional savings account that can be drawn on at later times by leaders. Thus, it should not be too surprising that leader consideration consistently emerges as a key behavioral competency in most taxonomies of leadership. We suggest here that it allows a leader to provide critical feedback without undermining the exchange relationship with subordinates so long as it is done in a task- rather than person-focused manner.

In short, these ideas regarding permanent changes in subordinate self-identities can be summarized in the following proposition:

Proposition 4.4. Leaders can produce permanent changes in subordinate identities by (a) making peripheral aspects of self-identities chronically accessible; and (b) by creating new chronically accessible identities through the subordinate's observation, experimentation, and evaluation of provisional selves.

Boundary Conditions on Self-Concept Change. Having utilized Ibarra's (1999) three stages as a framework, we would be remiss to ignore a potential boundary condition that is suggested by her work. In particular, Ibarra's research is based on the premise that the self is most susceptible to change during periods of transition or shock. Although incremental change across a lifetime is likely, the most dramatic shifts occur during periods of transition, such as starting a new job, obtaining a promotion, or changing workplace technology. This suggests that the ability of leaders to generate new schemas may be particularly critical early in a subordinate's job tenure. At this stage a paramount concern for organizations is the development of the shared organizational self-concept. A shared organizational self-concept will not only ease communication and coordination among members and between the organization and its members (Tindale, Meisenhleder, Dykema-Engblade, & Hogg, 2001), but it will also serve to legitimize organizational leaders who have, in all likelihood, ascended to their positions based on fit with the overall group prototype (Hains et al., 1997; Hogg, 2001). Thus, the menagerie of communications (e.g., sagas and stories), role modeling, mentoring, socialization and organizational rewards and punishments that leaders (and organizations) weave in their attempts to communicate possible selves to subordinates may be most successful if done early in the socialization process.

There is one other time when Ibarra's notion (1999) of provisional selves may apply. That is, during periods of reorientation and dramatic organizational change, such as when organizations adopt new technology or merge with another organization. During dramatic reorientations, the roles, status, social networks, competencies, and even jobs of many individuals may be threatened (Tushman & P. Anderson, 1986; Tushman & Romanelli, 1985). Identities may also need to change dramatically to accommodate new organizational realities. Here effective leaders need to realize that it is not just what subordinates do that changes, but who they are may change as well. Thus, a key aspect of leadership during reorientations may be to help subordinates develop more appropriate provisional selves and help mold these provisional selves into new organizational identities. It is unlikely that old identities will be discarded before new identities are clarified and accepted. Thus, appropriate identity management may be a critical aspect of avoiding resistance to change. This reasoning leads to our final proposition:

> Proposition 4.5. The development of new, chronically accessible identities
> is most likely during (a) employee transitions and (b) dramatic organization
> change.

Process Versus Content in Self-Identities.   Although this chapter has focused on the process associated with temporary and enduring effects of leaders that operate through changing the self-concept of employees, we have said little about the specific content. One exception was Brown's (2000) work that found that a leader's self-regulatory focus could be either promotion oriented, focusing on ideals to be attained, or prevention oriented, stressing the avoidance of undesired outcomes by conforming to ought self-guides. When leaders were visualized, these different promotion or prevention contents became accessible in subordinates and influenced their task behavior and task reactions.

Our two contrasting practical examples (GE and W. L. Gore) were chosen because both are consistent with the process-related propositions developed in this chapter and because they reflect management styles with very different content. Welch's style at GM was clearly prevention oriented, and it may have worked because GE was focused on efficiency and cutting costs. In contrast, the W. L. Gore style was promotion oriented, and it fit with the organizational orientation toward innovation and product development. In other words, the content of the underlying motivational orientation of these two leaders was consistent with their organization's strategy. Our main point is that both approaches fit with the same general process we have been describing although the content of the temporary and permanent changes that were fostered by these dynamic leaders were quite different though contextually appropriate.

There is, however, a tangential point that is worth mentioning. Both Jack Welch at GE and Bill Gore at W. L. Gore appear to have been successful at linking different organizational strategic orientations and compatible individual motivational orientation to the self-structures of organizational members. This approach to leadership may be an effective way to create a coherent and powerful strategy implementation system. This point should be examined by future leadership research that needs to consider both the potential of such self-based systems to function effectively in their specific environment as well as their capacity to adapt to dramatic environmental changes.

SUMMARY

In this chapter we have extended our structural model of a subordinate's self-concept to discuss the processes through which leaders may activate, create, and influence aspects of a subordinate's self-concept. Short-run effects influence the activation of elements of the WSC. As noted in this chapter, short-run effects can be understood through a consideration of the strength of the source, the strength of the linkage, and the pre-existing resting levels of activation for any given schema. On the other hand, long-term effects result either from the creation of associative links between leaders and the broader organizational setting or through structural changes to the self. Although discussed separately, these two processes may also work together in a complementary fashion.

The process by which these structural changes occur are particularly important for leadership scholars to understand given that knowledge which does not exist can neither be activated in the short run nor be linked with enduring features of the environment. We also noted that in highly effective organizations, the human resources management practices and the overall corporate strategy may also coalesce around the promotion versus prevention orientation of leaders and the level of identity they emphasize.

5

Generating a Mental Representation of a Leader's Behavior: Linking Perception to WSC Activation

To this point, we have identified the structure and operation of a subordinate's WSC (see chaps. 2 and 3), and we have suggested mechanisms that theoretically can link leaders to the activation of various selves within this structure (chap. 4). In effect, we have moved from the most proximal determinants of organizational outcomes—chronic or temporary activation within the WSC—to the psychological processes that lead to the activation of these proximal structures (e.g., priming). Building on the previous chapter, we now pose the following question: What is it precisely about leaders that results in WSC activation and change? In the previous chapter we noted that the manner in which the environment is categorized can have important implications for the aspects of the WSC that will be most strongly activated; we did not however, focus on the content of subordinates' mental representations. In addition, we did not address the relation of content to the basic processes that underlie the activation of these representations.

To address these concerns, we organized this chapter around three narrower themes. First, does it make sense to integrate perceptual categorization processes into our self-concept model of leadership; if so, how can we do this? In the previous chapter we briefly touched on the idea that perceptual processes and categorization were important; in the current chapter we present a more formal case for categorization processes as being essential

100

mediators between leader actions and WSC activation. Second, we present a heuristic framework that links leader behavior and action, subordinate perceptions and categorization, and the self-concept together. In addition, we also elaborate on the content of the perceptual layer, concentrating on one broad perceptual category that has formed the basis of our prior work: values (Lord & Brown, 2001). Third, we explicate our model through an in-depth examination of how the values implied by a leader's behaviors can lead to self-concept activation.

Before addressing these issues, it is worthwhile to reiterate at this juncture that although we continue to discuss the relationship between leaders and the self-concept in a unidirectional fashion, in reality we believe that the relationship is far more complicated. Not only are the self-concepts of subordinates influenced by leaders, but these same self-concepts may also influence what is perceived and attended to in the organizational environment. Social–cognitive researchers have demonstrated that the dimensions that characterize one's own self-definition are those that are used to evaluate others (Dunning & Hayes, 1996; Markus, 1977). As a result, the self-concept may assist us in understanding how perceptual (e.g., Lord et al., 1984) and behavioral (e.g., Bass, 1985) perspectives on leadership can be integrated.

DO PERCEPTUAL CATEGORIES MEDIATE BETWEEN LEADERS AND THE WSC?

What is it about leaders that causes self-concept activation and change? If readers are like us, the answer that springs most quickly to mind is that a leader's behavior or actions serve as the most proximal determinants of self-concept activation. A widely shared assumption among leadership scholars has been that leaders generate important organizational and group outcomes through their behaviors (Brown & Lord, 2001). Neophyte scholars are taught to approach leadership as a problem of identifying the behaviors or traits that make a successful leader. They are educated in the methodologies of the behavioral approach (e.g., behavioral surveys) and utilize them nearly exclusively. Similarly, practical leadership-training interventions have focused strictly on leader attitudes and behaviors (e.g., Barling, Weber, & Kelloway, 1996; Dvir et al., 2002; Eden et al., 2000).

The preeminence achieved by the behavioral approach within the leadership mosaic has met with little opposition. In fact, it is highly likely that most readers can trace their earliest fascination with leadership directly back to the study of one or more behavioral approaches. For more senior scholars, their earliest interest and excitement in leadership probably stems from reading about the Ohio State Leadership Studies and the Leader Behavior Description Questionnaire (e.g., Schriesheim & Stogdill, 1975) or the Michigan Leadership Studies (Likert, 1967). The resurgence of recent interest in leadership has been the result of developing behavioral measures of transformational leadership, such as the Multifactor Leadership Questionnaire (e.g., Bass, 1985; Bass & Avolio, 1990). Not only have behavioral approaches generated widespread excitement, but they have also inspired others in their efforts to isolate and bottle the essential elements of leaders. Since the Ohio State Leadership Studies took place, no fewer than 16 behavioral taxonomies have been suggested (Yukl, 2002, p. 62). Others have extended the behavioral approach by exploring the critical skills (Zaccaro & Klimoski, 2001), traits (Judge & Bono, 2000), and emotional regulatory skills (e.g., Chemers, Watson, & May, 2000) that account for a leader's behaviors.

In many ways the behavioral paradigm within the leadership field reflects normal science (Kuhn, 1970). In the tradition of normal science, fact gathering has continued for decades, culminating in the development of a full-range leadership theory (Bass, 1985) that consolidates the behavioral perspectives that have proceeded it. If democracy prevailed and our original question was voted on, scholars would, in all probability, vote overwhelmingly in favor of leader behaviors as the most proximal determinant of activation and change within a subordinate's self-concept. Initial polling of the early returns suggests as much (e.g., Lord et al., 1999; Shamir et al., 1993).

Yet, on further reflection, it seems that we too were myopic in our excitement to incorporate what is known about the self-concept with behaviorally oriented thinking about leadership. Although the gist of the behavioral process may remain accurate, an important elementary process has been neglected. Rather than a leader's behavior being the immediate precursor to WSC activation, it seems more consistent with a follower-centered perspective to focus on the mental representation or categorization of these behaviors as the most proximal influence on the self-concept change. In other words, subordinates' own internal sense-making processes mediate between a leader's behaviors and their WSCs.

The link between observed behavior and mental representation highlights an additional place at which organizational leadership may breakdown. Ineffectual leadership results not simply from the inability of a single individual to engage in the appropriate behaviors but also from any difficulty perceivers might have mapping those behaviors onto the intended cognitive categories. For instance, why are culturally transplanted leaders notoriously ineffective? Is it because they do not engage in leadership behavior, or is it because onlookers do not categorize the behavior in its intended fashion? Similarly, why is it that Americans have difficulty seeing radical Islamic leaders as possessing leadership qualities? Is it that these individuals do not behave in a leader-like manner, or is it because the behavior of these leaders does not resonate internally in the same fashion with an American audience? In our opinion, leadership models that do not explain the encoding of a leader's behavior effectively ignore the most basic psychological process that mediates the influence of a leader's behavior over subordinates. As we discussed at length in the previous chapter, the objective external world is translated into an internal, psychologically meaningful world—where physical wavelengths of differing amplitudes exist, humans see colors of differing intensities. As a result, social phenomena, such as a leader's behaviors, can only be understood in terms of the knowledge structures that they activate within subordinates (Brown & Lord, 2001). In articulating this perspective, we focus exclusively on cold cognitive structures in this chapter, and we discuss the role of hot affective processes in chapter 6. One brief example of affective effects nicely illustrates our general argument as well as the value of incorporating both affect and cognition in explanations of leadership.

Adopting the visualization methodology used by Brown (2000), Naidoo and Lord (2002a) had a sample of employed students visualize either a neutral setting (the student center) or their organizational supervisor. They then collected ratings of this supervisor on a number of behavioral (charisma) and perceptual dimensions (fit with leader prototype, LMXs, liking, and comfort with the leader). The most striking difference between these two conditions was that the affective state of subordinates, as assessed by the Watson, Clark, and Tellegen (1988) Positive Affectivity and Negative Affectivity Schedule (used as a state measure), strongly predicted ratings in the leader visualization conditions (e.g., $R^2 = .43$ for charisma) but was nonsignificantly related to leadership ratings in the neutral visualization conditions (e.g., $R^2 = .04$ for charisma). The point is simply that the internal meaning of leadership had a strong affective component in the visualization condition but not when subjects were simply asked to describe their leader without a vivid and accessible image of the person. Thus, we propose that the internal image and the associated affect strongly influenced perceptions of leader behavior and the subjects' relations with the leader. This idea leads to the following proposition:

> Proposition 5.1   Subordinate cognitions and affective reactions are the internal structures that mediate between leader behavior and subordinate responses.

Before continuing, it is worth reiterating that researchers in many other areas also focus on the interrelationship between the internal mapping of the external world and the self-concept. For instance, as we previously indicated, social psychologists liken the self to a digest, with key aspects of this structure linked to perceptions of environmental contingencies (Higgins, 1996). Similarly, neuroscientist Antonio Damasio (1999) wrote that the "neural patterns and images necessary for consciousness to occur are those which constitute proxies for the organism, for the object, and for the relationship between the two" (p. 20). Thus, consciousness depends on our cognitive capacity to map simultaneously the external environment, our self, and the relationship between the two. If we are to understand the influence of leadership on the WSC, we must first understand the internal mental representations that are formed by perceivers.

This raises an interesting question for leadership scholars: How are leadership behaviors mapped into internal representations of perceivers? A cursory examination of the leadership literature reveals that little information is available on this topic. In part, this difficulty arises from the bifurcation that currently characterizes leadership work. On the one hand, researchers who are interested in subordinate cognitive processes have not closely scrutinized how common behavioral taxonomies for leader behavior map onto underlying cognitive structures (e.g., Lord & Maher, 1991). On the other hand, leader-focused theories have given only passing consideration to the internal mechanisms that mediate the relationship between a leader's actions and observable outcomes. Instead, these behaviorally oriented perspectives have taken leadership behavior at face value, failing to consider the underlying processes that connect them to deeper meaning structures that exist within subordinates (Brown & Lord, 2001).

Strangely, although ignored at one level, the need to integrate the cognitive and behavioral perspectives seems widely supported by researchers. Scholars have discussed cognitive processes in their models (Conger & Kanungo, 1998) as critical mediating mechanisms (Yammarino & Dubinsky, 1994), as an important source of leadership ratings (e.g., Lord, Binning, Rush, & Thomas, 1978), and in terms of the content of perceiver's schemas of leadership (e.g., Offermann, Kennedy, & Wirtz, 1994). However, much of this work has not formally incorporated what is known about the psychology of person perception. Thus, despite over 50 years of behaviorally based leadership research and 30 years of cognitively based leadership research, these two approaches have not been adequately integrated.

To address this gap, in the next section we propose a two-step framework in which a leader's behavior is first encoded in terms of fundamental perceptual categories and then these perceptual categories directly influence a subordinate's self-concept. This framework will assist us in understanding how a leader's behavior connects to more basic psychological and social processes. In addition, it should help us understand the social–cognitive rationale for why leadership is by necessity contingent.

A FRAMEWORK FOR SELF-RELEVANT LEADERSHIP

To bridge the chasm between leader actions and subordinate self-concepts, we propose that the relationship between the external world and the internal self-system can be described by the process model outlined in Fig. 5.1. Al-

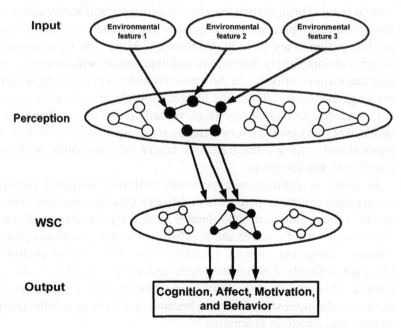

FIG. 5.1. A multilevel connectionist framework for self-relevant leadership.

(Thagard & Kunda, 1998). A positive constraint occurs when two units are positively related or when activation of one unit results in activation of a second unit (e.g., being insightful and intelligent). In contrast, two units have a negative constraint when the activation of one unit inhibits the activation of a second unit (e.g., being dishonest and open). The dynamic interplay between the sources of input and the interconnections among the knowledge or emotions that are activated results in the human information system settling into a particular schema or interpretation for an event or behavior. In terms of Fig. 5.1, this feature suggests that the perceptual schema settled on by perceivers will be a function of the positive and negative constraints that exist among the basic perceptual units.

Third, the amount of activation or inhibition that is transmitted between units depends on the weights linking these units. These weights are learned over time and reflect the strength of positive or negative constraints that underlie an individual's knowledge (see Hanges, Lord, Godfrey, & Raver, 2002). In large part, this third principle captures the accumulated history that an individual has with a particular supervisor, organization, context, or culture. In other words, knowledge or learning in connectionist systems is retained in the weights connecting units. It is regenerated again when these weights are subsequently used to interpret similar input. Through such learning, supervisory and leader actions have long-term consequences, consequences that extend beyond the immediate interactions they have with followers. Moreover, these connection weights are not simply due to personal experiences with leaders, but also they can form vicariously on the basis of how leaders treat fellow coworkers (e.g., Bandura, 1977). For instance, employee mistakes combined with leader anger and outrage (e.g., verbally chastising or firing the mistake maker) may lead to a very different meaning of mistakes within an organizational setting compared to a leader who responds with understanding to worker errors.

In short, in connectionist networks multiple, weighted constraints among units operate in parallel to construct a meaning that links a leader's qualities and actions with subordinates' WSCs. By simultaneously satisfying multiple sets of positive and negative constraints, perceivers produce a coherent, integrated, internal cognitive map of the social environment (Thagard & Kunda, 1998) that embeds leadership in a self-relevant, social context. This process automatically incorporates past learning related to the leader, the context, and the self, because this learning is reflected in the weights that constrain processing.

OPERATION OF THE HEURISTIC FRAMEWORK

Now that we have discussed the basics of connectionism, we return to our heuristic framework shown in Fig. 5.1 and its specific levels. In each of the following sections we discuss each of the precise links that we have hypothesized to underlie our model. In connectionist terms, Fig. 5.1 is multilayered feed-forward model with perceptions and the self-concept representing hidden layers.

Input to Perception

Conceptually, the first two layers of Fig. 5.1 involve basic person perception processes. A key distinguishing feature of our framework, relative to other leadership theories, is that we conceive of person perception and behavioral encoding as critical psychological processes. For leaders to function effectively, their actions, behaviors, policies, or words must be processed, understood, and encoded by an organizational audience. If actions are not seen, heard, or sensed, they cannot be encoded; therefore, they can have no influence over subsequent thought, behavior, or affect. Thus, for instance, although current leadership research suggests that environmental monitoring and vision creation are critical skills for senior-level leaders (e.g., Zaccaro & Banks, 2001), in our view these skills will be ineffectual unless they are coupled with mechanisms that allow for subordinate encoding.

At the heart of our framework is the most basic premise that behaviors are not the currency of social interaction and social perceptions. In our view, perceivers translate surface-level behaviors into more meaningful underlying cognitive structures (Brown & Lord, 2001). Consider for a moment the following quotes that were reported by ESPN Columnist Chris Mortensen (2001, Sept. 26) in an article entitled, "Jeff George Misjudged Importance of QB Leadership." In this article, written during the 2001–2002 National Football League season, Mortensen reported that many of the Washington Redskin players were disgruntled with Jeff George's team leadership after the team got off to a disappointing start. In this article several of the players were quoted as follows: "Plays like he is *scared,*" "doesn't *compete,*" "no *confidence,*" and "not *prepared.*" The important point of this example is not so much what the players stated but rather what they did not state. What we do not see in any of these player quotes is any explicit reference to behavior. Nowhere is there any direct scrutiny or discussion of the specific actions or behaviors displayed by Jeff George; instead, the players' descriptions of George's lack of leadership are communicated economically—in this case, in trait terms.

The fact that none of the players mentioned George's behavior is not surprising when considered in light of contemporary social–cognition research. Such work has documented that behavior is spontaneously and automatically encoded in terms of deeper cognitive structures. For instance, many scholars have examined the strong tendency of perceivers to encode behavior in terms of the underlying trait constructs that are implied by the behavior (e.g., K. Fiedler & Schenck, 2001; Uleman & Moskowitz, 1994; Van Overwalle, Drenth, & Marsman, 1999). Overall, this research suggests that perceivers automatically translate the behavior of other social actors into its underlying traits, a process that occurs unconsciously and regardless of the processing goals that the perceiver has in mind at any given instant (Uleman & Moskowitz, 1994).

It is surprising, given the state of basic social–cognition research, that, for the most part, leadership models have generally failed to incorporate psychological mechanisms that can account for how a leader's behaviors are encoded internally by perceivers. In fact, the only serious consideration of encoding processes has been restricted to cognitive leadership models. Rather than explicate how the encoding of leader behaviors occurs, these models have taken the encoding of behavior in terms of deeper structures as a given. For instance, Lord et al.'s (1984) categorization theory, suggests that the application of the label *leader* to a target depends on a two-stage process. First, the behaviors of a target must be encoded. Second, characteristics of the target must be compared to a prototype that exists in memory. Although categorization theory acknowledges the role of encoding, the importance of encoding has been overshadowed by concerns with the structure and content of the leader prototype (e.g., Lord, Brown, & Harvey, 2001; Offermann et al., 1994). Ultimately, however, the extent to which an individual will be perceived as a leader and impact followers depends not simply on the prototype that is currently in use but also on the strength with which prototypical traits and characteristics are applied to a target. An important implication of this suggestion is that impression management is essential for effective leadership (i.e., leaders must manage the impression that they are dedicated, intelligent, etc.).

It is clear from prior research that difficulties will arise for leaders at the encoding stage. In large part, the difficulties that arise are a function of the fact that social actions are not mapped internally in an analogous manner across subjects or across situations. Instead, action is replete with ambiguity and, thus, is subject to multiple interpretations. As Weick (1995) noted, all objects and events are defined within a context and meaning cannot be decided on unless a context is available to the perceiver (pp. 52–53). In contemplating the importance of context consider the following question: Which number is larger, 9 or 221? Before labeling the previous question as obvious, consider for a moment the counterintuitive results Birnbaum (1999) reported. Birnbaum randomly assigned participants in a between-subject experiment to either rate the number 9 or the number 221 on a 10-point scale that ranged from *very, very small* (1) to *very, very large* (10). Interestingly, Birnbaum found that 9 was judged to be significantly larger than 221 by subjects regardless of gender or education level. In explaining these effects, Birnbaum suggested that the two numbers bring to mind very different contexts. Whereas 9 is judged in terms of single-digit numbers, 221 is judged in terms of three-digit numbers. For Birnbaum, these results represent a scathing criticism of between-subject designs, at least when subjective decisions are made. Our intended purpose, however, is to demonstrate simply that human cognition is dependent on the broader context within which it occurs.

As with the numerical size judgments in Birnbaum's (1999) study, making sense of social actors is contextually driven. In most instances, multiple interpretations are available for any action. To circumvent the ambiguity inherent in this sense-making process, social–cognitive researchers have proposed connectionist models of human social perception (e.g., Read & Miller, 1998; E. R. Smith, 1996; Thagard & Kunda, 1998). Following the connectionist principles outlined earlier, these models maintain that perceivers simultaneously integrate multiple pieces of information from multiple modalities and that the meaning of the action emerges from the multitude of information that is available in a given context (Read & Miller, 1998). Clearly, this process suggests that "identical behavior may be interpreted differently in different contexts" (Thagard & Kunda, 1998, p. 8).

To understand the social–perceptual implications of this viewpoint, consider for a moment that you have witnessed one individual push a second individual (see Thagard & Kunda, 1998, p. 8). Although on the surface this action may appear simple to understand, it is, in fact, open to a multitude of interpretations. For instance, it may be interpreted as either a violent push or a jovial shove by the observer. What is your interpretation? Clearly, without contextual information the judgment is quite difficult, if not impossible. However, imagine that in addition to seeing the push you also see that the instigator of the shove was an African-American man, and now imagine that the same shove was instigated by a White man. How might the race of the instigator influence the meaning of the shove? Now imagine that you also see the facial expression of the instigator as he shoves his companion. Is he smiling or frowning? Perhaps you also know something about the instigator—for instance, he has just been released from prison or he has just become a circus clown. This simple example illustrates how context helps to determine meaning.

The need to consider the broader context within which a leader's behavior is observed should come as little surprise to leadership scholars who have known for some time that a key to being an effective leader is paying attention to situational contingencies (see Chemers, 2001). A moment of reflection indicates that our perceptions of leaders are influenced by a wide array of factors, all of which are simultaneously integrated by observers. Such factors have been examined in a piecemeal fashion by researchers showing that the categorization of leader behaviors is dependent on nonverbal behaviors (e.g., Awamleh & Gardner, 1999), gender (Hall et al., 1998), emotional displays (Naidoo & Lord, 2002b), situational crises (Emrich, 1999; Hunt et al., 1999), group performance (e.g., Rush, Phillips, & Lord, 1981), and culture (Jung & Avolio, 1999). Clearly, as is the case with general person perception, multiple sources of input are needed to understand and classify a leader's behavior. To capture the interpretive complexity that is inherent in social action, our model incorporates (see Fig. 5.1) multiple input sources, and it suggests that the interpretation settled on by perceivers depends, at least in part, on the complex array of factors that are simultaneously available. In effect, we are asserting that leadership is a situationally embedded process (Lord & Smith, 1999).

To understand the importance that context plays in encoding a leader's behaviors, consider for a moment a recently completed study by Brown, Scott, and Mattison (2002). These authors were interested in how the gender of the target leader interacted with the type of leader behavior displayed (agentic vs. communal) to influence the encoding of the behavior. To address this issue, they adopted a spontaneous trait inference methodology whereby perceivers were presented first with a leader behavior on a computer screen and immediately after with a word or nonword. Subjects then indicated whether the second stimulus was in fact a word (lexical decision), and their reaction times for this judgment were recorded. Critically, on many trials the word following the leader behavior was an aspect of the leader prototype that was implied by the behavior (e.g., *dedicated* or *intelligent*). For example, one behavior that was presented to participants was, "In a personal crisis Bradley gives time off to his employees" which was found in pilot testing to be indicative of "compassionate" behavior. Accordingly, the speed with which participants were able to make the word or nonword lexical decision served as an indirect index of the efficiency with which the perceiver was capable of translating the behavior into its underlying meaning, in this case the relevant aspect of the leader prototype.

The results of Brown et al.'s (2002) research revealed that no differences existed in participants' reaction times across three conditions: communal behaviors paired with a male target (CB–male), communal behaviors paired with a female target (CB–female), or agentic behaviors paired with a male target (AB–male). In contrast to these three conditions, participants were far slower at encoding agentic behaviors when they were paired with a female target (AB–female). This pattern of results suggests that participants were equally adept at encoding leadership behavior in terms of the underlying leader prototypical element for the AB–male, CB–male, and CB–female conditions. However, when presented with AB–female information, participants had difficulty encoding the behavior in terms of its underlying category. Following the rationale of spontaneous trait inference researchers, these findings suggest that the underlying element of the leader prototype was more strongly primed in the AB–male, and CB–male, CB–female conditions than for the AB–female condition. These results imply that perceivers had difficulty encoding the behavior into the prototypical element when women engaged in agentic behaviors.

These findings are interesting in two ways. First, they are fully consistent with the gender bias effects that have been reported for leadership evaluations (Eagly, Makhijani, & Klonsky, 1992). In their meta-analysis Eagly and her colleagues reported that women faced bias when they engaged in agentic behaviors but not when they engaged in communal behaviors. Moreover, no bias existed against men regardless of whether they engaged in communal or agentic behaviors. In fact, the results of Brown et al.'s (2002) investigation extend those reported in the meta-analysis, suggesting that bias may not simply arise at the time of evaluation or judgment but instead partially occurs when the behavior is encoded. That is, when a woman engages in a behavior that would be encoded as assertive, perceivers have more difficulty associating this behavior with a leadership prototype than they would for a male target. Second, and more pertinent to the current discussion, these results highlight the need to consider how multiple aspects of the context are utilized by perceivers when they encode and interpret leader behaviors. Participants in Brown et al.'s study clearly did not simply rely on the behavioral information that was available to them, instead they simultaneously considered both the gender and behavior of the target.

As a second example of how contextual factors influence the interpretation and reactions to leader behaviors, consider Casimir's (2001) recently published article. In his research Casimir examined how different combinations of leadership behavior influenced perceptions of the leader. In particular, Casimir created vignettes that varied the ordering and temporal spacing of socioemotional and task-oriented leadership behaviors, and he examined both individual preferences and liking for these different combinations. The results of this research indicated that particular combinations of leader behaviors were preferred and liked better by perceivers (e.g., support immediately proceeding pressure). Overall, Casimir's data suggest that the behavior emitted by a leader may generate a context within which subsequent behavior is interpreted by perceivers.

In addition to the need to consider leadership behavior within a broader context, it is also worthwhile to note the linkages that exist between the interpretation that is settled on by perceivers and more basic social–cognitive processes, such as the attributions that are drawn by perceivers. Consider Yorges et al.'s (1999) recent study conducted. Yorges et al. randomly assigned participants to read one of three vignettes in which the amount of self-sacrifice endured by a leader was manipulated—the leader benefitted, made personal sacrifices, or was unaffected (control condition). The impact of the self-sacrifice manipulation was then examined in terms of how much influence the leader would have over subordinates, assessed as the degree to which participants believed that subordinates should comply with the leader's request of donating money to a relief fund. Not surprising, a main effect was found for the self-sacrifice manipulation, such that participants indicated a greater willingness to comply with the leader's request in the self-sacrifice condition relative to either the benefitting or the control condition. Moreover, the effect of the self-sacrifice manipulation was mediated by the attributions that were drawn regarding the leaders' self-sacrificial behavior. As this example highlights, attributional processes may be an important consideration for understanding the interpretations that are settled on by perceivers. In our view, attributional processes will moderate the encoding processes of perceivers.

To this point, we outlined how the meaning and perceptions that are formed regarding a leader's actions are a function of the multiple stimuli that impinge on the perceiver. As a result, the meaning that leader behaviors generate within perceivers is dependent on the broader context within which the behavior occurs. Multiple factors are simultaneously considered and used by perceivers; as a result, the effectiveness of leader activities will, by necessity, be contingent (Chemers, 2001). In the following section, we move to the next layer in our framework and (a) reflect on the content of the categories that leaders activate and (b) consider how these perceptual schema may constrain activation in the WSC. Our thinking described in this section is summarized by the following proposition:

Proposition 5.2. The cognitive and affective meaning of leader behaviors constructed by a perceiver depends on the simultaneous consideration of multiple contextual constraints.

Perception to WSC

Although it should come as little surprise that we believe the perceiver's leadership prototype will serve as a key mediating perceptual category, our focus in this chapter is to explore how leader actions may be encoded in terms of the underlying values that are communicated by those actions. In this regard, we suggest that a leader's actions and behaviors activate different values within subordinates' perceptual systems. For instance, very different values will be communicated to subordinates when leaders make personal sacrifices for their work groups versus when they take personal liberties and advantage of their organizational position. As Chemers (1997) noted, a critical function of leaders is to model the normative expectencies that define the social norms and values within which a work group operates. In the current context we consider values not only because they are important in organizational life, but also because they represent fundamental truisms that are applied and processed in an automatic and unquestioned manner by perceivers (Maio & Olson, 1998).

The possibility that value activation is the direct outgrowth of leadership activities has important implications for the self-concept model that we developed in previous chapters. As noted by Cropanzano et al. (1993), the activation of self-structures occurs in part because of ties to more general normative constructs such as values that are implied by a given situation. Although direct evidence for this position is scant, two bodies of recent scholarly work do support this basic premise. First, data show that focusing individuals on the self results in the activation of an individual's core values (Verplanken & Holland, 2002). Second, theoretical work and research demonstrates that different self-identity levels may be tied to specific value structures (Oishi, Schmmack, Diener, & Suh, 1998; Rohan, 2000; Selenta & Lord, 2002; Triandis, 1989).

In recent work Verplanken and Holland (2002, Study 5) examined whether or not manipulating self-focus enhanced the accessibility of central values. In this research, individuals were preselected on the basis of whether altruistic values (e.g., helpful and equality) were central or peripheral. These two groups of subjects were then randomly assigned to either a high- or low-self-focus condition. Individuals in the high-self-focus condition searched for and circled words that were relevant to the self (e.g., *I* and *me*), whereas those in the low-self-focus condition searched for neutral words (e.g., *it* and *an*). Following the self-focus manipulation, individuals were provided with the opportunity to engage in an altruistic action (i.e., donating money). Not surprising, those individuals for whom altruistic values were most central and who had been primed to think about the self were more likely to act in accordance with these activated values (i.e., donate money). In effect, priming the self indirectly activated the core values that the individual endorsed.

Not only has research demonstrated links between an individual's conceptualization of self and values, but the available data also demonstrate that specific patterns of values may be related to specific self-concepts (e.g., individual, relational, or collective). In a correlational study, Oishi and his colleagues (1998) examined the relationship between dimensions of Schwartz's (1992) values taxonomy and individual differences in the independent–collective self-concept. Overall, Oishi et al.'s results suggest that, although the independent self was positively associated with valuing power, achievement, hedonism, and self-direction, it was negatively associated with valuing security, conformity, tradition, and benevolence. In contrast, scores on collectivism indicated precisely the opposite pattern with respect to these values. In addition to individual-level data, data at the level of societal cultures exhibit similar patterns, with cultures that are characteristically described as collectivist having values that are distinct from those that are characteristically described as individualist (Triandis, 1994).

Consistent with the available empirical data, recent value models have drawn similar conclusions regarding the connections between value systems and the self-concept. For instance, Rohan (2000) suggested that the path linking social value systems to social value priorities to social behavior may involve priming the collective self, and the path linking personal value systems to personal value priorities to behavior may involve priming the private self (i.e., individual). Thus, according to Rohan, identity level mediates the relationship between the values that are salient in a given context and outcomes. We elaborate on the importance of values within organizations and discuss the structure and content of values next.

Values. There is little doubt that values play an important role in organizational life. As but one example, consider the person–organization (P–O) fit literature (Kristof, 1996). P–O fit has been found to influence job seekers' choices of what jobs to pursue (e.g., Cable & Judge, 1996); the personnel judgments made by recruiters (Kristoff-Brown, 2000); and the ultimate satisfaction, commitment, and turnover intentions of employees (e.g., Bretz & Judge, 1994; Cable & Judge, 1996). Generally, positive outcomes for organizations are linearly related to the degree of overlap that exists between individuals and organizations. Although seemingly tangential, this research is relevant to the current context insofar as the P–O fit literature is largely premised on the value overlap that exists between individuals and organizations, suggesting that values are salient perceptual categories that guide organizational judgments and behavior. We also note that perceived values are likely to produce affective reactions as well. The fact that we do not address such affective consequences of values is simply because affect is covered in the following chapter.

The importance of values for organizational life is not surprising when viewed in light of the fact that stability is a key requirement for any social system (Schein, 1992, p. 282). There are a number of reasons to suspect that the communication and endorsement of a set of socially shared values is essential for the generation of stable and predictable internal organizational environments. First, because values are "desirable states, objects, goals, or behaviors, transcending specific situations and applied as normative standards to judge and to choose among alternative modes of behavior" (Schwartz, 1992, p. 2), they provide frameworks that generate the development of socially sanctioned purposes and coherence to behavior across situations. Second, because they are normative standards, values are a basis for generating behaviors that fit the needs of groups or larger social units. Third, several theorists (Rohan, 2000; Schwartz, 1992) have noted that values serve as standards that can be used to evaluate other people as well as to justify one's actions to others. Thus, it is not surprising that groups impose negative sanctions on group members who deviate from group norms (see Marques, Abrams, Paez, & Hogg, 2001) and that leadership assignment is at least partially dependent on fit with a group's prototypical beliefs (e.g., Hains et al., 1997; Hogg, 2001; Hogg, Hains, & Mason, 1998).

Although values have not been traditionally focal for leadership researchers, recent trends suggest that their interest in understanding how leadership is related to values is increasing (e.g., Dickson, D. B. Smith,

Grojean, & Ehrhart, 2001; J. L. Thomas, Dickson, & Bliese, 2001). For instance, Thomas et al. examined the relationship between a leader's values and evaluator's leadership ratings. Using a sample of 818 Reserve Officers' Training Corps cadets, they found that affiliation and achievement values predicted subsequent leadership ratings. Overall, Thomas et al.'s results indicate that values may be an important source of information used by perceivers when evaluating leadership targets. Others have extended this general notion, suggesting that not only are communications from leaders salient to perceivers but also that the organizational values that are most salient are a direct outgrowth of a leaders activities (Dickson et al., 2001; Lord & Brown, 2001).

In line with our previous work (Lord & Brown, 2001) and consistent with the suggestions of others (e.g., Rohan, 2000), we contend that leader behaviors activate different values in subordinates, and that the values that are activated are associated with different aspects of the WSC. Following our prior work, we utilized Schwartz's (1992, 1999) universal conceptualization of values to capture the content of the values that are likely to be activated by organizational leaders. According to Schwartz's empirical work, there are 10 underlying universal values that are shared by most of humanity: self-direction, stimulation, hedonism, achievement, power, security, conformity, tradition, benevolence, and universalism. These value types are arranged in a two dimensional space with a circular structure (see Fig. 5.2). Note that this circular structure conveys information regarding the dynamic interrelationships that exist among the values. In this regard, there are both compatibilities and conflicts among the values, with adjacent values tending to co-occur (e.g., achievement and hedonism) and values on the opposite sides of the circumplex being in conflict (e.g., self-direction or stimulation vs. conformity, tradition, and security).

In many respects the circular structure Schwartz (1992) outlined overlaps nicely with the connectionist framework we outlined earlier. Previously, we noted that meaning is created through the aggregate patterns of activation that, as a whole, represent meaningful mental processes (Hanges et al., 2002; Read, Vaneman, & L. Miller, 1997; E. R. Smith, 1996). Moreover, we suggested that, in part, the pattern that emerges is a function of the positive and negative constraints that exist among the basic units (in addition to the input). This perspective is fully consistent with P. B. Smith and Schwartz (1997) who highlighted the importance of value patterns, stating that the "meaning of a value is understood by its associations—positive, negative, and neutral—with other concepts" (p. 82). Thus, positive and negative constraints

FIG. 5.2. Organization of Schwartz's value types. Note: From "A Rose by Any Name? The Values Construct " by Meg J Rohan. 2000, *Personality and Social Psychology Review*, 4(3), pp. 255–277. Copyright © 2000 by Lawrence Erlbaum Associates. Reprinted with permission.

among values are crucial to constructing their meaning, with positive constraints occurring between adjacent values and negative constraints between values on opposite sides of Schwartz's circumplex model.

Consistent with this perspective, larger, more meaningful patterns or value schemas do emerge as four higher order factors underlie the 10 universal values Schwartz (1992) proposed. In this respect, Schwartz labeled these higher order factors as openness to change, conservatism, self-transcendence, and self-enhancement. Note that, although we utilized Schwartz's structure, in Fig. 5.2 we employed the dimensional labels that have been developed and applied by Rohan (2000). In large part, we utilized her labels because they make greater intuitive sense when overlaid with the self-concept dimensions discussed in previous chapters and because they may avoid evaluative misinterpretation (e.g., openness is better than conservatism). For our purposes, the key dimension in Fig. 5.2 is focus on social context outcomes versus focus on individual outcomes because the poles of this dimension distinguish among values that are likely to prime different self-structures—collective self-identities and individual self-identities, respectively.

On the basis of the internal structure of values, we draw two interrelated conclusions. First, we expect that the pattern of values that becomes most highly salient in an organizational context will be partially dependent on the compatibilities and conflicts that exist between the basic value types (i.e., positive and negative constraints). Second, as outlined elsewhere (Lord & Brown, 2001), networks of unorganized constructs will not provide as strong or enduring sources of activation as will highly organized networks. A direct implication of these two points is that a leader's effectiveness will depend on his or her ability to activate a coherent set of values within subordinates. As a result, leaders who simultaneously behave in ways that activate multiple value schema will undermine their own effectiveness. Alternatively, leaders whose behavior is out of alignment with other salient value sources in an organization may be equally ineffectual in their attempts to influence their subordinates. For instance, leaders who simultaneously emphasize individual achievement and benevolence values may be largely ineffective because such a pattern of behaviors activates incompatible value schemas within subordinates.

The ideas we developed in this section can be summarized as follows:

Proposition 5.3. Patterns of values activated by leader behaviors can be organized along an individual-collective dimension.

Proposition 5.4. Patterns of values mediate between leader behavior and WSC activation.

Proposition 5.5. Leader behavior has its greatest effect when it activates coherent patterns of values.

The argument we have been developing is abstract, but it can also be clearly seen in real examples. To illustrate, recall the very different leadership styles of Jack Welch at GE and Bill Gore at W. L. Gore. Welch's high-pressure style, in which he personally graded managers as A, B, or C, and advocated pushing the Cs out the door, conveys very different values than Bill Gore's approach of granting high autonomy to subordinates and tolerating mistakes as long as they do not sink the ship. We suspect that these different value systems activated very different WSCs among GE and W. L. Gore employees, which, in turn, produced prevention versus promotion-based motivational orientations.

To our knowledge, there is only limited direct scientific evidence to support the linkage between leader behavior and value structure activation.

Komar and Brown (2002) completed two investigations to test directly the idea that leaders can activate different value structures in subordinates. To test of the plausibility of this value activation hypothesis, they initially completed a two-session study. In this investigation, subjects were 24 students from an upper level psychology class who had recently returned from a work term. During the initial session, participants completed a series of individual difference measures and assessments of their work term. Critically, embedded within this initial booklet was the Multifactor Leadership Questionnaire (MLQ), an instrument designed to assess transformational leadership. Subjects were asked to rate their work term supervisor on this instrument. Three days following the initial session, participants completed a second, ostensibly separate questionnaire. Importantly, one component of this questionnaire required participants to write a physical description of the supervisor that had been rated 3 days earlier. The purpose of this paragraph was to prime the presence of their prior work term supervisor. Immediately following the completion of this written description, participants completed the Schwartz Value Inventory. Would the completion of the Schwartz Value Inventory be influenced by the degree to which the work term supervisor was deemed to be transformational? Surprising, the answer was yes! A very strong and significant correlation ($r = .63$, $p < .01$) was found between the MLQ ratings and the degree to which participants endorsed self-transcendent values as being personally descriptive. Self-transcendent values are values such as universalism and benevolence, which correspond to the focus on social context outcomes axis in Fig. 5.2. Moreover, no such relationship emerged between the transformational leadership ratings and participant endorsement of self-enhancement values ($r = -.02$, ns). These values (achievement and power) correspond to the focus on individual outcomes axis in Fig. 5.2.

Although Komar and Brown's (2002) Study 1 results provide initial support for the leader value activation hypothesis, critical readers may conclude that the nature of this effect is quite speculative given the absence of a control group or an experimental manipulation. To address this concern, Komar and Brown completed a second study that directly manipulated participant exposure to a transformational leader. In this instance, 30 participants were recruited and randomly assigned to either a transformational leader prime or control prime condition. Unlike Study 1 in which the impact of transformational leadership was assessed directly in terms of the degree to which participants endorsed self-transcendent values, Study 2 assessed value activation indirectly through a subsequent judgment task.

This task, which was performed following the transformational leader or control condition prime, required subjects to make promotion judgments for 15 hypothetical employees who differed along seven dimensions (e.g., reliability, work performance). After familiarizing themselves with the employees, participants were asked to select the two employees most deserving of promotion. Because values serve as standards that are used to evaluate people and events (Schwartz, 1999), Komar and Brown speculated that if transformational leaders do activate self-transcendent values, this effect would be detectable through the average scores of the selected employees along one dimension—team orientation. Coinciding with their expectation, a significant difference emerged such that participants in the transformational leader condition, relative to those in the control condition, selected employees who, on average, had higher team orientation scores.

In addition to this limited direct evidence that leaders activate values in subordinates, there is also indirect evidence that is consistent with this prediction. For instance, De Cremer and van Knippenberg (2002) manipulated whether a leader exhibited self-sacrificial behavior for the benefit of his or her group and examined the effect of this manipulation on cooperation, group identification, and belonging. From our perspective, we would anticipate that sacrificial leadership behaviors (which are group oriented) would activate self-transcendence or focus on social context outcome values in subordinates. Although De Cremer and van Knippenberg did not assess whether the activation of values mediated the relationship between their leadership manipulation and the outcomes, their results demonstrated a pattern that was consistent with this expectation. In this regard, relative to subordinates in the no self-sacrificial leadership condition, those in the self-sacrificial leadership condition were more likely to cooperate in the allocation of resources, were more likely to identify with the group, and expressed feelings of belongingness. Although the current study cannot be taken as a direct test of our framework, De Cremer and van Knippenberg's outcomes are fully consistent with our expectations, as are Yorges et al.'s (1999) results.

In addition to evidence that has established clear linkages between leader behaviors and outcomes, other research demonstrates that the salience of different values is consistent with the activation of different levels of self-identity (Korsgaard, Meglino, & Lester, 1996, 1997). For instance, Korsgaard et al. (1996, Study 1) found that individuals who were high in their concern for others were less predisposed to engage in rational decision making, as opposed to those low in their concern for others. That is, these individuals were less likely to consider their personal self-interest (i.e., ignore payoffs and risk) when making a decision. Furthermore, in a follow-up investigation Korsgaard et al. (1996, Study 2) found similar results when the value of concern for others was manipulated. Such results indicate that external sources (e.g., leaders) may be capable of influencing the values that are most salient and thereby influencing how individuals regulate themselves on a moment-by-moment basis. These findings suggest that typical response patterns that are consistent with the individual self are circumvented by activating collective values. Although previous work has not directly demonstrated the leader behavior to value perceptions to WSC linkages, the available data reviewed in this chapter are consistent with our general framework, suggesting that direct tests are warranted.

WSC to Output

The final consideration in our model is the linkage that exists between WSC activation and output. Because we highlighted this relationship in previous chapters (chaps. 2 and 3) we will not examine this linkage in great depth here. As noted earlier and elsewhere, those aspects of the most highly activated aspects of the self serve as the most proximal regulators of human activity (Cropanzano et al., 1993; Lord et al., 1999), and they do this, in part, through the type of task goals they activate. For example, De Cremer (2002) found that self-sacrificing versus self-benefitting behaviors of leaders activate collective versus individual identities and prosocial versus proself goals, respectively. Thus, both identities and the task goals primed by those identities will regulate the behavior, thoughts, and feelings that are produced in reaction to a specific situation. This idea can be stated more formally in the following proposition, which also represents the key idea behind several propositions developed in chapter 2 (Propositions 2.1 to 2.4):

> Proposition 5.6. Behaviors, thoughts, and feelings are regulated by the joint effects of identities (self-views or possible selves) and goals.

SUMMARY

As explained in this chapter, the impact of leader actions and behaviors on the self-concept are mediated by the activation of perceptual constructs that exist in the eye of the beholder. Unlike prior behaviorally focused models, which have largely ignored social–cognitive mediational mechanisms, our model suggests that social cognition is paramount for understanding the impact of leaders on subordinates. In addition, this chapter, in combination with previous chapters, highlighted our belief (Lord & Brown, 2001) that although value networks serve as general constraints on human self-regulation, such constraints need to be translated into more proximal constructs to understand immediate affective, behavioral, and cognitive functioning (Cropanzano et al., 1993; Kanfer, 1990). This occurs when salient values influence the likelihood that particular self-identities and associated goals will be activated.

In this chapter we focused on cold cognitive categories. In the next chapter we shift gears slightly and discuss the role of hot affective processes to understand how a leader's actions can influence a subordinate's WSC.

6

Leadership and Emotions

LEADERSHIP, EMOTIONS,
AND SELF-RELEVANT AFFECTIVE EVENTS

In prior chapters we showed that affective reactions to task performance provide an important metacognitive input that helps regulate effort and task engagement. We also found that affective reactions were an important medium for leader–follower communications and that liking as early as the first 2 weeks of interaction predicted the quality of leader/member exchanges up to 6 months later (Liden et al., 1993). Emotional reactions are also thought to be an important component of charismatic leadership (Yukl, 2002). Charismatic leaders are able to combine their vision with a strong emotional appeal to followers (Awamleh & Gardner, 1999). In addition, Dirk (2000) found that trust in one's leader, an emotional as well as cognitive evaluation, fully mediated the relation of past to future team performance. In short, affect is an important aspect of leader–follower reactions, and it is a critical aspect of leadership processes in general. Affective reactions are also likely to be an important consequence of the perceivers' mental representations of leaders, which were discussed in the previous chapter.

Need for an Integrated Cognitive–Emotional
Perspective on Leadership

Despite these persuasive findings showing the importance of emotions, leadership theories have generally focused on more cognitive elements—such as the development of leader vision, learning and problem-solving skills, a leader's centrality in interpersonal networks, the nature of leadership prototypes, or the model of mental representations of leadership developed in the last chapter. In contrast, the theory and measurement of affective processes has been ignored by leadership researchers or, alternatively, has been approached from a cognitive framework that emphasizes attitudes rather than basic emotional processes (Brief & Weiss, 2002). This focus on cognitions has greatly enhanced our understanding of many aspects of leadership processes, yet there are also sound reasons to believe that affective reactions structure all social interactions (Keltner & Kring, 1998; Levenson, 1994; Srull & Wyer, 1989), and that much of this process may be nonverbal and implicit. Thus, it may not be possible to have a full understanding of leadership processes if they are viewed only from a cognitive perspective. Consequently, in this chapter we develop an alternative emotion-based perspective on leadership, then we show how it can be integrated with more traditional, cognitively oriented leadership research.

Self-Relevant Leadership and Emotions

The perspective we have developed so far in this book provides an ideal foundation for considering emotional processes associated with leadership. There are many reasons for expecting a leader's impact on subordinate self-structures to have profound emotional consequences. First, self-structures have extensive and strong linkages to both cognitive and motivational processes as we illustrated in prior chapters. Second, emotional reactions are generally thought to begin with a primary appraisal process in which harm or benefit to the self and one's currently active goals are automatically assessed (Lazarus, 1991; Weiss, 2002), and such appraisals may structure perceptions of leaders as well as other organizational stimuli (L. A. James & L. R. James, 1989). Because leaders can facilitate both goal attainment and self-development, it seems likely that organizational members would respond more intensely to leaders than to other organizational stimuli, particularly when the self-relevance of a leader's actions is salient. Third, as we just explained, perceptions of leaders can be encoded in terms of value structures, and values show strong relations to the self (see the discussion of this issue in chap. 5) and to normative expectations. Both of these linkages should make representations of leaders affectively laden. Fourth, as we described in detail, leadership may have its greatest effect when it directly impacts the WSC of subordinates, and influencing the self-identities of subordinates is a strategy that is gaining increased attention in the leadership literature (Reicher & Hopkins, in press; Shamir et al., 1993; van

Knippenberg & Hogg, 2003). Fifth, Markus' (1977) seminal research shows that attempts to influence the core self-constructs of others are typically resisted. Hence, we might expect conflict and anxiety to center on explicit attempts by leaders to change organizational identities.

More research showing that emotions and self-structures are important comes from the justice literature. This literature indicates that interpersonal treatment that conveys dignity and social respect—interactional justice—has direct implications for the worth of the behavioral target (Bies, 2001). Bies also noted that interactional justice is strongly related to self-esteem and that it produces strong affective reactions: Interactional justice is described as a "hot and burning" (p. 90) experience. Consistent with this argument, a recent meta-analysis (Cohen-Carasch & Spector, 2001) found that interactional justice was strongly correlated with the quality of leader–member exchanges (mean $r = .66$) and satisfaction with supervisors (mean $r = .52$).

The importance of interactional justice is also illustrated by research on anger in the workplace (Fitness, 2000; Glomb & Hulin, 1997). For example, Fitness (2000) showed that anger can result from unfavorable treatment of the social self by leaders. Although intense hatred was not a common emotion experienced in Fitness's sample of workers, when it occurred, it tended to be in response to public criticism or humiliation of an employee from higher power members of an organization. Moderate to high levels of hate were also associated with unjust or demeaning treatment by one's supervisor. If such supervisor behavior is part of a continuing, abusive pattern, it is likely to result in voluntary turnover and low job and life satisfaction (Tepper, 2000). Thus, a lack of interactional justice is associated with supervisor behavior that undermines the self, and it produces extreme emotional reactions, lower job satisfaction, and greater turnover.

Finally, Tiedens (2000) conducted both laboratory and field studies showing that social status and emotions are strongly related, producing a vicious cycle in organizations. People expect different emotions from individuals of high status (anger for unfavorable outcomes, and pride for favorable outcomes) and low status (guilt for unfavorable outcomes and appreciation for favorable outcomes). Furthermore, people use emotional cues to infer status and gauge appropriate organizational roles and compensation. Thus, status, which indicates how the self is valued by others, affects emotions which, in turn, affect perceived status. This vicious cycle illustrates the role of emotions and social views of the self in creating or maintaining organizational hierarchies.

We think these arguments make a compelling case that self-relevant leadership is likely to provoke emotional responses in subordinates. Unfortunately, the literature on leadership and emotions is still in an embryonic stage (Brief & Weiss, 2002), and there is no comprehensive framework for analyzing a leader's effect on subordinates' emotions. Consequently, the central focus of this chapter is on adapting a widely used framework—the affective events theory (AET) (Weiss & Cropanzano, 1996)—to the leadership field.

Specifically, we propose that because basic emotions have a strong physiological basis that was developed through evolution, the structure of emotional processes provides a framework for understanding the structure of self-relevant leadership. This framework complements the more cognitively based analysis in the previous chapters. Furthermore, as already illustrated, we propose that the self-relevant actions of leaders are likely to produce strong reactions in followers, evoking responses that reflect basic emotions (e.g., anger, fear, happiness, sadness, surprise, and disgust).

Following AET, we also would expect there to be an important microlevel dynamic that builds on the basic emotions triggered by affective events and their appraisal to create strong action tendencies. For example, fear, a basic emotion, may trigger a fight or flight response, and a leader's role in such situations may be to orient followers toward one of these two responses while helping subordinates interpret and manage associated emotions. Interpretation, in turn, often demands integrating affective events with one's WSC and evaluating whether events are internally or externally caused. Causal assessment can then moderate the intensity of self-relevant emotions: Favorable outcomes can produce pride if internally caused but guilt or gratitude if produced by external factors; unfavorable outcomes produce sadness if internally caused but anger if produced by external causes (Cropanzano et al., 2000; Tiedens, 2000). Thus, AET helps us understand the structure of events, cognitions, and emotions in a manner that dovetails nicely with the perspectives developed in previous chapters.

Prior to discussing AET, we describe the perspective on emotions developed by evolutionary psychologists because it explains why emotions should be viewed as a fundamental aspect of social processes like leadership. Subsequent to this chapter's discussion of AET, we use this framework for developing a more integrative perspective on leadership that also incorporates cognitive processes. We then show why processes like courage (Worline et al., 2002), transformational leadership, and charisma produce emotional reactions in observers, and we discuss the practical implications of this perspective.

EMOTIONS: A FUNDAMENTAL SOCIAL PROCESS

Evolutionary View

The capacity to express and perceive emotions is often viewed as a critical factor in the evolution of the human species. Evolutionary psychology views specific emotions as solutions to adaptive problems confronted by our distant ancestors. Adaptive problems are evolutionarily long-enduring, recurrent clusters of conditions that pertain to either reproduction or survival (Cosmides & Tooby, 2000). However, as Cosmides and Tooby noted, reproduction involves a causal network that reaches out to encompass all aspects of human life. Therefore, adaptive solutions to reproduction problems, particularly those related to emotional processes, crosscut all facets of human life, providing a ubiquitous underpinning for social processes.

The broad impact of evolutionary adaptations can be seen in the central role afforded emotions in explaining human activity. Although emotions can be thought of as local, behavioral responses to specific problems such as instinctual behaviors in response to threat, emotions also function as higher order organizing devices. More specifically, emotions are seen as superordinate programs that direct the operation and interaction of other subprograms governing processes such as perception, attention, inference, learning, memory, goal choice, motivation, physiological reactions, motor systems, communication systems, energy levels, and effort allocation (Cosmides & Tooby, 2000).

The evolutionary viewpoint also structures current views regarding information processing. As Weiss (2002) noted, human cognitions are generally viewed as being modular in structure, having evolved to deal with specific types of problems. The brain, therefore, is not a general purpose computer but rather a set of domain-specific programs and structures designed to deal with different problems. Modern human behavior builds on the specifics of these programs and structures that have evolved over millions of years of human evolutionary history and billions of years of animal evolution. Because of the brain's modular structure, it is critically dependent on higher level coordinating devices such as emotions.

This argument echos our reasoning from chapter 2 regarding the WSC as being the currently active aspect of a confederation of selves that had a cen-

ual organism to other members of its species" (p.71). Information that directly affects these public and private selves often produces substantial emotional reactions because it has implications for a variety of socially mediated outcomes. Self-esteem thus may serve as an inner meter of one's interpersonal connections and access to socially mediated resources (Leary & Baumeister, 2000). Therefore, the self, one's social status, social rewards, and emotions are highly related. As we already showed, leaders who control many organizational outcomes can profoundly affect self-identities and self-esteem through their normal communications, and they have the formal power to change the organizational status of individuals. Consequently, leaders have the potential to produce strong emotions in followers through their actions that affect both subordinates' public and private views of themselves.

In summary, emotions can amplify symbolically based, verbal communications of leaders; they can directly infect followers with the emotions expressed by leaders; and they can convey information regarding one's potential for growth and rewards from group membership. Also, emotions are a particularly powerful basis for leadership because there are several basic emotions, which are thought to have innate and unique neural substrates (Panksepp, 2000), as well as unique and universal facial expressions (Keltner & Ekman, 2000). Emotions such as anger, disgust, fear, happiness, sadness, surprise, and contempt are generally seen as being basic and, therefore, are widely recognized across cultures (Weiss, 2002). Basic emotions also have associated action tendencies (e.g., fear is associated with a flight or fight response) that give rise to prototypical sequences of events (Russell & Feldman Barrett, 1999), and emotions can be used to infer status (Tiedens, 2000). This means that if leaders can evoke appropriate emotions in followers, they also evoke strong action tendencies that can be linked to the leader's vision or directives and can reinforce the higher status of leaders. Thus, when leaders trigger strong emotions in followers, they are initiating an affective event, with its own dynamics and a variety of potential outcomes. This perspective on leadership is developed in the following section.

LEADERSHIP AND AFFECTIVE EVENTS

Emotional Leadership as an Affective Event

To understand fully how basic emotions and leadership interact, we suggest that a new paradigm based on AET is needed for thinking about and examining the emotional aspects of leadership. Figure 6.1 shows the basic AET

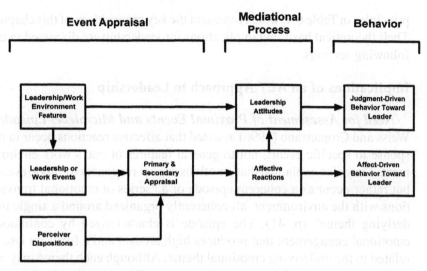

FIG. 6.1.   An AET model of emotional leadership.

framework adapted to leadership processes. Note that specific affective events pertaining either to a leader or to work tasks are the most proximal determinants of affective reactions, rather than general features of the work or leadership environment. This means that, although important, it is not task characteristics or organizational culture that directly influence affective reactions; rather, affect is determined primarily by the more microlevel social events that occur within this general context. A related implication is that leadership events should be studied as microlevel processes. Another important implication of the AET model is that a subordinate's appraisal of the leader–event and the emotions produced by that appraisal are critical mediational processes linking leadership events with attitudes and behaviors toward the leader. A fourth implication of this model is that the effects of an affective event, which may be the episode in which critical aspects of leadership occur, depends on how it is perceived and reacted to by subordinates. Thus, many individual difference variables associated with affective interpretation and reactions may need to be incorporated into leadership theories. A fifth implication is that the structure of leadership events may reflect the structure of underlying emotions. A final implication is that there are alternative routes to behavior toward a leader (or work task environment). In some instances, behavior is driven mainly by affective processes; whereas in other instances, behavior may have a more cognitive or judgmental basis. These aspects of an AET paradigm are summarized as six principles in Table 6.1, which represent the key propositions of this chapter. Their theoretical basis and implications for leadership are discussed in the following sections.

Implications of an AET Approach to Leadership

Need for Assessment of Proximal Events and Microlevel Episodes. Weiss and Cropanzano (1996) asserted that affective reactions occur in response to specific events, not to general features of one's work environment. They also explained that emotions are not responses to single events but rather occur as a coherent episode or a "series of emotional transactions with the environment, all coherently organized around a single underlying theme" (p. 41). The episode is characterized by continuous emotional engagement that produces high arousal and a focus on issues related to the underlying emotional theme. Although each theme may indeed have a meaningful aggregate level that reflects emotional valence or intensity averaged over time, there is also considerable variability over time, within episodes. Moreover, the variability of emotions within an episode may have different relations to outcomes such as performance or job satisfaction than does the aggregate emotional tone of different episodes. That is, change in emotions may sometimes be the critical factor causing organizational behavior. Consequently, if microlevel analyses were not examined, both important internal dynamics and important consequences of emotional episodes would be missed.

TABLE 6.1

Principles of Leadership Affective Events Theory

1. Affective events are proximal determinants of affective reactions toward leaders.

2. Microlevel assessment is required because affective reactions change over time in response to leadership events.

3. Primary and secondary affective appraisals are mediational processes linking leadership events and reactions to leaders.

4. Biologically based individual differences moderate affective reactions to events.

5. The structure of behavior and perceptions reflects the structure of basic emotions.

6. Behavior or attitudes toward leaders may be affectively or cognitively (attitudinally) driven.

This AET perspective implies that the emotional aspects of leadership may not just reflect general tendencies of leaders or subordinates but rather more complex episodes of leadership and subordinate reactions with important internal dynamics. For example, the leadership qualities of a military leader may become manifest in how he or she handles one specific combat episode and how that episode is appraised and reacted to by followers. Similarly, a CEO's actions in response to a specific business situation and the reactions of their followers may be crucial in understanding organizational leadership processes. Each of these episodes may have an overall affective theme, yet there may also be many cycles of leader behavior, subordinate appraisal, and leadership perceptions that occur within each episode. The emotional effects of such cycles would be lost if we only considered the aggregate effect of each episode on leadership processes. Similarly, they would be missed if we focused on enduring aspects of the environment rather than the microlevel processes related to emotions.

Appraisals as Mediational Processes.   The mediating role of appraisal in AET suggests that it is an important process in which some aspects of leadership perceptions are constructed. Although there has been extensive research linking leadership perceptions to cognitive processes such as prototype matching (see Lord & Maher, 1991, for a review), there is comparatively little research on how emotions affect leadership perceptions. We maintain that primary and secondary emotional appraisals are a key element in this process. Primary appraisals occur quickly in response to an event and assess the potential harm or benefit to the self or current goals. Secondary appraisals are more deliberate and assess the potential of a perceiver to cope with an event and to assign causality for an event.

L. A. James and L. R. James (1989) also noted that appraisals are relevant to leadership, but they developed a broader argument, proposing that primary appraisals produce integrated and parsimonious cognitive structures pertaining to emotionally relevant aspects of work environments. They tested this idea using multiple data sets from applied settings, finding strong support for a higher order factor in all data sets that they believed reflected a "higher order schema for appraising the degree to which the environment is personally beneficial versus personally detrimental (damaging or painful) to the self and therefore one's well being" (p. 740). We believe this higher order schema is merely the emotional context for cognitions created by emotional reactions to the affective events in a work environment. Importantly, L. A. James and L. R. James found cognitions pertaining to a leader's trust and support as well as a leader's goal facilitation to be strongly related to this higher order factor (loadings were generally near .90).

Laboratory research is also consistent with this argument that primary appraisals structure the meaning of environmental stimuli for perceivers. For example, Naidoo and Lord (2002b) found that the changes in positive affectivity produced by exposure to a leadership stimulus were strongly related to perceptions of charismatic leadership. This effect is consistent with the operation of automatic primary appraisal processes with respect to leadership, even though subjects knew that they would not be harmed or helped by the leadership stimulus they evaluated.

Secondary appraisals also have important linkages to leadership processes. Secondary appraisals require that one integrate situational information about an event with the event's outcomes. Thus, they require both more time and more cognitive resources than primary appraisals, but they can still be completed quickly for most events, requiring only a few seconds. Considerable evidence indicates that one aspect of secondary appraisal—attributions of causality to leaders—is an important determinant of leadership perceptions. For example, experimentally provided information regarding a leader's performance has been widely shown to affect perceptions of leadership. (For a review of this literature, see Lord, 1985.) However, this performance cue effect only occurs when perceivers appraise the leader as having been causally responsible for the performance outcome.

This appraisal of causality may involve careful causal reasoning that assimilates situational information with outcomes, or it may be based merely on perceptual aspects of an event such as how central a leader was in one's field of view, as shown by Phillips and Lord (1981). Subsequent research (M. R. Murphy & Jones, 1993) indicates that the schemas used to encode events (person vs. situational schemas) can also affect causal assessments to leaders and the outcome of secondary appraisals. Interestingly, high arousal focuses attention and memory on central rather than peripheral details of events (Deckers, 2001, chap.6). Because leaders are likely to be central in many affective events while situational details are peripheral, this focusing process is likely to increase the use of person rather than situational schemas; therefore, causal attributions to leaders are likely to increase as emotional arousal increases. As Tiedens (2000) noted, the emotions expressed by leaders can also serve as cues for competence and status, which may have implicit effects on secondary appraisal.

In short, both primary and secondary appraisals of subordinates are likely to be important in influencing their affective reactions to an event and in constructing leadership assessments. We suggest that this process provides both an immediate affective indicator of leadership stimuli as being potentially beneficial or harmful (the change in the perceivers own affective state) and an attribution of personal responsibility for outcomes to potential leaders. In slower paced and less emotionally intense situations, this affectively based information is then likely to be integrated with cognitive information about the leader; but in faster paced, emotionally intense environments, behavioral responses are likely to be driven by one's affective reactions as created by ongoing primary and secondary appraisals of social stimuli, as suggested by AET (see Fig. 6.1).

Individual Differences in Appraisals.   Research regarding individual differences in the orientation of both affective and motivational systems is beginning to coalesce into a coherent picture. One type of difference pertains to the intensity of an individual's reactions to positive events, and it is associated with an approach-related motivational orientation. Variability on this dimension can be assessed with one of the Big Five personality dimensions, *extraversion*, and also with the highly correlated Positive Affectivity Scale of the Positive and Negative Affect Schedule (PANAS)(Watson et al., 1988). Higher scores are indicative of greater reactivity to positive events, which has been confirmed by functional Magnetic Resource Imaging neuroimaging studies (Canli et al., 2001; Davidson, 1992). As Carver (2001) noted, this dimension also relates to the behavioral activation system (Gray, 1990), and it is associated with approach-related motivation.

A second type of individual difference concerns reactivity to negative events. This dimension, which is independent of reactivity to positive events, can be assessed with the Big Five dimension of neuroticism, which is highly correlated with the Negative Affectivity Scale of the PANAS. Neuroimaging research indicates that the intensity of reaction to negative stimuli is correlated with neuroticism (Canli et al., 2001; Davidson, 1992), and individual differences on this dimension are associated with Gray's (1990) behavioral inhibition system for avoidance motivation. One prediction based on assimilating these individual difference effects with our prior discussion of secondary appraisal would be that attributions of a leader's causal role in an affective event would vary with individual differences in perceivers that influence the intensity of their affective reactions. Intense reactions should produce greater focusing on central details such as leaders and increased tendencies to encode in terms of person rather than situational schemas. Consequently, causal attributions to leaders in negative affective events should increase with perceiver neuroticism because neuroticism will affect the intensity of reactions to negative events; whereas attributions of responsibility for positive events should increase with extraversion because it influences the intensity of reactions to positive events. As Tiedens (2000) noted, the emotions used by a leader such as anger are also cues indicating status and potential competence. Emotions such as sadness or guilt imply lower status and competence. Individuals high in neuroticism should be most sensitive to such negative emotions.

The implications of such differences for appraisals of leadership need to be systematically investigated, but our preliminary research indicates some intriguing possibilities. The previously referenced Naidoo and Lord (2002b) study suggests that changes in positive affectivity are strongly associated with charismatic leadership perceptions. Thus, it shows that emotional reactions can translate directly into charisma and leadership perceptions. Few effects were observed for negative affectivity in Naidoo and Lord's study. This may occur because positive affectivity has stronger relations to social processes than does negative affectivity as suggested by prior research (Barsade et al., 2000). However, the minimal effects for negative affectivity found by Naidoo and Lord may also reflect the nature of the experimental context. That study did not involve any personal threat or potential harm to subjects. In more negative situations, one might expect negative affectivity to predict appraisals of affective events; consequently, reductions in negative affect might be associated with leadership. Indeed, experimental research shows that perceptions of charismatic leadership tend to be higher in crisis situations (Emrich, 1999; Pillai, 1996). Thus, one important function of leaders may be to reduce a perceiver's anxiety in crises by making positive rather than negative outcomes more salient. If individuals high in negative affectivity react more intensely to crises, then they have more potential to be positively affected by charismatic leadership. Effective leadership in crises may reduce negative affect as well as increase positive affect, suggesting a role for both positive and negative affectivity measures in understanding appraisals of and reactions to affective events related to leadership.

Subsequent research with real organizational leaders (Naidoo & Lord, 2002a) nicely illustrates the role of negative affect. This research compared subjects' descriptions of their organizational supervisors after two different types of visualization instructions. In one condition, subjects were asked to visualize their supervisor, imagining what he or she looked like, what his or her voice sounded like, what it would be like if the supervisor were present in the room and so on. In the neutral condition, they were asked to visualize the student center. After visualization, subject's ratings of their supervisor on several popular leadership scales and measures of subject's state and trait positive and negative affectivity were collected. In the neutral visualization condition, there were few significant correlations between perceiver affect and leadership ratings; but in the leader visualization condition, both positive and negative affectivity were significantly correlated with leadership perceptions. Positive affectivity effects tended to be redundant with rated supervisor effectiveness, but the effects of state negative affectivity were independent of rated performance and affected almost all dependent variables. Thus, as we suspected, ratings of leadership for supervisors in actual organizations are also highly dependent on the degree of negative affect associated with a leader's image.

The two Naidoo and Lords' (2002a, 2002b) studies also illustrate an important principle of AET that was discussed previously. In the first study (Naidoo & Lord, 2002b), subjects listened to a specific event (a charismatic speech), and it was the change in affect from subjects' baseline level (state positive affectivity minus trait positive affectivity) that predicted leadership perceptions. This is the type of microlevel event we suggested leadership researchers should examine (see Principle 2 in Table 6.1). In contrast, in the second study (Naidoo & Lord, 2002a), subjects visualized their actual work supervisor and then made leadership ratings. Such ratings, which are typical of most leadership research, would reflect average reactions across many events. Although still related to perceiver affect, these aggregate leadership ratings reflected only the level of affect created by the visualization procedure (state positive affectivity or state negative affectivity). Thus, change in affect had little effect on ratings. These ratings reflected time-aggregated reactions to leaders, not the microlevel processes of AET. Taken together, these two studies provide strong evidence for the value of considering individual differences in reactivity to affective events as an important factor in leadership processes. Thus, as we previously proposed, leadership depends on perceivers' reactions, not just a potential leader's behaviors.

Affect as an Underlying Structure to Leadership Events. We explained earlier that emotions operate as higher order organizing devices for many cognitive and behavioral processes. Consequently, one might expect the structure of emotions to serve as an underlying structure to affective events related to leadership. Emotions are often thought to have a circumplex structure in which different emotions are arranged around a circle with two axes: one related to a positive–negative valence distinction and the other to the intensity of emotions (Diener, 1999). The circumplex model is shown in Fig. 6.2.

This model is relevant to leadership in several ways. One way is that it provides a means for analyzing the effects of individual differences on emotional and motivational processes. Watson et al.'s (1988) measures of positive and negative affectivity are obliquely related to the circumplex dimensions as shown by the dashed lines in Fig. 6.2. Thus, they relate to how strongly people are likely to experience positive and negative emotions, respectively, as our previous examples (Naidoo & Lord, 2002a, 2002b) illustrated. Carver (2001) made a compelling case that these same dimensions reflect the tendency to engage in approach versus avoidance motivational systems. Thus, the circumplex model shows how emotions and motivations tend to be aligned.

We suggest that, to be effective, leaders need to be sensitive to this alignment of emotions and motivation and that many leadership activities may function to move subordinates within this structure. For example, some leaders may tend to emphasize promotional motivational activities, and others emphasize prevention (Brown, 2000), and this orientation may need

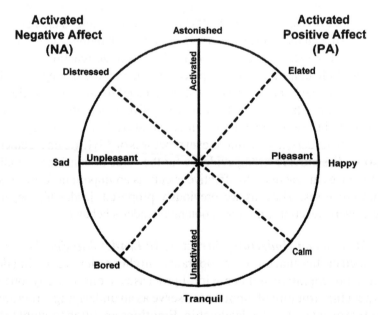

FIG. 6.2. Circumplex model of emotions.

to be matched to followers' positive affectivity or negative affectivity, respectively. Other leadership activities may be directed at managing emotional intensity. In crisis situations, when emotions are typically intense, leaders may need to manage emotions prior to addressing substantive issues. In contrast, during normal times, when most subordinates experience emotions on the bottom portion of the circumplex model, leaders may need to create stronger emotions to gain attention and motivate subordinates. Emotional valence may also need to be managed by leaders. Individuals who see circumstances (or themselves) too negatively may need to be encouraged by leaders to prevent disengagement from tasks or organizations; whereas individuals who are too far toward the positive side of the circumplex may need leadership that develops more realistic appraisals of situations (or themselves). In short, diagnosing the location of subordinates and current situations in terms of the circumplex model may be helpful in indicating the type of leadership that is required.

The circumplex model may also be useful for understanding the cognitive underpinnings of many types of routine behavior. Russell and Feldman Barrett (1999) maintained that core affect, which is defined by conscious feelings of activation and pleasantness or unpleasantness, is associated with prototypical emotional episodes. Thus, prototypical emotional episodes and core affect can be located on the perimeter of the circumplex model. Prototypical emotional episodes involve discrete emotions that have different structures and routinized behavioral tendencies. In more general terms, core affect tends to trigger specific behavior and cognitive scripts. Thus, the way we think and respond to situations may depend on strong emotional cues. If leaders want to change subordinates cognitions or behaviors, they may first need to address the core affect of subordinates.

It may also be useful to think of a leader's own responses in terms of core affect. Wofford and Goodwin (1994) maintained that leadership can be understood in terms of metacognitive processes, such as the leadership scripts, that organize and generate leader responses to situations. Although they tend to emphasize cognitive assessments of causality in explaining which scripts leaders will use (Wofford et al., 1996), it may also be useful to investigate core affect that leaders experience as a potential cue to activating their leadership scripts. For example, Norris-Watts and Lord (2002) examined the effects of stereotype threat (which we view as a negative emotion) on female leaders' decision making, finding that stereotype threat not only produced more autocratic decisions, but it also shifted the basis for these decision processes from the leader's underlying self-schemas to social norms.

Affect- and Judgment-Driven Routes to Behavior. The AET maintains that behavior can be a direct result of affective reactions to an event or it can result from a more deliberative process that makes use of attitudes and judgment processes. Our generalization implies that affective reactions, leadership perceptions, and behavior toward a leader may also have either a more affective or attitudinal basis. One way to understand this process is to use Scherer's (1994) perspective on the affect–behavior linkage. He suggested that emotions decouple the stimulus and behavioral response, which is equivalent to saying that emotional appraisals and reactions mediate between affective events and behavior. However, Scherer went on to say that for intense emotions, there is an evolutionary-based need to have rapid and reliable responses released by the affective stimulus. Consequently, for intense emotions, the action tendencies are very strong and are highly dependent on the nature of the emotional event; for less intense emotions, however, behavioral systems can be more flexible, and the mediational role of appraisal is increased. Applied to leadership, this argument implies that with intense episodes, leadership may be closely tied to the structure of underlying emotions (e.g., anger, fear, sadness, and joy), and subordinate responses may be affectively driven by responses to prototypical emotional events; with less intense episodes, more cognitively based attitudes may predict responses.

Lord and Harvey (2002) adapted this principle to an information processing-perspective. They argued that emotional processing is much faster than symbolically based cognitive processing. With intense emotions, there is often a need for an instantaneous response, and there is not much time for careful thought. In such circumstances, strong emotions coupled with preconscious categorization processes (based on the connectionist architectures discussed in chap. 5) directly cue behavior. With less intense emotions, more flexible conscious processes associated with secondary appraisal have time to intervene between a stimulus and response. In such cases, appraisals can be more complete, including knowledge retrieved from memory or constructed on the spot through reasoning processes. Secondary appraisals can modify or suppress the responses initiated by primary appraisal, although cognitive load and high emotional intensity make suppression of emotions very difficult (Wegner, 1994; Wenzlaff & Bates, 2000).

Cognitive and Affective Encoding of Leadership Events

Cognitive Assessments of Emotional Processes. Although information given in the previous sections suggest that emotions are an important part of leadership processes, they also suggest that there will be substantial problems using traditional questionnaire-based methodologies to investigate the specifics of emotional leadership processes. One problem is that emotions are automatic, often having effects that are unrecognized, and they involve primitive, nonverbal mechanisms. Consequently, the specifics of emotional processes associated with leadership are unlikely to be symbolically represented in a way that can be accessed directly through the questionnaire methodology generally used to describe leadership processes. For example, the emotions of charismatic leaders may influence followers by an emotional contagion process that involves facial mimicry and the effects of facial expressions on emotions that were described earlier in this chapter (Cherulnik et al., 2001). Subordinates are likely to be unaware of such processes. Furthermore, charismatic leaders maintain more eye contact with followers, which makes these leaders more central in followers' visual fields. Visual salience, in turn, affects followers' assessments of leader causality for outcomes (Phillips & Lord, 1981). Thus, emotion-relevant, nonverbal behavior can affect more cognitive aspects of secondary appraisal such as assessment of causality. In short, even though the overall result of emotional episodes will affect many types of questionnaire-based ratings of leadership behaviors, this does not mean that the nature of emotional processes can be revealed by questionnaire methodologies. Thus, new ways of thinking about and assessing leadership are required.

The inability of subjects to describe the specific emotional processes associated with leadership adequately is clearly shown in an experiment conducted by Naidoo and Lord (2002b). They had subjects listen to a prerecorded speech that was either high or low in imagery. While listening to the speech, subjects also viewed a picture of a leader who had a neutral emotional expression, and they made continuous ratings of this leader's charisma. Unbeknownst to subjects, in some experimental conditions, the neutral leader picture was replaced by a picture of the same leader smiling or showing an angry expression. This was done by presenting the smiling or frowning picture for only 33 ms, which is too fast for conscious perception. Subliminal smiles or frowns were presented every 20 s. Results showed that individuals who were especially sensitive to negative stimuli (subjects high in negative affectivity) responded to the frown condition with reduced trust of the leader, less time looking at the leader, and a more negative overall affective response. Subjects who were more sensitive to positive information (subjects high in positive affectivity) responded to the subliminal smile condition with more time looking at the leader, less overall negative affect, and a more favorable response to the high-imagery speech, provided that they understood the speech's meaning. In other words, charismatic leadership ratings and subjects' emotional responses were directly affected by the subliminal facial expressions that were present for only one six-hundredth of the time subjects viewed the stimulus leader. This experiment illustrates the power and subtlety of the emotional aspects of leadership. It also implies that subjects would be unable to describe the specifics of the underlying processes because they had subliminal effects.

Of course, in real-life situations, perceivers often would be aware of their affective response and many of the stimuli that produced this affect. However, many specific details of task or social stimuli can still be lost when we automatically create a personal meaning for social stimuli through affective appraisals. As suggested by AET, this personal meaning is the proximal determinant of both affective and cognitive responses to leaders. Individual differences in the tendency to respond intensively to positive or negative stimuli (positive or negative affectivity) may be as important as differences in knowledge related to leadership (implicit leadership theories) in constructing this personal understanding of a leadership event. Thus, both leaders and perceivers provide important components in affective events related to leadership, and the components they provide are both affective and cognitive in nature.

Cognitively Based Theories of Leadership. Our focus on affective events and leadership does not mean that more cognitive processes are unimportant. Many crucial aspects of leadership can be explained by cognitive theory (see e.g., Lord & Maher, 1991). Furthermore, even highly emotional events are often analyzed from a cognitive perspective by both leaders and followers who seek to understand why they felt or behaved in a certain manner. It might also be reasonably argued that most normal leadership is more cognitive than emotional. Such leadership reflects the application of both explicit and implicit theories about leadership by leaders and followers. Followers use extensively developed cognitive structures and metacognitive processes to understand and remember a leader's behavior (Lord, Brown, & Harvey, 2001). Similarly, the enactment of leadership behaviors can be explained by the implicit theories, self-schemas, and metacognitive processes of leaders that are used in reacting to subordinates or leadership situations (W. Smith, Brown, Lord, & Engle, 1999; Wofford & Goodwin, 1994; Wofford, Goodwin & Whittington, 1998; Wofford et al., 1996).

Cognitions, Emotions, and Extraordinary Leadership. Although cognitive explanations of leadership are critical, there is also clear support for the argument that extraordinary leadership—leadership that changes people and organizations in fundamental ways—has a strong affective component. By definition, extraordinary leadership is only needed periodically (Tushman & Romanelli, 1985), but it may be critical for the successful development of individuals or for the appropriate evolution of organizations. It is during reorientation periods that charismatic leaders leave lasting imprints. Our point is simply that such reorientations are affective as well as cognitive shocks, and they should be analyzed as both an affective and cognitive phenomena. Our use of Weiss and Cropanzano's (1996) AET as a template for such leadership processes provides a necessary complement to more cognitive explanations of reorientations (Lord & Maher, 1991; Porac, Thomas, & Baden-Fuller, 1989). Although not emphasizing leadership directly, Worline et al. (2002) provided a model of courage at work and the changes it produces that embodies many of the elements of AET. Because extraordinary leadership is often courageous, we take a brief look at their theory in the following section.

Courage and Leadership Behavior. Worline et al. (2002) addressed a process that many would argue is central to leadership—courage. By courage they meant behavior that breaks with expectations and normal organizational routines to create a new structure for higher performance. Courageous events are perceived by actors as being risky, but they are carried out in spite of associated fear to achieve an important underlying value. Courageous events have many consequences that involve both cognitive and emotional factors: They change the agency of both actors and observers and the quality of connections among the individuals involved, and they can often change organizations as a whole. Thus, they produce effects often associated with charismatic leadership, but the underlying process described by Worline et al. is more general.

One key aspect of courageous events is that they break with prior routines and expectations and, therefore, are appraised as being risky by both actors and observers. Thus, like AET, emotional appraisal processes are central in courageous events. Careful cognitive processing is also important, in part, because courageous events are unexpected. Another key factor is that courageous events are socially embedded; therefore, they often change the nature of connections among individuals. Worline et al. (2002) also noted that courageous events tend to be encoded in terms of stories rather than abstract principles. This factor suggests that they have more of a basis in episodic than semantic memory. As mentioned previously, Allen et al. (2002) explained that episodic memory has a more central emotional component than semantic memory, so it makes sense that courage is story based rather than analytic.

Although courageous events evoke fear in observers, observers also see that actors have successfully managed fear by responding with courage. Thus, courageous events often have an inspirational aspect that enhances the perceptions of worth and agency for observers. Coping with fear becomes a catalyst for enhanced competence, and leadership is associated with transforming this fear into positive self- and organizational perceptions. In other words, through primary appraisals, observers recognize that potential harm is associated with courageous actions. This reaction in observers initially activates fear responses, garners attention, and makes courageous acts more memorable. Successful resolution of events through courageous actions then changes emotions in observers, and it changes attributions of the personal qualities of courageous organizational members (e.g., leaders). Seeing this pattern makes observers believe that they too can respond to fear with courage, thereby enhancing their own perceived competence and agency. We already noted that others (Naidoo & Lord, 2002b) found that increased positive affect is strongly associated with perceptions of charisma in perceivers. What Worline et al.'s (2002) perspective adds is the recognition that this process also transforms the observer's self-perceptions, resulting in enhanced self-worth and greater agency.

The Connection of Affective Events to Self-Structures

As noted at the outset of this chapter, there are several types of research indicating that leadership events that engage the self-structures of followers are likely to produce strong affective responses. One argument that has already been developed is that primary appraisals assess the relevance of stimuli to the self and to current goals. A second argument, which is a central point of this book, is that subordinates learn about their self-identity from the affective reactions of others, and leaders are important sources of feedback. A third argument comes from the extensive literature on charismatic leadership. Simply put, charismatic leaders are thought to have emotional impacts on subordinates, in part, because they engage self-structures of subordinates (Shamir et al., 1993).

An additional point is that self-esteem can indicate social belongingness and be a meter indicating the quality of interpersonal connections and the likelihood of garnering externally mediated resources. As Tice and Baumeister (2001) noted, the four qualities that form the basis for self-esteem—competence at task performance, likeability of personal traits, physical attractiveness, and moral goodness—are also the criteria used by groups to exclude or include individuals. Thus, leadership that relates to these four qualities is likely to produce strong self-relevant emotions.

Finally, as noted in the previous chapter, the values that a leader embodies can activate identities at different levels, some implying individual-level identities and others activating collective-level identities. Values, in turn, are likely to be closely related to affect. Consequently, the value-based meaning the followers attach to a leader is also likely to activate particular emotions as well as particular WSCs.

Levels of Self-Identity and AET. Another central point of this book is that behavior and cognitions are generally regulated by one's WSC, and the WSC can be defined at alternative levels of identity. Our application of AET explains that leader behavior that potentially harms or benefits the self can produce strong emotions. Integrating these two perspectives implies that the type of behavior that is self-relevant varies with level of identity. When the WSC is based on individual-level identities, leader behavior that compares one individual to another, either directly or indirectly through allocating rewards, is likely to produce emotional reactions in subordinates. This is because such behavior has implications for the self-worth and self-esteem of subordinates and, in turn, their probability of attaining socially mediated rewards. When this is done in front of other organizational members, emotional reactions are likely to be particularly strong. Thus, leader behavior with implications for task competence, personal traits, physical attractiveness, or moral goodness, which influence self-esteem, should be particularly likely to trigger affective events and strong emotions when individual-level WCSs predominate. We would also expect that leader behavior with relevance to individual-level values would produce affective reactions when individual-level WSCs predominate. Our prior discussion of Jack Welch at GE again provides a compelling example of such processes.

When the WSC is based on relational identities, leader behavior that conveys a change in affective evaluations of subordinates is likely to trigger affective events, particularly when the change is in a negative direction. Again, the precipitating leader behavior may be direct, such as expressing displeasure at a subordinate, or it may be indirect such as changes in the nature of leader–member exchanges. When the WSC is defined at the collective level, we suggest that evaluations of one's focal group or comparisons of one's group to other groups are likely to produce affective reactions. It is also likely that information that bears on inclusion or exclusion in groups would also produce affective reactions. Finally, values relevant to WSCs at either of these collective-level identities may also produce affective reactions.

Although interesting theoretically, one might ask how such a synthesis would be relevant to a practicing leader. One answer is that it specifies the type of leader actions that are likely to produce strong emotional reactions in subordinates and, according to AET, are also likely to produce affectively rather than more cognitively driven behavior. In such cases, leaders must deal with emotions of followers as well as their cognitions. Indeed, emotions must often be dealt with before cognitive messages can be adequately processed by subordinates. Others have argued that effective leaders may be particularly sensitive to subordinate emotions (Goleman, Boyatzis, & McKee, 2002), but we argue that such sensitivity needs to be coupled with an understanding of how identity level can constrain the micro-processes in affective events.

Feedback and AET. Thinking of AET in terms of levels of identities and one's WSC also yields benefits for understanding feedback processes between leaders and subordinates. Although most models of motivation or self-regulation indicate that feedback is critical to producing effective behavior, increasing the amount of feedback available to subordinates can often reduce organizational performance (Kluger & DeNisi, 1996). One possible explanation for such negative effects of feedback suggested by Kluger and DeNisi is that the feedback is interpreted at too high a level, being interpreted in terms of its meaning for self-worth of subordinates. Based on the material covered in this chapter, we would recast these findings by suggesting that such self-relevant feedback is likely to trigger self-relevant affective events in subordinates, which in turn require resource-demanding emotional regulation that interferes with feedback-based learning. Furthermore, we would argue that the identity level of subordinates would help specify what type of feedback is likely to be seen as self-relevant. For example, feedback on task performance level, particularly if presented in relation to other workers, could be interpreted in self-relevant terms with an individual-level WSC, but this is less likely with relational- or collective-level WSCs. Kluger and DeNisi argued that feedback that is interpreted at levels below the self that either deal with metacognitive issues or provide task relevant information are more likely to improve performance. A critical issue for leaders who attempt to provide feedback, particularly negative feedback, at these levels is to avoid self-relevant implications.

Although we described the WSC as a metacontrol structure that guides cognitions, motivation, affect, and behavior in previous chapters, this does not mean that performance feedback, particularly negative feedback, should be framed at the level of self-structures (e.g., " You didn't do very well"). Feedback at the strategic (e.g., "Coordination with coworkers needs to be increased") or task level (e.g., "Refer problems with product quality to Mr. Smith") may be much more effective. Feedback that undercuts a subordinate's self-worth can lead to task disengagement as a means to cope with the perceived threat (Carver & Scheier, 1998). In other words, subordinates may tune out such feedback and the tasks to which it relates. Another useful strategy that has been shown to minimize such effects is to frame feedback in terms of the future rather than the present, thereby engaging possible selves rather than self-views (see Fig. 2.1). Other research also shows that framing tasks in terms of ideal rather than ought or feared selves (Kass & Lord, 2002) produces significantly higher performance.

Meaning and AET.   A more general answer to the question of what type of events produce affective reactions is provided by revisiting the theoretical perspective developed in chapter 5. In this chapter, we argued that patterns of values can be used to activate particular identities, and we suggested that these patterns are processed by networks of neuron-like units. These neural networks allow one to construct personal meanings from external stimuli and current goals. Thus, in very general terms, one might argue that it is the personal meaning of stimuli that provokes affective reactions, and this personal meaning is constructed from networks that involve self-structures. Indeed, as noted in chapter 5, Damasio (1999) argued that the core of human consciousness is the cognitive capacity to represent the external environment, the self and to see the relationship between the two. Thus, any leader action that directly influences the self or changes the relation of the self to key task, social, or organizational environments is likely to produce affective reactions. We also noted in various places that humans have a very specific memory system—episodic memory—for storing and accessing context-specific, self-relevant information and for time travel within this system. Therefore, the meaning that leaders help construct can be a past, present, or future self-relevant episode.

One additional function of neural networks may be to mediate between very fast-acting emotional architectures, which produce the microlevel cycles in emotional episodes, and much slower acting symbolic-level architectures, which register and store the time-aggregated level of positive or negative valence for an episode. Emotional architectures are genetically based processing systems that can operate in very fast time frames (10 to 50 ms) and are quite independent of cognitive load; whereas symbolic architectures use rule-based processes that are much slower (500 to 10,000 ms), are generally serial in their operation, and are quite sensitive to cognitive load (Lord & Harvey, 2002). Neural networks are capable of extracting structure from environments through automatic, implicit learning. Thus, they can detect patterns in emotional episodes or in longer term interactions with familiar others. In addition, because they operate in an intermediate time frame between emotional and symbolic architectures (typically 250 to 500 ms), they are ideal mechanisms for automatically integrating momentary emotional reactions in affective episodes into more meaningful and enduring affective assessments of stimuli.

To see how such automatic integration may work, consider, for example, processes involved in listening to the speech of a charismatic leader. Research suggests that a charismatic leader frequently will use emotion-evoking images, facial expressions, and eye contact to infect followers with emotions. However, these are only micolevel events that need to be integrated into lasting assessments of the leader in terms of trust, comfort, liking, and acceptance of his or her vision. This can be done through two processes that involve neural networks. First, as already mentioned, neural networks may register underlying statistical patterns in environments so that episodes with a predominant positive theme are experienced and re-membered as being positive, and those with a predominant negative theme are represented negatively.

Second, neural networks can be tuned by emotions that operate on bias-ing factors that make specific types of networks easier or harder to activate. (See Lord, Hanges, & Godfrey, 2002, for an explanation of this process.) Thus, very strong emotions can make some networks more likely to be acti-vated, whereas others are unlikely to be used as perceivers construct endur-ing meanings for events. For example, when charismatic leaders evoke fear in followers, it may automatically activate prevention-related self-guides and inhibit promotion-related motivational structures. Prevention-related motivational structures may then structure the theme of emotional episodes and perceivers' reactions to them. This orientation can, in turn, affect many motivational processes in subordinates such as their willingness to think creatively and try new options, their level of performance anxiety, their willingness to take risks, or their tendency to maintain full task engagement when challenged or when momentary setbacks are encountered. Further-more, all of these effects may occur implicitly as emotions prime specific types of self-relevant motivational processes. Our contrast between Jack Welch and Bill Gore provides an applied example of such processes, whereas Naidoo and Lord (2002b) provided a scientific example. They found that subliminally presented angry faces undermined trust in the leader for subjects who were high on negative affectivity and were in high-imagery conditions.

Thus, connectionist systems can serve three important functions: They extract statistical regularities in environments; link emotional and sym-bolic systems; and, as noted in chapter 5, represent patterns of values that underlie meaning. Thus, they can link internal patterns of cognitions and emotions with external regularities in environments. Chapter 5 notes that leaders can operate through such processes to change WSCs. This is a highly individual process that can be closely related to stable individual differences like personality, but note that it has a more aggregate analog in terms of organizational culture (Schein, 1992). Indeed, the schemas that develop from consistencies in organizational environment may be the source of the deep structure for cultures as noted by Lord and Maher (1991). The important point for leaders to recognize is that at both the in-dividual and the organizational levels, the affective basis of such struc-tures may make them difficult to change through cognitive processes. Considerable research (Fabrigar & Petty, 1999; S. T. Murphy & Zajoc,

1993) shows that affectively based attitudes are influenced more by affective than cognitively based persuasion. If the same principle applies to structures like scripts or schemas, then it implies that affectively based aspects of personality or organizational culture may be most susceptible to affectively based leadership.

Crisis and AET. One final implication concerns the relation between AET and crisis. Crises are, by definition, affective events, and a critical requirement of leadership is to steer organizations and followers through crisis-related circumstances. Crisis also fosters both the selection of charismatic leaders (Pillai, 1996) and the perceptions that potential leaders have high leadership qualities (Emrich, 1999). One critical aspect of this process may be the use of emotions by leaders to elicit particular types of responses by subordinates. Although the emotional impact of charismatic leaders may be carefully orchestrated by their use of rhetoric, gestures, eye contact, and facial expressions (Emrich et al., 2001), it is also possible that the underlying emotional and motivational tendencies of leaders are revealed through the microlevel processes in these affective events. As we described at the outset of this chapter, humans have hard-wired, genetically based capacities to perceive and react to emotions much faster than conscious processes can operate. Furthermore, as we just explained, through cultural experience and unique learning histories, perceivers can develop connectionist networks that can implicitly integrate fast-acting emotions in creating personal meanings for affective events. Thus, leaders who experience fear and focus on preventing loss in crises are likely to convey emotions that evoke the same responses in followers; whereas leaders who respond courageously to crises are likely to increase both their own sense of agency and that of followers (Worline et al., 2002). Indeed, as some laboratory research suggests, charismatic leadership may be strongly associated with the ability of leaders to enhance followers positive affect during periods of crisis (Naidoo & Lord, 2002b). We believe that our AET model coupled with microlevel assessment of emotional processes associated with leadership can be very helpful in understanding such processes.

Implications for measuring leadership. Leadership research has generally used methodologies based on the implicit assumption that subordinates' reactions to leadership could be understood as reactions to overall behavioral tendencies of leaders. Thus, common behavioral questionnaires such as the Leader Behavior Description Questionnaire (Stogdill, 1963) or the MLQ (Bass, 1985) ask about the extent to which leaders engage in specific types of behavior across situations. However, as one generalizes from AET to leadership, one might expect considerable variability over time in one's affective assessment of leadership (or any other social perception for that matter). Furthermore, that variability may be associated with important effects of leadership on subordinate processes such as motivation or satisfaction. Such effects would be missed with just the summary reactions to affective events or behavioral styles.

Of course, an AET perspective also implies that we cannot just ask leaders or followers to describe affective events and their reactions long after they occur. Rather, these events, and subordinates' reactions to them need to be measured in real time, as they occur, ideally using information rich methodologies (physiological measures or audio and video recordings) not just verbal descriptions. Furthermore, if dyads rather than individuals are the appropriate unit of analysis for AET, it may be necessary to link such methodologies for measuring leadership to measures of subordinate reactions to leaders. This is because, ultimately, leadership involves the meanings created by subordinates for affective events, not just the behaviors or visions of specific leaders. We know of no studies that use such real-time methodologies, but they are feasible from a technical perspective. Retrospective, verbally based methodologies may be useful for helping to identify some events as being central to leadership, but it is unlikely that they can provide a full understanding of the dynamics of leadership processes within particular episodes, such as how leadership may change affective reactions of subordinates or how subordinates create emotionally based meanings from a leader's actions and expressions.

SUMMARY

In this chapter we explained that emotions are faster acting but less flexible types of processing systems than more conscious cognitions. Emotions arise from evolution-based brain structures that coordinate many other types of processes, particularly those needed to respond to external events that threaten the self. For this reason, we suggested that an emotion-based structure underlies many social events and cognitive structures. Conse-

Schriesheim, & Williams, 1999; Tyler & Caine, 1981), organizational citizenship behaviors (OCBs) (Moorman, Blakely, & Niehoff, 1998; Skarlicki & Latham, 1996), reactions to selection procedures and decisions (Ployhart & Ryan, 1997; Ployhart, Ryan, & Bennett, 1999), performance appraisal (Cawley, Keeping, & Levy, 1998), and workplace retaliation (Skarlicki & Folger, 1997; Skarlicki, Folger, & Tesluk, 1999). This partial listing of organizationally relevant outcomes shows the importance of justice considerations in organizations. Moreover, focusing on organizational justice helps to illustrate the applied relevance of the theoretical framework that we developed in this book.

TYPES OF JUSTICE

The notion of justice has intuitive meaning for most individuals, yet researchers have shown that there are several facets to organizational justice. A two-factor approach to organizational justice has distinguished between distributive and procedural justice. Distributive justice focuses on whether outcomes are consistent with norms for outcome allocation (e.g., equity or equality; Colquitt, 2001), whereas procedural justice pertains to the fairness of the methods used to produce outcome distribution decisions. Distributive and procedural justice are each important in their own right, yet as we discuss in a subsequent section, considerable research suggests that they also interact (Brockner &Wiesenfeld, 1996), with high procedural justice compensating for low outcomes.

Although the two-factor approach to organizational justice has been useful, Bies (2001) and Bies and Moag (1986) argued that the nature of the interpersonal treatment one receives from another person reflects a third type of justice—interactional justice. Moreover, because leaders often interact directly with subordinates, interactional justice should be particularly important for understanding leadership processes. Bies (2001) provided extensive evidence showing that people can distinguish interactional from procedural justice. More interestingly, he linked interactional justice to one's sense of self, that is, one's self-identity. Indeed, we argue that each of the three types of organizational justice are linked to one's self-identity and that it is through an understanding of the self-identity issue that leaders can affect particular justice perceptions.

At a basic level, the importance of organizational justice to leadership processes is shown by Fitness' (2000) study of anger in the workplace. She examined anger-inducing events in the workplace, finding that 69% of the anger-inducing events instigated by a superior involved unjust treatment, whereas only 28% of coworker- and 16% of subordinate-instigated events involved unjust treatment. Although Fitness' operationalization of unjust treatment was not limited to a specific type of justice, the results demonstrate the importance of justice for understanding leadership in relation to a basic-level issue such as emotional processing. This fundamental nature of organizational justice and leaders' role in it merits an analysis of a more proximal determinant of justice perceptions—the self-concept.

ORGANIZATIONAL JUSTICE THROUGH THE LENS OF THE SELF-CONCEPT

Perception is a key element in defining organizational justice as it highlights the subjective, and thus idiographic, nature of fairness—what may seem fair to a particular person, relationship, or group may not necessarily be considered fair by another person, relationship, or group. The subjective nature of organizational justice, however, raises the question of what mechanism determines different justice perceptions.

We believe that perceptions of organizational justice are regulated, in part, by one's WSC (Markus & Nurius, 1986; Markus & Wurf, 1987). More specifically, the linkages between the WSC and justice-related events at work are responsible for the meaning attached to justice. This is because it is through the WSC that justice events at work are linked with underlying personal, relational, or social-collective values that give meaning to events. For example, when others treat a person unfairly and the individual level of the WSC is active, injustice may imply that others have a low evaluation of one's abilities or worth. When the WSC is defined at the relational level, injustice may indicate that one's dyadic partner will not consider what is best for the relationship and cannot be trusted. When the collective level of the WSC is salient, injustice may be linked to the self through more general, collective values, indicating a lack of concern for organizational norms and values.

Throughout this book we maintained that leaders are an important element of the social context in organizations. Consequently, leaders are in a position to activate implicitly or communicate explicitly different values by priming the WSC which, in turn, moderates the processes that drive justice perceptions. An overarching proposition of this chapter is that both the justice dimensions (distributive, interactional, or procedural) relevant to an assessment of justice and the standards for fairness on each dimension will change as identity levels vary.

These processes are discussed in detail in the following sections in terms of two interrelated mechanisms by which leaders can indirectly affect organizational justice. Specifically, leaders can affect both the justice dimensions that are salient and the standards by which distributive, interactional, or procedural justice are evaluated. We believe such processes have powerful effects on organizational justice perceptions and are achieved through the mediating mechanism of a subordinate's WSC (i.e., Leadership → WSC → Organizational Justice (OJ). However, perceived justice also likely reflects underlying values communicated by leaders so that justice processes also feed back to the WSC, either reinforcing or undercutting an identity that has been activated (i.e., Leadership → WSC_t → OJ_t → WSC_{t+1}, where t indexes time) For example, as previously discussed in chapter 5, when a leader advocates group-oriented values but is seen as unfairly benefitting from group actions rather than being self-sacrificing, this action undercuts any existing group-level identity and suggests that individual-level "me-first" values are more important. These values then determine what type of justice becomes relevant for interpreting justice-related events through their impact on the WSC.

We turn now to a discussion of the two interrelated mechanisms by which the self affects organizational justice perceptions. The first mechanism influences whether distributive, interactional, or procedural justice dimensions receive the most weight in determining evaluations of fairness. The second mechanism pertains to the development of standards of comparison for evaluating justice-related events.

MECHANISM 1: DIFFERENTIAL WEIGHTING OF JUSTICE DIMENSIONS

A critical issue in understanding overall assessments of fairness is to know how distributive, interactional, and procedural justice are differentially weighted by individuals. Most analyses of justice perceptions use group data with weights for a given dimension of justice being determined by some statistical procedure such as multiple regression. However, although multiple regression analyses represent group averages, they may not be an accurate description of any specific individual. People are generally thought to be limited information processors who simplify perceptual and evaluative processes; thus, they are unlikely to use all three dimensions (Lind, 2001). Instead, people are more likely to use only one or two justice dimensions, with the use of these dimensions varying across time and across individuals. Group data represents an amalgamation of these cross-time and cross-person processes that may be an inaccurate representation of specific individual processes because such an amalgamation ignores individual preferences or tendencies to process justice-related information in terms of outcomes or interpersonal or procedural aspects.

What is needed to better understand how individuals function in evaluating justice is some way to sort individuals who emphasize the same aspects of justice into groups. We propose that the individual, relational, and collective levels of the WSC provide a good basis for such sorting of individuals, because they orient individuals toward factors consistent with either distributive, interactional, or procedural justice. The WSC varies with context; thus, it could reflect the contextual factors that accentuate specific aspects of justice in specific situations. In addition, the WSC also reflects chronic differences across individuals; thus, it could indicate consistent tendencies of individuals to emphasize certain aspects of justice events.

The following sections explicitly analyze how the WSC level that is active should influence the importance of the distributive, interactional, and procedural justice dimensions. We propose that for each of the three self-concept levels—individual, relational, and collective—there is a corresponding type of justice that is made salient by contextual influences on one's WSC and, therefore, should be more central in one's evaluation of justice. More specifically, we expect a focus at the individual level of self-construal to be related primarily to distributive justice concerns, whereas a focus at the relational level of self-construal should be related primarily to interactional justice concerns. Finally, a focus at the collective level of self-construal should entail concerns with procedural justice. We discuss each of these three linkages in the following sections.

Individual Level Identity and Distributive Justice

Each of the self-concept levels was covered in detail in chapter 3, so here we briefly review the elements that characterize each level (see also Brewer & Gardner, 1996; Markus & Kitayama, 1991; Triandis, 1989) as they bear on organizational justice. At the individual level, individuals engage in interpersonal comparisons based on their traits, abilities, and other relevant characteristics. This process essentially serves to differentiate an actor from others, such that self-worth is determined through favorable comparisons to relevant others (Brewer & Gardner, 1996; Lord et al., 1999). The individual-level WSC may become manifested through various organizational practices, such as performance appraisal and formal reward structures, that have the effect of differentiating among organizational members (Lord et al., 1999).

The tendency at the individual level toward differentiation with regard to others based on elements in the social context becomes more interesting when viewed in light of distributive justice. Distributive justice refers to people's perceptions that the outcomes they receive are fair (Cropanzano & Greenberg, 1997). We expect that employees focused at the individual level will view outcomes, such as pay, promotions, or benefits, as important bases for self-evaluation. In addition, because leaders often administer outcomes, the outcomes symbolically represent the employee's position relative to other coworkers as communicated by the leader.

This perspective has two important applied implications. First, because individuals are motivated to maintain a favorable view of the self (Deckers, 2001), from an equity perspective they will see their ability and contribution to a task as being greater than they actually are, predisposing them to expect greater-than-average outcomes and, most likely, creating perceptions of injustice. Kruger and Dunning's (1999) empirical research has shown that even people who are in the lowest quartile of performance see themselves as being above average. Therefore, we could expect that almost all individuals would believe they warrant greater than average outcomes.

The second implication is that the meaning of injustice will also have implications for self-worth, implying lower levels of self-worth than one's biased ability perceptions suggest. Negative affective reactions are one likely consequence of this justice-based self-relevant meaning because it represents a threat to the self that would be detected by primary appraisals (see chap. 6). In addition to negative affective reactions, we would expect that lower self-worth has other consequences, such as lower task self-efficacy, more difficulty engaging in difficult tasks, and greater vulnerability to temporary task setbacks. Leaders who generally cannot provide sufficient rewards to achieve perceived fairness from the perspective of all subordinates solely on the basis of distributive justice need to support the self-worth of subordinates and achieve organizational justice through other means related to interactional or procedural justice. Such actions would minimize the indirect, ripple effects of low-perceived distributive justice on work behavior and attitudes, but this approach may not work for individuals who are chronically focused at individual levels and are primarily concerned with distributive justice.

Relational-Level Identity and Interactional Justice

The self can also be defined at a more social level in which one's motivation involves concerns for the welfare of specific others (Brewer & Gardner, 1996; Markus & Kitayama, 1991). When the WSC is defined at the relational level, individuals are focused on fulfilling their roles in relationships with other people, with the other person's welfare being a salient social motive. Self-worth arises from appropriate role behavior as conveyed through the reactions of the other (Brewer & Gardner, 1996). Furthermore, when others are close, their identities may be incorporated into the self (Aron & McLaughlin-Volpe, 2001).

This interpersonally oriented level of the self is congruent with work on interactional justice, which refers to the interpersonal treatment that one receives from another person (Bies, 2001; Bies & Moag, 1986). Acknowledging that interactional justice was initially couched within a decision-making context, Bies (2001) more recently argued that interpersonal concerns are distinguishable from the decision-making processes that characterize procedural justice. Indeed, this emphasis on interpersonal concerns is consistent with research indicating that people have a fundamental motivation to maintain interconnectedness with other people (Baumeister & Leary, 1995).

The prominence of interpersonal concerns should be most salient when an individual's WSC is defined at the relational level. Such an interpersonal focus should lead individuals to be sensitive to aspects of fairness reflecting the extent to which their relationship with a significant other (e.g., the leader) is successful. This success is likely evaluated by the degree to which an individual perceives the absence of threats to the self (e.g., derogations, disrespect, and deception) when interacting with another individual (Bies, 2001). Indeed, Van den Bos and Lind (2002) recently argued that trust in authorities, such as supervisors, is derived from justice-based heuristics. As such, interactional justice is likely to convey to members of role relations that their dyadic relationship is beneficial rather than exploitive or harmful and that the self-concept they develop within this relationship is safe. Thus, interactional justice would seem to be a prerequisite for the full development of role relationships such as dyadic-level leadership.

The developmental aspects of interactional justice have been considered by two recent theoretical articles (Lord et al., 1999; Scandura, 1999). Scandura suggested that social justice affects the nature of the leader–member exchange that develops between superior–subordinate dyads. She noted that interactional justice evaluations are critical early in the role-making process because subordinates evaluate initial exchanges with leaders. Justice may be particularly important at this stage because it serves a broad heuristic purpose in resolving uncertainty (Lind, 2001; Van den Bos & Lind, 2002). Thus, interactional justice signals to subordinates that leaders and authority in general can be trusted and that efforts will be rewarded. In Scandura's model, over time, subordinates are differentiated into in-groups and out-groups with distributive justice contributing to out-group membership and procedural justice contributing to in-group membership. Moreover, in-group membership is determined by interactional justice. Lord et al. (1999) independently reached similar conclusions, maintaining that relational identities and interactional justice would be particularly important early in dyadic relations. They also suggested that interactional justice was a critical bifurcating variable, with low-interactional justice fostering individual-level identities and high-interactional justice setting the stage for the development of collective-level identities. The main implication of both of these theories is that organizational justice, particularly interactional justice, is an important aspect of employee developmental processes in organizations. Issues such as the development of leader–member exchanges or the acceptance of a collective organizational identity cannot be fully understood without incorporating an understanding of social justice processes.

The idea that social justice is important from a developmental perspective is also consistent with research on the group-value relational model (Lind & Tyler, 1988; Tyler, 1997; Tyler & Lind, 1992). Briefly stated, the rationale of the model is that individuals are sensitive to procedures because they are indicative of the group's values, as well as the extent to which the individual is valued by the group or authority enacting the procedure (Tyler & Lind, 1992). Although the model deals with groups, it also applies to the quality of interaction with the authorities who represent the group. Consequently, followers focused at the relational level are likely to monitor their interactions with leaders for signs of interpersonal fairness that, in turn, validate their relationship with the leader and the entire organization.

Tyler (1997) reviewed several studies supporting the group-value relational model. Specifically, in several large surveys he found that the perceived legitimacy of a leader depended on instrumental issues pertaining to the favorablity and control over outcomes received by employees. Legitimacy also depended on relational issues involving the communication of identity-relevant information through neutrality, trustworthiness, and status recognition (dignity and respect). Although both instrumental and relational concerns were important, relational concerns had larger and more general effects. Furthermore, the importance of relational issues increased with factors that enhanced either a subordinate's personal bonds with the supervisor or identification with the organization as a whole.

Although Tyler's (1997) work is important and relevant to our concern, he did not distinguish between relational- and collective-level processes. Consequently, it is hard to disentangle the leadership-related aspects of his studies from effects at the more collective, organizational level. This distinction may not be so important for testing justice theory, but it is critical for understanding where to apply justice theory to change organizational practices.

A practical issue related to such research is whether leaders should focus on interactional or procedural justice. We argued that this depends on a subordinate's identity level, but our coverage of justice and relational identities also suggests that interactional justice will be particularly important when employees are new to either an organization or their work unit. For such employees, we would expect both procedural and distributive justice information to be lacking. Consequently, their leaders should pay particular attention to interactional justice. Leaders should be particularly careful to treat new employees with dignity, respect, and politeness. Furthermore, this issue is likely to be particularly important for new female employees who tend to emphasize relational concerns (Gabriel & Gardner, 1999). One additional issue related to employees who lack information on procedural or distributive justice is that they also may use heuristics based on interactional justice to draw inferences about these other justice dimensions as implied by the work of Van den Bos and Lind (2002) on the substitutability of justice dimensions.

Collective-Level Identity and Procedural Justice

As a social self, the collective level of the self-concept differs from the relational self in that the social relationships move beyond the dyadic level to a more inclusive orientation of the group as a whole, with less of an emphasis on personalized attachments. Thus, when focused at the collective level, individuals should be concerned with the extent to which leaders represent the prototype of the in-group as research has shown (Hains et al., 1997; Hogg, 2001; Hogg et al., 1998). Self-worth at the collective level arises from favorable intergroup comparisons (Brewer & Gardner, 1996).

As discussed in the section on the relational self and interactional justice, social identity models can be used to explain why procedural justice may be more important when a collective self-representation is active in the WSC. When focused at the collective level, an individual should be most concerned with the procedures that are enacted for the whole group because they are representative of the group's values and the extent to which an individual is valued by the group or organization (Tyler & Lind, 1992). Interestingly, this concern may have more of a cognitive than affective basis, whereas relational identities may place more relative emphasis on affect (Lord et al., 1999).

Support for the Level of Identity and Justice Dimension Linkages

Our alignment of relational identities with interactional justice and of collective identities with procedural justice is congruent with other research that has attempted to distinguish between interactional and procedural justice based on person- and organization-oriented mechanisms. For example, Masterson, Lewis, Goldman, and Taylor (2000) argued that interactional justice perceptions should influence supervisor-oriented attitudes and behaviors through LMX (the quality of the leader–follower relationship), but they maintained that procedural justice operates through a more collective variable, perceived organizational support (POS), which reflects the quality of the employee–organization relationship. Because LMX reflects a dyadic, role relationship with one's supervisor, we believe it may be most important when relational identities are salient, whereas POS should reflect more collective factors because it pertains to treatment from the organization as a whole. Because of the potential parallel with our framework, we discuss the Masterson et al. study in more detail.

Masterson et al. (2000) analyzed responses from 651 employees using structural equation modeling (SEM). Two of their findings are critical to our argument. First, they found procedural justice to predict POS but not LMX, whereas interactional justice predicted LMX but not POS. Second, mediational hypotheses were generally confirmed: LMXs mediated the effects of interactional justice on supervisor-directed OCBs and job satisfaction, whereas POS mediated the effects of procedural justice on organization-directed OCBs, organizational commitment, job satisfaction, and intentions to quit. Together, these results are suggestive of two separate routes—relation-oriented and collective-oriented routes—for understanding interactional and procedural justice. If LMX and POS are most important with salient relational and collective identities, respectively, then Masterson et al.'s mediational results are exactly what our theory would predict. Similarly, Moorman et al. (1998) also found POS to mediate the relationship between procedural justice and several OCBs, which again shows the relationship between procedural justice and more collective, organization-directed behaviors.

Pillai et al. (1999) provided additional support for this theoretical framework. Using SEM, they examined the mediating effects of organizational justice and trust of supervisor in the relationship of leadership to several dependent variables. Using economic exchange- and social exchange-based arguments, Pillai et al. theorized and found support for the relationship between transactional leadership and distributive justice, as well as the relationship between transformational leadership and procedural justice. In addition, as expected from our theoretical framework, links that are inconsistent with salient identity had no significant effects in Pillai et al.'s study—neither transactional leadership and procedural justice nor transformational leadership and distributive justice were significantly related in their SEM model. Among the other results, transformational leadership had an indirect effect on trust, mediated by procedural justice, as well as a comparatively larger direct effect on trust. Although Pillai et al. did not assess self-identity, these results are consistent with our theoretical framework. In other words, the primed identity should affect the salience of procedural and distributive justice. Unfortunately, Pillai et al. did not distinguish between interactional and procedural justice in their measurement of procedural justice, which precludes a better understanding of the role of interactional justice.

Although the latter research provides indirect support for our ideas, research by Brockner, Chen, Mannix, Leung, and Skarlicki (2000) and Kwong and Leung (2002) provided some direct support for our ideas concerning the Brockner and Wiesenfeld (1996) interaction of distributive and procedural justice. Brockner and Wiesenfeld reviewed results from 45 independent samples in which justice was examined in both laboratory and field studies. They found an interaction between procedural and distributive justice such that distributive justice mattered most when procedural justice was perceived as being low. Specifically, outcome favorability was positively related to the favorability of participants' reactions when procedural justice was low; but reactions were favorable regardless of the outcome favorability when procedural justice was high. This result was quite consistent across samples and across a variety of dependent variables such as satisfaction, organizational commitment, acceptance of court decisions, task productivity, theft, and trust in and satisfaction with supervisors.

One practical implication of the Brockner and Wiesenfeld (1996) interaction is that when distributive justice is low, attention to procedural justice can have a broad positive impact on many organizational outcomes. This approach is likely to be a low-cost solution for organizations trying to be fair to employees (Brockner & Wiesenfeld, 1996). This implication is more informative, however, in light of recent research showing that individuals operating at a relational or collective level may be more amenable to interactional or procedural justice manipulations, which is consistent with our contention that justice dimensions will be differentially weighted depending on the level of the WSC that is active.

As such, across three studies, Brockner et al. (2000) found that the Brockner and Wiesenfeld (1996) interaction depended on the level of self-construal. More specifically, their results revealed that high-procedural justice mitigated the effects of low-outcome favorability on participant reactions for those participants with an interdependent self-construal. The rationale Brockner et al. developed for these effects was that procedural justice indicated that authorities could be trusted, which means that low current outcomes will eventually be redressed in the future. Trust, in turn, is more important when social exchanges are more important, which is likely with interdependent compared to independent self-construals. Although Brockner et al. did not distinguish between relational and collective interdependent identities, their logic seems to apply equally well to these two social identity levels.

More recently, Kwong and Leung (2002) examined the extent to which relational and collective orientations moderated the Brockner and Wiesenfeld (1996) interaction. Interestingly, they also examined the extent to which interactional justice interacted with outcome favorability. In the first of two studies, Kwong and Leung found that closeness of a specific other moderated the interaction of interactional justice and outcome favorability on feelings of happiness in light of an interpersonal dispute. The results showed that, for those who viewed the dyadic agent as a close other, interactional justice compensated for poor outcomes. In a second study, Kwong and Leung used organizational commitment to represent the importance of the organizational relationship—that is, a collective orientation—for employees. Prior organizational commitment moderated both the interactions of procedural justice and outcome favorability as well as interactional justice and outcome favorability in terms of reactions to a salary freeze or reduction.

Thinking in terms of Brockner et al.'s (2000) theory, the Kwong and Leung (2002) results seem to imply that trust can be inferred from interactional as well as procedural justice; therefore, either of these justice dimensions can convey a sense that future outcomes will compensate for current injustices. They also showed that the importance of the interaction party (whether an individual or an organization) moderates the interaction of justice dimensions, with importance depending on the level of a participant's self-construal. This research adds further credence to the suggestion made earlier that justice may be important in developing high-quality exchanges between leaders and subordinates (Lord et al., 1999; Scandura, 1999) and that this process is also dependent on subordinates' identity level. What is now needed is an experimental study that directly manipulates identity level and directly establishes trust as an important mediational process that is inferred from justice as suggested by Van den Bos and Lind (2002). These results also show the value of our prior suggestion that sorting individuals into groups who emphasize the same aspects of justice would help advance our understanding of justice processes. As we suggested, this research shows the effectiveness of grouping individuals based on identity level.

In sum, the preceding research suggests that the conceptual distinction between interactional and procedural justice, based on interpersonal and collective mechanisms, has substantial merit and that different justice dimensions are likely to receive differential weighting, in terms of information processing, depending on the level of the WSC that is active. Our theorizing regarding identities and justice dimensions can be summarized by the following proposition:

> Proposition 7.1. Identity will influence the dimension of justice that is salient, with individual level identity priming distributive justice, relational-level identity priming interactional justice, and collective-level identity priming procedural justice.

Use of Justice Dimensions in a Dynamic Model of Justice Evaluation

Thus far, we argued that different dimensions of justice are likely to align with different WSC levels. In this section, we discuss how this idea can be used to develop a fairly simple dynamic model of justice evaluation, shown in Fig. 7.1. In Fig. 7.1 we show three possible feedback loops, with each corresponding to a specific justice dimension and a specific level of the WSC. We maintain that these loops generally are not active at the same time, partly because this would create an excessive information-processing demand, and fairness processes may be used to reduce not increase uncertainty and information processing (Lind, 2001; Van den Bos & Lind, 2002). Instead, different dimensions may be used by different people or at different times to evaluate organizational justice. Therefore, the issue of differential weighting of justice dimensions translates into the information-processing question of which justice evaluation loop is currently active. That issue, in turn, depends on the specific level of the WSC that is active.

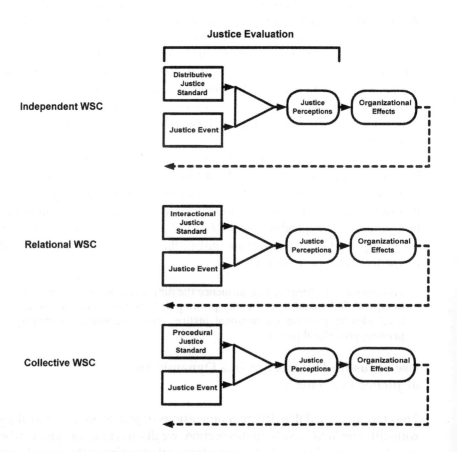

FIG. 7.1.   Levels of WSC and justice dimensions.

To specify dynamic processes in Fig. 7.1, we adopted the standard conventions from control theory to show how self-regulatory systems function. In this figure, time and information flow from left to right, and the triangles depict comparators that compare sensed feedback from relevant environments to standards from higher level systems. Sensed feedback is always an input on the lower, left side of the comparator triangles, and standards are shown on the upper, left side of each comparator. Output from the comparators is shown on the right of each triangle as a standard for a lower level system or for determining perceptions, affect, or behavioral reactions. Each comparator, along with input and output connections, thus provides a negative feedback loop that senses discrepancies of perceived inputs from standards and responds in a cognitive, affective, and/or behavioral sense. Discrepancies are a key motivational construct in motivational and cognitive self-regulatory theories (Carver & Scheier, 1998; Lord & Levy, 1994).

Each justice evaluation feedback loop in Fig. 7.1 begins with a standard derived from the WSC. Justice events are then compared against this standard to assess their consistency with the standards. When justice events meet or exceed standards, we perceive justice and react positively; but when standards are higher than actual events, we perceive injustice and react negatively. Thus, justice events are also affective events, and the AET model discussed in chapter 6 is also relevant. These positive or negative reactions then have consequences for organizations in terms of the attitudes and behavioral outcomes noted at the beginning of this chapter. An additional consequence is that these reactions also feed back to self-views (see Fig. 7.2) to impact perceived self-worth and, ultimately, have a delayed, second-order effect on justice evaluations and affective reactions. This process reflects a dynamic, contextually sensitive approach to evaluating justice-related events that is regulated through the self-concept.

For example, consider an individual focused at the individual level of the WSC who views pay as a relevant basis for self-evaluation and, consequently, has a salient distributive justice standard. This individual would then be expected to focus on and evaluate justice-related events such as pay, promotions, and formal recognitions vis à vis the salient standard. The end result of this justice evaluation process is a justice perception that is then manifested in terms of organizational effects either through affectively driven or more attitudinally driven processes.

Despite its initial complexity to one not familiar with control or self-regulatory theories (e.g., Carver & Scheier, 1998), an important advantage of this model is that it is relatively simple in terms of the information processes in-

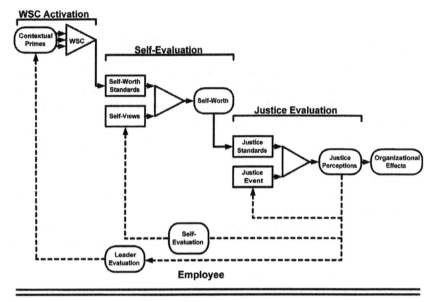

FIG. 7.2.   A dynamic model of organizational justice evaluation.

volved and, consequently, does not require extensive information-processing resources from individuals. In most cases, a quick and narrowly focused evaluation will likely reveal that organizational practices are fair, and workers can then focus on other issues. However, when one perceives injustice, complexity can be increased in two ways to provide a more comprehensive evaluation of justice. One way is to reconsider one's abilities and worth to determine if one's initial expectations were too high. This means of resolving injustice, however, may require a reorientation of self-views that threatens self-esteem and worth. Another means of extending one's assessment of justice is to consider a second justice dimension.

Evaluating a second justice dimension is likely to occur when the initial assessment indicates unfairness or, as already discussed, when one lacks sufficient information to make judgments on one aspect of justice, because one may substitute judgments from other dimensions (Lind, 2001; Van den Bos & Lind, 2002). For example, a person guided by an individual-level WSC who perceives that he or she is receiving insufficient outcomes using the top feedback loop in Fig. 7.1 may then consider more relational or collective issues assessing whether interactional or procedural justice exist.

That is, the person may make two or possibly three sequential justice decisions—Are my outcomes fair? Does my boss respect me? Or are organizational procedures fair? A similar sequence may occur for individuals who simply lack information regarding distributive justice.

Each of these decisions may involve simple judgments from a single loop shown in Fig. 7.1, which consumes few processing resources. Thus, we suggest that each loop is still considered in isolation, but that fairness may at times involve more than one sequential decision. However, certain combinations of judgments—for example unfairness on each decision considered—are likely to be particularly troubling to individuals. Moreover, if the original level of self-identity remains activated, we would expect that, over time, an individual will periodically return to the corresponding loop to reevaluate the particular justice dimension in a process of rumination.

Although we are positing that justice dimensions are considered sequentially and in isolation (this suggestion can be tested using process-oriented methodology), when aggregate, group-level data is analyzed, the consequence of such sequential processing may look like an interaction of justice dimensions. Extensive research supports such interactions among justice dimensions, but we again stress that there is no reason to assume that results from aggregate analyses of group data precisely describe individual-level processes. By this, we mean that the existence of statistical interactions does not necessarily imply that each individual jointly considers justice dimensions in a multiplicative manner. These interactions could just as easily result from the simpler, sequential consideration of justice dimensions. Indeed, many of the studies showing interactions between distributive and procedural justice use independent experimental manipulations of these dimensions that may be processed as discrete, dichotomous judgments (e.g., fair–unfair outcomes and fair–unfair processes) rather than as multiplicative assessments of fairness.

Simpler processes also have the advantage that they are more general, being plausible in environments that tax information-processing resources as well as those that do not. Organizational justice judgments seem almost ubiquitous in organizational environments based on the number of factors they have been shown to affect; thus, it seems likely that they are produced by relatively simple, general processes. Consequently, although justice dimensions may interact or substitute for each other, they are still likely to be considered sequentially by individuals. This reasoning is summarized in the following two propositions:

Proposition 7.2. Evaluation of organizational justice will involve sequential evaluation of justice dimensions, beginning with that dimension most closely associated with the current level of the WSC and terminating when a dimension indicates that fairness has occurred.

Proposition 7.3. There will be interactions among justice dimensions such that negative reactions to organizational justice will be most extreme when all dimensions that are considered indicate a lack of fairness.

MECHANISM 2: DIFFERENT STANDARDS FOR JUST LEADERSHIP

Standards

Up to this point, we discussed the weighting of organizational justice according to which level of self-identity is currently active. Moreover, in Fig. 7.1 we expanded the differential-weighting issue to incorporate a justice evaluation process in which a justice event is compared to a justice standard (e.g., distributive) corresponding to a specific level of the WSC (e.g., individual) resulting in a more dynamic model. In this section, we address more directly the development of these justice standards in terms of the WSC.

We believe that the justice standards depend on perception of one's own self-worth, which means that justice is dynamically regulated around different levels for different individuals. Individuals with unfavorable self-assessments may accept lower levels of outcomes, dyadic exchanges, or group identities than individuals with more favorable self-assessments. Consequently, the actual judgments produced by the justice evaluation processes shown in Fig. 7.1 can vary across individuals with similar types of identities, depending on their perceived self-worth. This issue, then, concerns the operation of comparison processes across each of the three panels of Fig. 7.1, whereas the issue of differential weighting of standards pertains to which of the three panels would be used by a particular individual or at a particular time.

Linking standards to self-worth, of course, raises the question of how self-worth is determined. We believe that the nature of the standards is likely to vary with the level at which the WSC is defined. Based on our earlier discussion, we expect that at the individual level, self-worth is determined by evaluating one's traits and characteristics in comparison to others; at the relational level, self-worth is determined by the fulfillment of one's role in the relationship; and at the collective level, self-worth is determined in terms of the favorability of intergroup comparisons (Brewer &

Gardner, 1996). Comparison of self-views to these different standards, therefore, creates a basis for self-worth and justice expectations, as well as for assessing the meaning of justice-related events.

The process we just described can be represented by three hierarchically nested feedback loops of the type already described. This organization, which is shown in Fig. 7.2, is a common way to represent self-regulatory processes (Carver & Scheier, 1998; Lord & Levy, 1994; Powers, 1973). This figure has three types of feedback loops—one associated with justice evaluation, one associated with self-evaluation, and one associated with WSC activation. This system is still efficient in terms of information processing because each loop creates minimal processing demands, and higher level loops are used less frequently than lower level loops, which are used only when lower level loops fail to resolve discrepancies.

The evaluation of one's leaders is also shown in Fig. 7.2 as part of a larger feedback loop flowing from justice perceptions. The latter loop feeds back into the WSC because a leader's actions in a justice event symbolize values that influence the WSC. For example, when subordinates are asked to accept a salary freeze, but management gets large raises, values supporting a collective orientation toward an organization are undercut, whereas an individual-level, everyone-for-themselves orientation is primed. As such, the three-level feedback system shown in Fig. 7.2 graphically illustrates how the WSC is embedded in a social context of which a leader is an important part. This framework also shows how the WSC helps determine perceived self-worth, which then creates an idiosyncratic self-regulatory context for understanding justice events with ultimate consequences for both the wider organization and for exchanges with the leader connected to the justice event.

Justice Standards at Different Identity Levels

Having laid out the underlying dynamics in Fig. 7.2, we are now in a position to discuss how this system would operate differently with different levels of the WSC. At the individual level, one's position along the self-worth dimension depends on whether one sees himself or herself (called self-views in Fig. 7.2) as being better or worse than comparison others (called standards for self-worth in Fig. 7.2), which then creates different standards for expected outcomes and for justice. An individual who sees himself or herself as being relatively worse than others would require less favorable outcomes for an exchange to be defined as fair. Conversely, someone who sees himself or herself as better than others would have more stringent outcome standards for evaluating the fairness of social exchanges. For example, a manager whose unit ranks in the top 5% of a company's performing units will have different contract expectations than one whose units are in the bottom 5%. Thus, at the individual level, self-worth affects the amount of organizational rewards that a subordinate needs to achieve or maintain perceptions of justice.

At the relational level, one's evaluation of self-worth depends on whether one sees oneself as deserving a close bond with the leader, based on what he or she considers to be suitable behavior in the role relationship with that leader. An individual with high self-worth would require a lot of consideration from and social interaction with the leader, whereas someone with low self-worth would require less consideration from and social interaction with the leader in an interpersonal sense. Thus, in the former case, an individual would require a higher level of LMX with the leader and greater consideration for the leader to be seen as fair. The meaning of justice or injustice would also reflect back on the value of one's role and one's ability to fulfill it as shown by the dotted line to self-views in Fig. 7.2. When justice is lacking in role relationships, it is likely that a relationship-oriented individual will denigrate the role as a means to minimize the affective consequences of injustice. Therefore, low-perceived justice may undercut existing levels of LMX or satisfaction with one's leader, as the employee disengages from the role relations with one's supervisor. It is also likely, as discussed earlier, that one would consider other aspects of justice, reacting most negatively when they all indicate unfairness.

Lastly, at the collective level, one's position along the self-worth dimension is based on the extent to which one views the respective in-group favorably in comparison to other groups. An individual who is high on this dimension views his or her in-group as having high worth and would have a stringent definition of what is considered as fair to the group. They should use this stringent standard in evaluating themselves, other group members, and a group's leader. As such, to be seen as just, a leader may need to be seen as representative of the in-group (relative to the out-group) before followers with strong collective identities will accept their acts as just (Hogg, 2001; Tyler, 1997). For example, a prototypical leader should serve as an effective symbol of the larger collective and thereby prime a more collective identity. With such a collective identity in place, followers may be more likely to emphasize procedural aspects that are likely to affect the group as a whole (De Cremer, 2002; De Cremer & van Knippenberg, 2002).

As explained in the previous section, most individuals are motivated to see their contributions to a social exchange as greater than average. Therefore, we predict that at the individual level, subordinates are likely to require greater-than-average outcomes to meet their definitions of fairness, which are grounded in upwardly biased, self-worth standards. Similarly, when the WSC is defined at the relational level, subordinates will require greater-than-average consideration and interaction from the leader to meet their definitions of fairness. Lastly, those with a collective WSC will require greater-than-average conformity to group prototypes, both for themselves, other group members, and their leaders. Our expectations concerning the level of standards are summarized in the following propositions:

Proposition 7.4. The level of justice standards will depend on evaluations of self-worth, and evaluations of self-worth will depend on the level of the WSC that is activated.

Proposition 7.5. Fairness judgments will show an upward bias with an individual-level identity yielding greater-than-average expected outcomes, a relational-level identity yielding greater-than-average expected consideration and interaction with one's leader, and a collective-level identity yielding expectations of greater-than-average conformity to group prototypes.

LEADERSHIP AND INJUSTICE: PRACTICAL IMPLICATIONS

Leaders as Managers of Injustice

Figures 7.1 and 7.2 show how employees are likely to integrate their active self-identity with justice perceptions, with the consequence of this regulation being not only reactions to organizational justice but also changes in attitudes and work behaviors. Thus, many important work outcomes may require an understanding of organizational justice processes for leaders to be effective, and this understanding, in turn, requires an understanding of how justice evaluations are embedded in self-structures. These issues are particularly important when leaders are dealing with new employees or are attempting to manage change. Similarly, a major problem for leaders is that of managing perceptions of injustice so as to avoid the many negative consequences that can result. How should this be done?

We suggest that although high-perceived self-worth can lead to perceived injustice, maintaining subordinates' views of high self-worth is essential not only for their health and happiness but also because self-worth is a basis for successfully managing challenging tasks. Thus, leaders must convey to subordinates that the lack of sufficient outcomes reflects real constraints on outcome distribution, not low assessments of subordinate self-worth. This can be done by being particularly careful to combine information on low-outcome distribution with high-interactional and procedural justice. Such an approach would indicate that although outcomes are lower than self-based expectations, leaders and organizations can still be trusted and are still concerned with employee welfare.

When Not to Use E-Mail

Consider the following example of how not to handle this process. In an attempt to create a more efficient allocation of resources within his college, a dean at one of our universities unilaterally proposed eliminating a doctoral program. This was done without prior discussion of this option with relevant faculty members in the affected department and without a face-to-face meeting to explain this decision. Instead, the message was conveyed by e-mail near the end of the semester when everyone was naturally working harder than normal to finish academic year activities. Not only did this decision produce strong emotional reactions, but the eventual decision was not accepted by many department members, producing a 2-year struggle with university administrators to reverse the decision or find an acceptable alternative, which is still ongoing.

Why were reactions so strong and persistent when the dean was a legitimate administrator whose responsibilities include resource allocation decisions? First, interactional justice was low because the dean chose e-mail rather than a face-to-face meeting. Low-interactional justice can indicate that individuals are not valued by the authority. Furthermore, because the change created high uncertainty, individuals were particularly likely to pay attention to justice processes as a means to judge the trustworthiness of the dean, just as Van den Bos and Lind's (2002) fairness heuristic theory would predict. Second, faculty members were given little voice in the initial proposal, although they did provide a counterproposal that was not accepted. Hence, their perceptions of procedural justice were also low. Third, given the heavy workload near the end of the semester, distributional outcomes were also low relative to required inputs. Thus, no matter how this initial decision was evaluated, it was perceived as being unfair, and trust of the dean was undermined.

Life is full of unexpected and unfair events, so why should an event such as this persist unresolved for almost 2 years? One reason undoubtedly is the slow pace of academic decision, but another has to do with the model shown in Fig. 7.2. In this model, justice events are not evaluated in isolation, but instead they are considered in the immediate context of self-views and self-worth. Consistent with this model, the self-views of affected faculty members were threatened. Their immediate response was to arrange a face-to-face meeting with the dean where they presented comparative data on publications, citations, and the grants they had obtained. This meeting can be viewed as an attempt to reaffirm their self-worth both to each other and to a relevant authority by maintaining high self-views. Indeed, one positive outcome of this meeting was a reaffirmation on the part of the dean that the faculty were indeed of very high caliber.

But again, the issue was not resolved, and again, one reason can be seen in a further examination of Fig. 7.2. Note that in this figure the bottom line goes through leadership perceptions to contextual primes that activate the WSC. The critical contextual factors at this level are values, which tend to be personal values when individual-level identities are salient, and social values when collective identities are salient, as they were in this case. In fact, the doctoral program in question had been a major focus of the six faculty members involved for several years, and their group identity had coalesced around this issue. In terms of Cropanzano et al.'s (1993) study, the program had become a self-relevant personal project linking immediate task activities with higher level identities and values. Thus, the program served to integrate the identities of these individuals into a social and professional academic world. Without this program, the basis for an important aspect of the faculty members' identities and their connections to an important social group was eliminated. We believe it was this higher level linkage that made it so difficult for the faculty members to give up this program. Indeed, consistent with this reasoning, their current activities are focused at transforming this program into one that is more acceptable to the administration and still consistent with the professional identities, research interests, and social relations of the faculty members involved. In other words, they are actively constructing an alternative WSC that has more institutional support. In Ibarra's (1999) terms, they are creating group-level provisional selves. As this rather long example clearly illustrates, the application of organizational justice in organizational decision-making processes is a complex issue, in part, because justice is both a proxy for trust in authorities and a means of linking identities to organizational activities.

What should the dean have done to avoid these problems? Rather than just making and communicating decisions, he should have developed a pro-

chapters 2 and 3. It is well recognized that task goals and task performance feedback serve to create self-regulatory systems that can be nested hierarchically (see Carver & Scheier, 1998) within self- and value systems. And, it is also well-known that such systems are immediate determinants of task performance. Thus, Fig. 7.3 reflects accepted theories of self-regulation that were previously discussed.

What is not widely recognized is that such systems are also exactly the type of systems that determine social fairness evaluations. Indeed, a comparison of Fig. 7.2 and 7.3 show that they differ primarily in terms of the feedback loops on the far right, which involve justice evaluation loops and task regulation, respectively. The models are quite similar in that both the justice evaluation and the task regulation feedback loops are embedded within the same type of WSC activation and self-evaluation loops. This offers the possibility that the linkage between justice evaluation and task behaviors can be understood by considering the potential interaction of the same Self-Evaluation feedback loop (the middle feedback loop in Fig. 7.2 and 7.3) with the feedback loops on the far right sides of these two figures.

We offer two brief examples to show how this process might work, but our objective here is simply to show, on a more detailed level, how justice and task performance could be dynamically linked rather than to offer a formal theory. For example, consider again the equity theory finding that when subjects are paid by the hour but are undercompensated, they lower inputs to restore justice. What is unspecified in this theory is precisely how inequity produces lower performance. However, if we consider the effects of injustice on self-views as shown by the middle feedback line in Fig. 7.2, we can see that lower-than-expected compensations could lower task-relevant self-views through feedback processes. For example, despite the need to maintain a favorable self-image, some employees may reason, "If I get less pay than Bill, I must not be as good at my job as he is." However, when the same conclusion, "I'm not as good at my job as Bill is," is translated into revised task performance goals, lower self-views also lower performance standards. Performance is regulated around goals (Locke & Latham, 1990), so these new task goals naturally produce lower performance. This example makes sense primarily for one who has an individual-level WSC, because it orients one toward social comparisons to determine worth and distributive justice issues.

When a collective-level WSC is involved, the dynamic linkages are similar, but the content can be expected to vary substantially. Consider, for example, the effect of a leader's self-sacrificing versus self-benefitting behavior on group member cooperation (De Cremer & van Knippenberg, 2002). The organizational justice model of Fig. 7.2 shows that the perceptions of unfair benefits are likely to affect leadership perceptions negatively in the bottom feedback loop of this model. This, in turn, feeds back to influence contextual primes for the WSC. Figure 7.3 is more specific on these contextual primes, differentiating primes that activate individual-level identities and personal values from those that activate social identities and social values. Thus, we might expect a leader's self-benefitting behavior to activate an individual-level WSC, whereas self-sacrificing behavior would activate a collective level WSC. As shown in Fig. 7.3, these general self-orientations can become translated into self-relevant projects and then eventually into task-oriented goals. As De Cremer (2002) noted, task goals can be either proself or prosocial, and these different types of goals can affect the occurrence of cooperative task behaviors. Thus, the interpretation of the justice-relevant behaviors of leaders shown in Fig. 7.2 can explain the basis for task goal transformations in Fig. 7.3 because of their common linkage through values and the WSC.

Our main point in these two examples is that the feedback effects of organizational justice evaluations may operate through self-relevant processes and may be responsible for translating justice effects into task-relevant organizational behaviors. Such explanations are possible because we have an integrated model explaining how the self regulates task behavior in Fig. 7.3 which corresponds to our justice model in Fig. 7.2. The practical value of such a model, then, is that it can help specify the likely consequences of leader actions. Many of these consequences would not be clear without a specific dynamic model as a guide. Without such an understanding of motivational processes, leaders would operate much like our dean in the previous example of an e-mail-communicated organizational change, with no way to anticipate the self-evaluation or self-activation effects of their intended organizational decisions.

EMPIRICAL SUPPORT
FOR AN IDENTITY-BASED JUSTICE MODEL

In this chapter, we laid out a rather complex model of organizational justice and identities in Fig. 7.1 through 7.3 We also discussed both the fit of this model with existing literature and the practical implications of this perspective. In this final section of this chapter, we comment on how the model can be tested empirically. Our initial approach to the issue of empirical support was to examine preexisting data from 191 employed students collected by Johnson et al. (2003). As we would expect from our model, justice and identity interacted in predicting satisfaction with leaders or management. Specifically, the effects of interpersonal justice on several dependent variables (e.g., satisfaction with leaders, management in general, and interpersonally relevant OCBs) increased with the extent to which subjects reported strong relational identities. Neither the interaction of individual identities with distributive justice nor the interaction of collective identities with procedural justice were significant, but this may largely reflect the effects of the student sample, which consisted of mostly new employees and a predominance of part-time employees.

We also found that gender interacted with interpersonal justice, with the relationship between satisfaction with leadership and interpersonal justice being higher for women than men. This result is consistent with Gabriel and Gardner's (1999) research indicating that women tend to put more emphasis on interpersonal relations, whereas men emphasize more group-oriented collective identities. Thus, both individuals high in relational identities and women, place more weight on interpersonal justice in predicting satisfaction with their leader. These are important results because they indicate that an individual's identity level moderates the effects of interpersonal justice on relations to leaders. In addition, we found no significant interactions of interpersonal justice with collective identity, which confirms our expectation that these two dimensions of identity should be treated separately. Interestingly, when looking at organizationally relevant OCBs, we found an interaction between gender and procedural justice that indicated men placed more weight on procedural justice than women in determining collectively oriented OCBs. We did not find this for individually oriented OCBs or satisfaction with management. This again is consistent with Gabriel and Gardner's research showing that women and men emphasize relational and collective identities, respectively.

Although encouraging, as noted previously, weights from regression analyses on aggregate data provide only a rough test of the type of model developed in this chapter. A better approach would be to use reaction time data to investigate the speed with which justice- or performance- related constructs could be accessed. For example, based on Proposition 7.1, we might expect positive associations between reaction times for justice dimensions and associated identities such that reactions to distributive justice questions would be faster when individual-level identities were primed or were chronically accessible, reactions to interactional justice questions would be fastest with salient relational identities, and responses to procedural justice questions would be fastest with salient collective identities.

Similarly, the substitutability of justice dimensions suggested by Proposition 7.2 implies that the availability of justice dimensions that are not central to an identity level will be higher when injustice exists for prior justice evaluations. For example, individuals with salient individual level identities should rely first on distributive justice information in judging fairness of organizational practices, and their evaluations should incorporate procedural or interactional justice information only when distributive justice is low. Thus, procedural or interactional justice information should be more accessible when distributive justice is low than when it is high. The logic linking performance and justice evaluation systems as depicted in Fig. 7.2 and 7.3 could also be tested by examining whether low-distributive justice led people to lower task goals, as implied by some equity theory research, or whether a leader's emphasis on self-sacrifice rather than self-benefit makes prosocial goals more accessible than proself goals, as De Cremer's (2002) research suggest.

SUMMARY

This chapter extended the consideration of identity level to the area of organizational justice. The distinction between distributive, interactional, and procedural justice was explained. and a natural relation among identity levels and types of organizational justice was proposed. Specifically, we proposed that distributive justice should be most salient when an individual-level identity is activated. interactional justice should be most salient when a relational-level identity is activated, and procedural justice should be salient when a collective-level identity is activated. We also suggested that justice dimensions that matched the current level of the WSC will be evaluated first in appraising justice events; but when evaluations of these dimensions suggest unfairness, additional justice dimensions will be evaluated.

We also explained that the linkage of organizational justice and identities can be represented by a system of three hierarchically nested feedback loops in which justice is evaluated, self-worth is assessed, and the currently active identity is aligned with the organizational context. In such control systems, effects flow in both directions, with the WSC constraining personal projects and justice standards through top-down, feed-forward processes, and justice evaluations feeding back to justice standards, self-views, leadership perceptions, and activated values. Such control systems were used to show how justice evaluation and leadership perceptions are part of dynamic systems of values and identities in organizations. We also noted that organizational justice, particularly interactional justice, has heuristic value because it symbolizes many things to employees, such as trust and value by one's leader and organization.

8

The Value Added by a Second-Order, Subordinate-Focused Approach to Understanding Leadership Processes

We began this book by arguing that, despite extensive research, the scientific understanding of leadership was incomplete because leadership researchers, like most naive observers, focused on the perceived qualities of leaders, especially the behavior of leaders. The problem with that approach is that leaders are thought to affect organizational outcomes largely through their impact on subordinates. Thus, leaders may initiate the leadership process, but they do not complete it. Subordinates do! Because leadership effects are largely mediated by follower self-regulatory processes, we maintained that it made sense to focus on subordinate self-regulation as the source of a second-order, scientifically grounded theory of leadership processes and then work backwards, by using reverse engineering, to obtain a more comprehensive understanding of leadership processes. In simpler terms, understanding leadership demands more than understanding leadership traits or behavior; it also requires an understanding of how followers perceive those behaviors; how these perceptions make followers feel and think about themselves; and, ultimately, what these thoughts and feelings make followers want to do.

To understand subordinate self-regulatory processes, we introduced the construct of a working self-concept, and proposed that the WSC operated as a self-regulatory, control system. Like other self-regulatory systems (e.g., Carver & Scheier, 1998), we suggested that the WSC guided thoughts and actions by comparing sensed input to internal standards and then responding both cognitively and affectively to the perceived discrepancy of sensed input from standards. We elaborated this simple idea by noting that the WSC could shift among three types of self-regulatory systems concerned with proximal motivation, distal motivation, or self-development (see Fig. 2.1); we extended this idea further by noting that the content of the relevant self-regulatory system (self-views, possible- selves, and current goals) also changed when the WSC was defined at individual, relational, or collective levels (see Fig. 3.2). Self-regulatory feedback loops are often viewed as being embedded in hierarchies of feedback loops that vary in abstractness (Carver & Scheier, 1981, 1998; Lord & Hanges, 1987; Powers, 1973) as we showed in Figs. 3.1 and 7.3. We argued that the self provided the most useful level of abstractness for understanding leadership processes because it could be influenced by leaders and yet was internal to subordinates. Importantly, the self was also robust in the sense that it pertained to a wide spectrum of follower psychological processes that were social, cognitive, affective, and motivational.

In the prior chapters we showed how this perspective could be elaborated to understand a number of issues: the relation of self-regulatory systems to subordinates' motivation, cognitions, and affect; how this system could be linked to leaders and the values that their actions symbolized; and how such a system could be applied to understanding complex social processes such as social justice. In the current chapter, we step back from the content of the theory we developed and evaluate three related issues that pertain to the value added to the scientific literature by this approach to understanding leadership processes. Specifically, we address the potential yield of this approach in terms of scientific ideas that can guide further theory development; we explain how this theoretical approach could be used to develop more successful applied interventions that are grounded in a scientific understanding of leadership processes rather than more commonsense ideas about leadership; and, finally, we discuss ways that future research could more fully develop this approach. We turn now to those issues.

FOLLOWER-CENTERED LEADERSHIP PROCESSES
AND LEADERSHIP THEORY: VALUE ADDED

Capacity to Integrate Prior Theory

Theoretical Richness or Theoretical Confusion? In a commonly expressed axiom, some leadership scholars have suggested that there are as many approaches to leadership as there are leadership researchers (Yukl & Van Fleet, 1992). Although there can be little doubt that this statement exaggerates the heterogeneity of perspectives that can be found in the leadership literature, there also can be little doubt that, as a discipline, we are in no danger of experiencing a theoretical shortfall. The breadth and diversity of opinion that has characterized the social scientific investigation of leadership over the last 100 years has served as both a strength and weakness of the field. Simultaneously, leadership scholars have created a theoretically rich, vibrant discipline, as well as one that has become a confusing array of constructs, propositions, theories, and results.

Consider for a moment how the varying perspectives and approaches to leadership interconnect. For instance, what is the relationship between transformational leadership, LMX and self-sacrificial leadership? How do contingency perspectives fit with other theories of leadership? How can subordinate focused social–cognitive models be integrated with behaviorally focused leader models? How do leadership processes vary across culture? To date, the task of answering such questions has been nearly impossible, in large part, because no general overarching framework exists.

One motive that guided us while writing this book was our hope to create a leadership framework, one that could assist researchers and practitioners who have been as puzzled as we have by how the different pieces of the leadership puzzle fit together. To this end, we began this book by suggesting that the investigation of leadership should emanate from an understanding of subordinates, rather than leaders, because subordinates produce the outcomes that are most often credited to leaders. In particular, we suggested that advances could be made in terms of understanding how subordinates' self-concepts mediated leader actions. In our view, the self provides a fundamental psychological context within which contemporary leadership theories can be organized, integrated, and understood. In the following sections, we concretely operationalize this objective by discussing how the self-concept framework that has unfolded throughout this book can be heuristically used to organize and connect seemingly disparate leadership perspectives. In subsequent portions of this chapter we move beyond specific theories and discuss the self framework in terms of its more general implications for understanding basic leadership principles (e.g., contingency views) and broader contextual issues (e.g., culture).

Identity Level as a Heuristic Framework for Leadership: Individual Identity.   One way in which leadership theories can be systematically organized is in terms of their common focus on subordinates' individual self-concepts. As we outlined in previous chapters, the individual-level self is characterized by attempts to differentiate the self from others, leading individuals to evaluate their worth in a contingent manner. A number of viewpoints on leadership appear to be particularly applicable to this identity level. For instance, one might situate at the individual-level leadership theories that have focused on monitoring, feedback, and contingent rewards (Komaki, 1986; Larson & Callahan, 1990; Podsakoff, Todor, & Skov, 1982); transactional exchanges (Hollander, 1964); and distributive justice (Tyler, 1997). In each of these cases, a leader's activities establish an environment that accentuates the need for an individual to be focused on his or her own personal responsibilities, performance, and outcomes. Similarly, we suspect that, outside of any formal theory of leadership, any leader activities that are perceived as self-benefiting by subordinates should function in such a way as to increase the salience of individualistic identities within subordinates (De Cremer, 2002).

Relational-Level Leadership Theories.   In addition to situating theories in relation to the individual self, some theoretical positions on leadership share a common focus in terms of a subordinate's relational-level self-identity. As the reader may recall, a relational perspective suggests that the self is the result of interpersonal processes that unfold between a leader and a subordinate. It is at the relational level that our perceptions of how others perceive us, which have been termed reflected appraisals (Shrauger & Schoneman, 1979), serve as the primary determinant of our self-views and, thus, how we will regulate ourselves. Perhaps most exemplary of this level is the self-fulfilling prophecy work (SFP) laid out by Dov Eden and his colleagues over the past 20 years.

In numerous field experiments with the Israeli military, Eden (1992) repeatedly demonstrated that a leader's expectations for a subordinate influence the subordinate's subsequent work performance. For instance, in the first experiment conducted with the Israeli military, Eden and Shani (1982) manipulated the expectations that boot camp instructors held for the soldiers who would be participating in basic training. Four days prior to the soldiers arrival at basic training, the instructor's expectations for each soldier were manipulated by informing each instructor of the soldier's potential (high, average, or low). Unbeknownst to the instructors, the information regarding each soldier's potential was an experimental manipulation that was independent of each soldier's true ability. The effect of this manipulation was evaluated at the end of basic training by assessing soldiers' performance on four dependent variables—achievement on multiple-choice exams in three subjects and weapons proficiency, as rated by an impartial evaluator who was unaware of the expectation manipulation. Impressively, the results of this field experiment revealed that those designated as high performers significantly outperformed the low and average performers on all four dependent variables under investigation. Findings such as these are interesting within the current context because they suggest that reflected appraisals are a potent tool available to organizational leaders.

Interestingly, we think that similar theorizing about the relational self and reflected appraisals may provide useful insights into leader effects that emerge at the group or organizational level. Although Eden's (1992) work primarily focused on the direct communication of a reflected appraisal to a subordinate, it seems quite plausible that similar mechanisms can account for how leaders impact larger groups of subordinates through organizational climates. Several scholars have noted that a leader's impact on subordinates may lie in the creation of different organizational climates. For example, in reviewing laboratory research conducted by Kurt Lewin, George Litwin and Robert Stringer (1968) concluded that the climate created by Lewin's leaders "proved to be more powerful than previously acquired behavior tendencies, and it was able to change the observed behavior patterns of group members" (p. 36). More recent research with charismatic leaders continues to support such linkages between leader behaviors, organizational climates, and organizational performance (e.g., Koene, Vogelaar, & Soeters, 2002). Despite such work, the influence mechanism remains somewhat mysterious. Why is it that an organizational climate should change individual behavior?

In our view, the influence that is derived through climate stems from a combination of several key characteristics of the self that allow for the occurrence of anticipatory reflected appraisals. Ultimately, climates communicate to individuals the norms and values that are broadly shared throughout a group. As with any normative structure, these norms both communicate descriptive information to individuals (how people are) as well as prescriptive information (how people should behave). Thus, when combined with an individual's capacity to project himself or herself into the future (see Tulving, 2002), climates allow the individual to anticipate the reflected appraisals of others for any given attitude or behavior. Conceptualizing leadership in broader terms, the mechanism outlined here recognizes that any member of an organization can act as an agent of leadership (Lord & W. G. Smith, 1999), instilling appropriate role-based behavior for any other organizational member. That is, leader effects become routinized when the anticipated reflected appraisal of one's coworkers acts to constrain and regulate behavior within the acceptable prescriptive bounds that are dictated by an organization's climate. Andersen and Chen's (2002) theory of the relational self, which is discussed in a subsequent section of this chapter, makes a very similar point, maintaining that there are as many selves as there are significant others. Their work suggests that significant coworkers may have effects that are similar to leaders.

Collective-Level Leadership Theories.   In many domains, effective leadership depends on the ability of leaders to construct collective identities for their subordinates. For instance, the success of many sports teams hinges on a coaches' ability to shift players from being internally focused on their own welfare (e.g., personal performance bonuses) to being externally focused on advancing the group's agenda (e.g., winning). In recent years, a number of leadership theories have been proposed that can be integrated in terms of their common focus on creating collective-level identities within subordinates. Most salient in this grouping are the transformational, charismatic, and self-sacrificial leadership approaches that have grown in popularity in recent years. In contrast to transactional leadership, which we noted appeals to an individual's self-interest, transformational, charismatic, and self-sacrificial leadership styles are thought to have their effects on organizations because they transform individuals to move beyond their own self-interests (Yukl, 2002). That is, subordinates working with leaders who display these behaviors come to identify more strongly with the organization and the people they work with, oftentimes leading them to work counter to their own best interests for the good of the company.

Although previous frameworks have not organized these theories in terms of their relationship to the collective self, the available data suggest that integrative efforts may provide useful insights into the similarity that exists among these approaches. For instance, research on self-sacrificial leadership has shown that self-sacrificial leaders are perceived to be more charismatic (e.g., De Cremer, 2002; Yorges et al., 1999) and that these types of leaders transform subordinates to adopt a social orientation (De Cremer, 2002). Similarly, transformational leadership research has shown that it is related to collective outcomes, such as affective organizational commitment and organizational citizenship behavior (Lowe, Kroeck, & Sivasubramaniam, 1996; Podsakoff, Mackenzie, Moorman, & Fetter, 1990), and that it is related to subordinates' collective identities (Conger, Kanungo, & Menon, 2000; Paul et al., 2001). Moreover, transformational leadership research has shown that this leadership style exhibits stronger effects among individuals who already hold collective-level identities (Jung & Avolio, 1999).

In combination, the available empirical data lead us to conclude that self-sacrificial, charismatic, and transformational leadership styles operate similarly through subordinates' collective identities. In addition, we suspect that many of the relationships that exist between these theories and other leadership theories can be easily understood in terms of a common linkage with subordinates' collective level identities. For instance, consider LMX theories of leadership. LMX focuses on dyadic relationship that emerges between a given leader and a follower (Gerstner & Day, 1997). Yet, previous research has demonstrated that LMX and transformational theories are very highly intercorrelated (Gerstner & Day, 1997), at least when measured by questionnaires. In our view, such findings are not surprising given that high LMXs may also help create collective-level identities. In this regard, the pattern of treatment received from a supervisor not only reflects the dyadic relationship that exists within a given supervisor–subordinate pair, but it also communicates how valued the subordinate is to the larger group (Tyler & Lind, 1992). Thus, just as transformational leadership behavior or self-sacrificial behavior on the part of the leader can lead subordinates to define the self in collective terms, so too can a high-quality exchange with a supervisor. As a result, both theories may simply reflect alternative pathways to activating a subordinate's collective identity.

In short, we showed that many leadership theories can be organized in terms of the identity level at which they operate or their effect on identity levels. Additional details relating leadership theories to identity levels and specific aspects of the WSC are presented in Lord et al. (1999).

Capacity to Generate Novel Insights

Leadership Processes and Meaning.   Johnson-Laird (1989), a noted cognitive scientist, argued that people do not respond to the environment directly but, instead, to the internal meaning they construct from environmental cues. Meaning, in turn, is often derived from mental models of the environment and how it works. We suggest that a powerful type of mental model is the representation people have of themselves in particular situations. As already noted, the self is constructed in a context-sensitive way that highlights an environment's potential to harm or benefit an individual. It is this aspect that makes environments meaningful. Individuals continually monitor and react to this aspect of meaning through primary appraisal processes, and they use emotional reactions as an alert system to indicate when environments offer high potential benefit or harm. One important theoretical insight our perspective provides is that it is not leader behavior per se that is important to understand, but rather it is the meaning of that behavior for subordinates as interpreted through their mental model of the self in a current context or, as we defined it, their WSC. The WSC, then, is an important mediator of leadership effects, translating them into emotional reactions, cognitions, and self-regulatory processes.

By now, this perspective is likely to be so familiar to the reader that it does not seem novel; however, it is worth restating that such follower-centered perspectives on leadership processes are rare. Furthermore, we articulated this concept at a broad, abstract level in differentiating among individual, relational, and collective WSCs. We also showed how this broad level can be translated into more specific proximal, distal, or developmental motivational systems (see Fig. 2.1) and how these systems, in turn, can be tied to self-regulation in terms of context-specific tasks (see Figs. 3.1 and 7.3). Thus, our theory specifies how leaders can influence a subordinate's intended meaning in a particular context through very general interpretive systems (the WSC and its level) or through more focused, self-regulatory hierarchies. It also explains why framing tasks in terms of potential gains or losses (Kahneman & Tversky, 1979) can have such powerful effects on thoughts and behavior, namely, because it transforms the subjects' meaning and self-regulatory system from one form to another (from gain- to loss-oriented WSCs).

Integrating Cognitions and Emotions.   As noted in chapter 6, much of the prior leadership literature is cognitively oriented in either its methodology or its substantive focus. In that chapter, we made the case for considering the emotional side of leadership in terms of affective events and how they were perceived and reacted to by others. A novel benefit of our perspective is that the self-identity and, particularly, the WSC automatically integrates both emotions and cognitions, melding them into a self-regulatory system that produces behavior and is then guided by behavioral effects as reflected in feedback from task and social systems. Primary appraisals, the resulting emotions, the self-guides associated with learning versus performance goals, and the goal hierarchies that forge links to specific environments all have both emotional and cognitive components that are integrated with respect to a nexus provided by the WSC. What this perspective offers to leadership theory is a way to understand how emotions and cognitions are integrated by followers and a way to see how both the cognitive and emotional activities of leaders influence this process.

Multiple Selves and Midrange Theories. A problem shared by both personality and leadership theory is one of finding *mid-range theoretical perspectives*—theories that are broad enough to generalize across situations yet are specific enough to yield reasonably accurate predictions or guides to behavior. For example, in a compelling but overly specific view on personality, Mischel and Shoda (1995) argued that personality is comprised of situation-specific self-regulatory processes that generalize within situations across time, but not across situations. Taken to their extreme, contingency theories regarding leadership provide a similar perspective.

Our perspective suggests that there may be a way to organize contexts into larger units that still have coherence at a deeper level. We suggest thinking of differences in WSCs in a coherent way provides this deeper level of analysis that can generate midrange theories of both personality and leadership. In the previous section of this chapter we showed how this perspective can help organize leadership theories. With respect to personality theory, we will simply sketch out a general argument.

We agree with Mischel and Shoda (1995) that self-regulation requires context-specific productions (if–then statements), but rather than seeking the context as the source of the conditions satisfied by the if component of productions, we believe it is more fruitful to define the if component in terms of the internal meaning of the context for subordinates as suggested by Johnson-Laird (1989). As we already argued, internal meaning can be explained in terms of the nature of the self-system or WSC that is developed. This meaning may generalize across contexts, suggesting areas in which the effects of personality will also generalize.

J. R. Anderson's (1983, 1987) Adaptive Control of Thought (ACT*) architecture is also production based, and he demonstrated that goals provide a deep structure that can trigger the automatic application of skill across contexts. We simply maintain that this same principle can be applied one or two levels up in a subordinate's goal hierarchy. To carry this analogy a bit further, activating a WSC then would correspond to activating a specific type of personality in subordinates, and changing WSCs (either temporarily or permanently) would correspond to changing a subordinate's operating personality. Thus, leaders can be thought of as influencing subordinates by changing the aspects of their personality that are active in work contexts. S. M. Andersen and Chen (2002) extended this same idea to the effects of significant others on self-regulation by positing that the activation from significant others spreads to a companion self-with-significant-other representation that guides behavior.

Leaders as Regulators of Individual–Society Connections.   We argued that leaders can change the WSC of subordinates by activating different sets of values. Schwartz (1992, 1999), however, argued that societal values reflect societal solutions to enduring problems. Thus, by altering the pattern of values that is salient to individuals, leaders also change the connection of individuals to larger societies and the societal problems they are oriented toward solving. A prototypical example of such leadership is illustrated by John F. Kennedy's challenge from his inaugural address, "Ask not what your country can do for you—ask what you can do for your country" (Kennedy, John Fitzgerald, Microsoft Encarta Encyclopedia, 1999). This simple challenge effectively moves followers from individual to collective orientations and from a focus on getting to giving.

Seeing leadership as regulating the connection of a subordinate's self-regulatory system to society also shows how leaders can address social problems while still allowing maximum autonomy to followers. Rather than ordering subordinates to behave in a manner that benefits society or creating social norms for desired behaviors, effective leaders activate a WSC that produces desired behaviors through subordinates' own self-regulatory structures. Through such processes, leaders are likely to gain commitment to addressing societal problems rather than superficial compliance. As Yukl (2002, pp. 142–143) noted, effective leadership is not controlling. We add that effective leadership is more likely to be inspiring and that inspiration comes from helping subordinates see how they are connected through common values to a larger society.

Capacity to Integrate Broader Social Science Research.   Although not a specific insight, we believe a novel benefit of the perspective on leadership processes that we have developed is its broad capacity to integrate social science research. In addition to the burgeoning literature on self-identity, we included thinking on evolution, emotions, cognitions, social cognitions, social perceptions, motivation, self-regulatory systems, individual differences, personality, social justice, and values. In addition, we discussed how specific theoretical findings in these areas have implications for leadership. To give but one brief additional example, consider Gabriel and Gardner's (1999) finding that women tend to develop collective identities at the relational level, whereas men tend to develop collective identities in terms of larger social units. Our theoretical perspective transforms this curious fact into an understanding of how men and women are likely to differ in their self-regulatory systems, the meaning they construct in a particular context, and their leadership requirements.

VALUE ADDED TO THE PRACTICE
OF LEADERSHIP

Moving Leadership Theory Closer
to the Source of Effects

As we discussed in chapter 1, one problem that plagues leadership interventions is that they are typically focused on leaders, whereas the hoped-for effects of interventions are created by followers' responses. The leader only initiates a process that is completed by other organizational members. Considerable variance in the effects of interventions can be created by variability in the meaning of these interventions to followers and followers' reactions to the meaning they construct. Without a clear understanding of these follower-centered aspects of leadership processes, the effects of interventions are unlikely to be very predictable. In other terms, follower meaning construction and reactions are mediating processes for a leader's effects, and mediators explain more variance in dependent variables than antecedents because they are closer in a causal sense to the intended effect.

Based on this logic, we expect that one important applied value of the theory that we developed is that it moves leadership theory closer to the source of a leader's effects. By understanding how leadership affects subordinates' feelings and cognitions, practitioners should be able to design interventions that are more effective, and they have a better idea what to examine when interventions do not produce their intended effect. For example, practitioners may want to understand what an intervention means to subordinates rather than just how it is viewed by leaders. Answers to these questions might be helpful: Does an intervention engage promotion versus prevention orientations in subordinates? (This may be as much a function of individual differences in subordinates as differences in leader skills or behavior.) Does this intervention activate self-views versus possible selves? (This again may be a function of differences in subordinates, not differences in leaders.)

By understanding mediating as well as antecedent leadership processes, practitioners can also consider other ways to produce the intended effect. For example, an individual's WSC may be as dependent on the values stressed by an organizational culture as it is on the values primed by a leader's actions. Thus, if our concern is with creating a collective rather than an individual WSC, practitioners can compare the effectiveness of leadership interventions to those involving culture change. Leadership change may not be the best solution to all types of organizational problems. Without a focus on subordinate-centered mediating processes, such comparisons would not be as clear.

Robust Theory and Robust Practice

At the outset, we noted that one advantage to using the self-concept as the theoretical mortar that binds leadership together was the self's robust capacity to link leadership and organizational events. Leaders affect many processes and outcomes and; as a result, any theoretical mechanism that attempts to explain leadership should be capable of accounting for similar variation in the outcomes that are of interest to organizational scholars. Our reading of the self-concept literature suggests that it fits this criterion, as it has been linked to a broad spectrum of psychological processes and outcomes (Banaji & Prentice, 1994). Throughout this book we noted numerous linkages between aspects of the self and outcomes; however, given that these examples were dispersed throughout the entirety of our book, it may be worth revisiting this issue—examining a single self-construal.

Consider for a moment just the individual level of the self. We suggested throughout this book that the individual self is one of the pathways through which organizational leadership operates. What outcomes might organizational leaders and organizations anticipate if this is the chosen leadership pathway? How might this pathway change the nature and operation of our organizational theories? How might this pathway shift the weight we assign to different factors when forming a decision? We consider some of these issues next, exploring how leaders who activate the individual self may change the very nature and determinants of subordinate behavior, motivation, and perception.

As a starting point, we begin with the most basic issue of how the activation of the individual self can shift the determinants of an organizational actor's behavior. According to the theory of planned behavior (Ajzen, 1991), behavior is proximally regulated by behavioral intentions, which, in turn, are a function of an individual's attitude toward the behavior and social norms. Attitudes comprise an individual's beliefs about the behavior in question, whereas subjective norms capture the expectations that others may hold as to which behaviors should be engaged. Although prior work has indicated that subjective norms do not consistently predict behavior, more recent work has indicated that the level at which the self is defined may be an important moderator of the weight assigned to subjective norms (Ybarra & Trafimow, 1998). In this regard, Ybarra and Trafimow found that although the activation of the collective self led participants to weigh subjective norms more heavily in deciding behavioral intentions, the activation of the individual self led participants to weigh attitudes more heavily. How might such effects bear out in an organizational setting for leaders who operate through the individual self? Illingworth (2001) and Venkatesh, Morris, and Ackerman's (2000) work provides two examples.

As the reader may recall, Illingworth (2001) found that an individual's own attitudes tended to be much better predictors of OCB intentions when individual-level identities predominated than when interdependent (relational or collective) identities were elicited. The importance of situational norms in predicting OCB intentions showed the opposite moderating effect, being higher under interdependent than independent conditions, but this effect varied more with specific OCBs. In line with Illingworth's findings, Venkatesh et al. (2000) found that the relationship between attitudes, subjective norms, and the adaptation of software by employees depended on the gender of the employee, a demographic variable known to coincide with self-construal (Cross & Madson, 1997). Venkatesh et al.'s results suggested that although men's adaptation of the software was determined by attitudes, women's adaptation to the software was influenced by subjective norms. Venkatesh et al.'s study did not directly investigate the self, but their results are consistent with men being oriented toward more individual identities and women emphasizing collective identities.

Results such as these highlight how the antecedents of behavioral intentions can shift when different components of the self are salient. Practically, these findings, once integrated with our leadership model, suggest that when leadership operates through the individual self, organizationally based attempts to implement change must be targeted at changing attitudes. Interestingly, this perspective also suggests that interventions that are designed to change organizational actors' behavior by shifting individual attitudes may have little efficacy when the leadership process that is in operation occurs through the activation of the collective self.

As a second example of how the self may determine important outcomes, consider the issue of intrinsic motivation and how it can be altered when the self is shifted between different levels. In line with contemporary wisdom noted earlier in this book that although motivation can be externally maintained, such a basis for motivation may, over the long run, rob individual's of the joy and intrinsic motivation that they derive from a task (Ryan & Deci, 2000). From this perspective, motivation derives from an actor's need to exercise personal control and self-determination over his or her environment. In the end, we are motivated, persist, and enjoy tasks that provide us with control and the ability to determine our own destiny. In contrast, when we are robbed of self-determination and control, several negative outcomes result, such as lowered intrinsic motivation, lower life satisfaction, and poorer health (Ryan & Deci, 2000). It seems evident, given discussions of empowerment, employee participation, and employee ownership, that organizational scholars too have accepted the importance of self-determination. Yet, will self-determination transcend different leadership pathways?

Although we have no doubt that self-determination is an important consideration within organizations that implement leadership through the individual self, self-determination may become less relevant as collective leadership pathways are utilized. Consider for a moment the cross-cultural findings reported by Iyengar and Lepper (1999). In their investigation, Iyengar and Lepper compared American students who are known to be individualistic and Asian American students who are known to be collectivistic in terms of their intrinsic motivation to engage in a mathematics task under one of three conditions. Here, students were assigned to a condition in which they had full and personal control over the environment, the environment had been established by an in-group (i.e., students from one's class), or the environment had been established by an out-group (i.e., students from another school). According to the logic of self-determination theory, one might predict that the highest level of intrinsic motivation should occur in the full control condition. Consistent with this expectation the intrinsic motivation of American students was at its highest when personal choice was accentuated as compared with the in-group and out-group conditions. In sharp contrast, the Asian students exhibited the highest intrinsic motivation when an in-group determined the work setting. Results such as these suggest that although the principles of self-determination may be an important determinant of employee motivation within organizations, their applicability may be bounded by the leadership and self-systems that are in place within an organization.

As a final example of how the different leadership pathways might change fundamental psychological processes, consider attributional processes. Attributions are clearly an important aspect of organizational life, influencing the development of trust (Korsgaard, Brodt, & Whitener, 2002), self-esteem (Schroth & Pradhan, 2000), disciplinary decisions (Liden et al, 1999), and motivation (K. M. Thomas & Mathieu, 1994), to provide but a few examples. Basic psychological research that has examined attributional processes has indicated that observers oftentimes make the fundamental attribution error whereby they underestimate the degree to which behavior is shaped by the situation and overestimate the extent to which it is influenced by a person's disposition (Ross, 1977). As Dan Gilbert (1989), a noted social psychologist, outlined, this process occurs unconsciously and spontaneously. According to Gilbert, perceivers automatically categorize behavior (e.g., that is an aggressive behavior) and characterize the actor (e.g., he or she must be aggressive), and it is only when sufficient cognitive resources and motivation exist that perceivers will take situational influences into account (e.g., perhaps the excessive heat caused the aggressive act). As a result of the fundamental attribution error, as perceivers we infer that social agents are personally responsible for workplace events.

Despite its robustness, is the inference of personal agency and responsibility an inherent aspect of our psychological makeup, occurring equally for all perceivers? As readers may already suspect, a key determinant of the degree to which perceivers make the fundamental attribution error is the level at which their self-concept is defined (Morris & Peng, 1994; Newman, 1993; Zarate, Uleman, & Voils, 2001). Newman (1993), for instance, found that degree of individualism reported by participants was associated with their tendency to infer traits from behaviors. Similarly, Morris and Peng (1994) demonstrated that the attributions that are made by perceivers vary as a function of a culture's level on an individualism–collectivism dimension. Despite the fact that leadership scholars have not investigated whether differing leadership styles can influence attributions, we see little reason to suspect otherwise.

In summary, because the self is the fundamental regulator of human activity, thought, and affect, it can serve as a powerful integrative umbrella for leadership researchers, allowing them to understand how a wide spectrum of psychological, social, and cognitive outcomes may co-occur with different leader orientations. Furthermore, as we demonstrated through the previous examples, by understanding leader influence through the self, we can, as researchers and practitioners, develop a better understanding of the psychological context that will evolve within an organization. Leaders who influence organizational outcomes by activating an individual self-construal within their subordinates should anticipate that this influence will be widespread, altering the precursors of behavior, the locus of intrinsic motivation, and the very perceptions that guide subordinates.

Improving Organizational Leadership: Fundamental Assumptions

Throughout this book we approached the integration of leadership and the self-concept primarily through the eyes of a researcher, laying out a model that can be both subjected to empirical validation and used to form a meta-framework. Theory is, of course, not neutral. As with any leadership theory, our framework is premised on certain fundamental assumptions regarding human nature, the meaning of leadership, the appropriate modes of investigation, and the nature of the questions that should be addressed. The influence of the assumptions that embody leadership theories does not, however, end at the doors of researchers' labs.

Instead, these assumptions permeate practice and implementation throughout our discipline. For instance, the dominant behavioral perspective of leadership has not only served to guide most research throughout the discipline's history, but the basic assumptions of the approach have trickled down and influenced current interventions and organizational practices (Day, 2001). That is, if our theories assume that CEOs and senior managers are the direct cause of organizational outcomes, then, by extension, we might also suggest that, in practice, senior-level mangers should be compensated handsomely and that training budgets should be skewed toward providing training opportunities to these same managers. Although the direct application of our model remains a distant goal, one dependent on the outcomes of future empirical tests, we too have assumptions, and, as such, it may be worthwhile to highlight how some of these assumptions may play out practically.

One basic premise of our model is that leadership is a social influence process and that leaders are simply one component of a system. As we emphasized throughout this book, the most immediate cause of many of the outcomes that are valued by organizations result from the diligence, hard work, and ability of subordinates. Unlike some approaches (e.g., Meindl, 1995; Meindl, Ehrlich, & Dukerich, 1985), we do not question that leaders are important; they are simply one aspect of a larger system. Effective organizational leadership is dependent on how well all components of the system are operating in tandem. Although executives may conceive of a better product, it will be ineffectual if the right people with the appropriate skills are not in place to produce and sell the product; similarly, a better executive vision requires people to enact the vision.

An important implication that derives from this systems view of organizational leadership is that effective leadership is dependent on the investment that organizations make into both understanding their people and the tasks that they perform. In essence, effective leadership is contingent on the human resource practices that are engaged in by an organization—without competent and skilled employees, leaders cannot be effective. As a result, we suspect that organizations that invest heavily in their employees and human resources, particularly in industries in which skill change is rapid, will have the most effective leadership system. Front line employees must have the necessary skills and training to complete the tasks that are required of them. Similarly, selection, job analysis, and placement become essential elements in the implementation and creation of effective organizational leadership processes, as people must be appropriately positioned into jobs that fit their unique constellation of skills. In the end, we assume that leadership effectiveness is about the functioning of a system, and, as such, leadership interventions must be targeted at improving all components of the system, not any single component.

A second premise of our model is that subordinate perceptions are an important determinant of effective organizational leadership. In our view, leadership is truly in the eye of the beholder. As we noted previously, subordinates do not react to the behavior that is engaged in by leaders but rather to the meaning that this behavior creates. This has two important implications for the creation of effective organizational leaders. First, to function effectively, organizational managers must be trained in terms of the meaning that they need to create through their actions. A direct corollary of this premise is that interventions directed at leaders should not focus on training specific behaviors because, as we noted previously, meaning is context dependent. Instead, training should be focused on the content of the meaning that will be projected to subordinates and the skills that are needed to regulate meaning in terms of this image. In many respects this position converges with others who have independently arrived at the same conclusion regarding the centrality of meaning creation in leadership (e.g., Gardner & Avolio, 1998). A second implication of this premise for organizational practice is that effective leadership must be coupled with feedback systems. That is, as with any other control system, if a leader is to adequately regulate meaning creation, he or she must be aware of whether his or her behavior matches or deviates from this intended standard (Carver & Scheier, 1998). Given this, it comes as no surprise to us that social sensitivity plays an important role in leadership (e.g., Zaccaro et al., 1991) and that the implementation of upward feedback systems are associated with increases in subordinates' perceptions of leadership (Atwater, Roush, & Fischthal, 1995).

Although our discussion has centered on the practical implications of two of the components of our model, others could be discussed just as easily. For instance, if, as we assume, self-concept change is most likely during periods of transition, then how might organizations create processes that will simultaneously minimize disruptions while maximizing the influence of organizational leaders (e.g., job rotation or job enlargement)? If, as we assume, the salience of organizational leaders is associated with the degree of influence that is exerted over subordinates, then how might organizations take advantage of this process (e.g., small span of control)? The point that we wish to stress is not that we have drawn assumptions about the nature of leadership, but that, as with any theory, the assumptions outlined in our model have practical implications that extend beyond research questions.

Multilevel Views of Leadership: Moving Up, Moving Across, Moving Down, and Moving Through Time

It is widely recognized that leadership is a multilevel process (Dansereau, 1995; Dansereau & Yammarino, 1998; Hall & Lord, 1995), with leadership often crossing boundaries as one moves from organizations to groups, to dyads, to individuals, and to intraindividual processes. This multilevel aspect of leadership has raised two nagging problems for both theory and practice. The first problem pertains to the level at which data should be analyzed whether testing theory or evaluating interventions, and the second problem concerns the level at which theoretical variables should be measured or interventions should be focused to be most effective. Early approaches to such issues focused on the appropriate analysis of data (Dansereau, Alutto, & Yammarino, 1984), whereas later approaches (K. J. Klein, Dansereau, & Hall, 1994) stressed that this was a problem of theory formulation as well as data analysis. A practical strength of our approach that focuses on the follower's WSC is that it provides a theoretical system for moving beyond the follower level or the leader level when considering appropriate applied practice. In this section, we briefly illustrate how our theoretical system could be used as a guide to apply at four alternative levels of analysis associated with moving up, moving across, moving down, or moving through time.

Moving Up.   We use the term *moving up* to mean leadership practices that consider the effects of higher level entities such as organizational or societal culture on leadership practice. For example, it is widely recognized that organizations are becoming multinational and that expatriate managers have substantial difficulties and high rates of failure (Shaw, 1990). Such problems have often been understood in terms of cultural variation in the way leadership is defined by perceivers (Den Hartog et al., 1999; Hanges et al., 2000) or in terms of the value structures that differentiate cultures (Hofstede, 1980). Our theoretical perspective provides a more integrated framework for this practical issue.

Specifically, by providing a microlevel cognitive model of how leaders use the values they espouse and symbolize to activate a WSC in followers, as we did in chapter 5, we provide a common mechanism for both culture and leadership to influence followers: the effect of values on the follower's WSC. Furthermore, we suggested a three-level distinction—collective, relational, or individual—that is affected by the values represented by leaders and cultures. What this system implies for practice is that congruence in the identity level implied by cultural values and leader values is required for leaders to have a powerful effect on subordinates' WSC. This is basically an extension of Propositions 5.3, 5.4, and 5.5 that includes culture as another source of values. For example, leaders who have been successful by espousing values that prime an individual-level WSC in followers are likely to have problems moving to collective cultures because the values they espouse and the self-regulatory systems they engender in followers are inconsistent with the higher level culture.

In the context of Fig. 3.2, leaders may be operating at the top of our triangular column, whereas subordinates are located at the bottom of this column. What this means in more concrete terms is that the proximal motivational systems stressed by leaders and culture are likely to be inconsistent: Leaders are likely to stress values and WSC components that elicit self-views based on differentiating the self from others, or they may emphasize goals that are proself; whereas subordinates are likely to be most receptive to self-views that show how the self is part of a larger group, and they may emphasize goals that are pro-social. Such issues are natural outgrowths of follower-centered views of leadership, and they contrast with leader-centered views that would stress how leadership prototypes changed with culture (e.g., Gerstner & Day, 1994; Hanges et al., 2000).

What are the practical implications of this issue? First, they suggest that cross-cultural training of expatriate leaders needs to focus not just on how leadership prototypes differ across cultures but also on how leaders need to adjust the values they espouse and the identities they prime to be consistent with workers in the host culture. If our focus is on selection or job assignment instead of training, similar principles apply—the match between the host culture and a leader's value–identity orientation should be considered as a potential part of a selection or job assignment system. The same issues operate in reverse when leaders remain in their original culture but workers come from cultures where different identity levels predominate. In both cases, the overriding issue is that many leadership effects are likely to be mediated by the WSC and the associated self-regulatory systems of followers.

Certainly, the notion of situational contingencies is not a new idea in the leadership field (e.g., Fiedler, 1964; 1971). Our point is simply that leaders, being a linkage between cultural values, subordinate identities, and self-regulatory processes, need to be oriented towards these contingencies. A similar argument could be developed at the level of organizational rather than national culture. For instance, as already suggested, the values of Jack Welch and GE prime different identities and self-regulatory orientations than do those of Bill Gore and the W. L. Gore company. However, we leave elaboration of such organizational-level applications to the reader.

Moving Across.   We use the term *moving across* to describe dyadic levels of analysis that pertain to the cross-person processes involved in LMXs. The theories developed in chapter 4 described both short- and long-term effects that leaders can have on subordinates' WSC. The notion of reflected appraisal and, particularly, our emphasis on relational identities also help to specify important dyadic-level processes. Thus, our theoretical perspective complements the extensive work on LMXs (see Gerstner & Day, 1997, for a review of this literature).

The major practical benefit of our theory is that we specify how leaders can impact on the subordinate's WSC in Propositions 4.1 through 4.5. These are testable propositions that could be examined in a particular organizational context and, if supported, could be used as a guide to effective leadership influence. In these propositions, we lay out a theory of how and when leaders can alter the way subordinates self-regulate. We think this may have immense practical benefits for understanding effective dyadic-level leadership. Of particular importance is that we suggest specific processes by which identities are developed: the observation, experimentation, and evaluation of provisional selves by subordinates. We also describe how this process varies with level of identity (see Table 3.1). Essentially, we specified how leaders can contribute to employee development and socialization processes and how this process varies with identity level. However, rather than focusing on socialization in terms of norms or specific roles, we took a more employee-centered approach that stresses the development of identities and employee self-regulation. Although we avoided popular terms such as *empowerment,* it is worth noting that this approach to employee development has the potential to create autonomous, empowered employees who satisfy organizational needs because organizational needs are consistent with employees' identities.

Moving Down.   We use the term *moving down* to reflect levels of analysis that are within specific individuals. The WSC is a linkage to such intraindividual processes (Markus & Wurf, 1987), which can be both cognitive and affective. In level of analysis terms (Hall & Lord, 1995), these intraindividual processes reflect parts rather than entity relations, because these processes change over time within a specific individual (an entity). For example, we noted how a shift from using self-views to possible selves as standards in a control system shifts orientations from proximal to distal motivational processes. Similarly, a shift in orientation from positive to negative affect can provoke a change from

promotion- to prevention-oriented self-guides, reframing many motivational processes. The main practical point here is for leaders to recognize that the WSC is a continually changing self-regulatory system that
both guides and is guided by affect as well as cognitions.

In other words, employee behavior and thought is a microlevel process
that is guided by these dynamics. Although selection, training, job assignment, and socialization may be oriented toward stable differences across individuals (entity-level effects), actual behavior is more dynamic and
variable. We provided a theoretical system that addresses these momentary
dynamics in terms of affective events, for example, or in terms of hierarchically oriented self-regulatory processes. Understanding employee self-regulation at this level, and the potential role of leaders in this process can then
provide a guide for leaders in terms of how they should behave to be effective as circumstances change with respect to a particular employee.

Consider for example, the issue of an unfavorable reaction of an employee (or employees) to an organizational or leadership event. Most leadership theories provide no guidelines as to how a leader should react at this
microlevel of analysis. Our approach, however, suggests several diagnostic
issues that might be explored such as: Was the reaction driven by cognitive
or affective processes? (Speed of response may be one cue.) If affect seems
critical, was the reaction in response to potential threats (real or only perceived) to the subordinate's self or to goals that are central to the self? (A
clear grasp of identity levels and their translation into organizational goals
may help one understand this issue.) Was the subordinate's response reflec-
tive of organizational justice considerations or their implications for the
self-worth of the subordinate? (Here again the perspective given in chap. 7
would be helpful.) Alternatively, if responses were more attitudinally
driven, is it possible that the wrong level of identity was used by the subordinate to interpret organizational events or that leadership activities symbolized the wrong values to subordinates?

The point of such questions is simply to illustrate that, because it is inher-
ently dynamic, the theory we developed has value at the microlevel in terms
of understanding within-person variability in terms of the interaction of
self-regulatory processes and leadership or organizational events. Practicing leaders have to deal with such moment-to-moment issues, and most
leadership theories provide little help because they treat subordinates as
constant entities. Our approach extends to followers and follower's
self-regulatory processes; thereby, it provides a framework for thinking
about and addressing within-person processes.

Moving Through Time. We use the term *moving through time* to describe a final level of analysis because it affects the potential aggregation of effects across leaders of the same subordinate. By moving through time we mean that people do not exist only in the present, but they have the potential to time travel, revisiting past selves and situations and projecting into the future. It appears that only humans have the unique capacity for time travel (Roberts, 2002; Tulving, 2002). The practical point here, as noted in our discussion of the self-development face of Fig. 3.2, is that perceived movement toward desired possible selves is a source of emotions and drive for individual, dyadic, and societal entities depending on the level of the WSC. Thus, leaders can have powerful effects on such units by influencing subordinates' views of the future or their perceived capacity to move toward desired selves.

However, to do this effectively leaders either have to be oriented toward the current WSC levels of their subordinates or they must first prime the appropriate level in those subordinates. Our framework makes it possible to see how a leader can tap into the projected movement of entities over time as a means of exerting influence. In addition, as we will briefly explain, it may be extended to see how the effects of various leaders can also cumulate over time. We do this by generalizing S. M. Andersen and Chen's (2002) recently proposed theory on the relational self to the leadership domain.

S. M. Andersen and Chen (2002) developed a social–cognitive theory that maintains that past assumptions and experiences in relationships with significant others tend to resurface in relations with new people, a process they called *transference.* Our extension is merely to suggest that leaders are one type of significant other. In S. M. Andersen and Chen's theory, significant-other representations are chronically accessible (as leader representations may be at work) and are highly laden with affect. They proposed that when the significant-other representation is activated, a companion self-with-significant-other representation is also activated, through spreading activation from the other representation to the self-representation. This spreading activation infuses the WSC with knowledge that is associated with the relevant relational self. In other words, significant others, like leaders, make different aspects of the subordinate's WSC accessible in the presence of leaders or when a mental image of leaders is salient to subordinates.

Three aspects of this self-with-significant-other relationship are noteworthy. One aspect is that the standards held by the significant other for the self and the memories of one's ability to meet those standards are particularly important. This idea is quite consistent with Higgin's (1989, 1996) self-discrepancy theory, which is central to both our theory and that of S. M. Andersen and Chen (2002), and it implies that standards can suggest a promotion or prevention orientation. A second aspect is that the relation of significant others with the self likely occurs through connectionist architectures because many aspects of the other—looks, smell, gestures, facial features, behaviors, habits and attitudes—can prime multiple productions within an individual and thereby automatically affect behavior. Productions are merely simple if-then relationships, in which particular configurations of environmental cues (the *if*) define the conditions necessary to trigger a behavioral, cognitive, or affective reaction (the *then*). The third aspect of S. M. Andersen and Chen's theory is that not only are idiographic aspects of the self activated by this process, but socially shared constructs such as social identities or social categories can also be activated. Thus, a leader who is sexist may activate not only the thoughts and feelings in female subordinates that are associated with that specific relationship, he or she also can activate stereotypic beliefs about the abilities of women and can make stereotype threat salient.

In sum, S. M. Andersen and Chen (2002) describe many of the properties we already discussed, but they did not do so in the context of leadership. Given the many similarities between their theory and ours, we believe that it makes sense to discuss their notion of transference in terms of its applied implications for leadership. This generalization of S. M. Andersen and Chen's theory would predict that when new leaders share many aspects with prior leaders, they automatically activate some of the same facets of a subordinate's WSC that prior leaders did. In other words, transference allows prior relations to travel through time, reactivating relevant aspects of the WSC when similar leaders are encountered. For example, the effects of a drill sergeant on one's WSC and all the skills and competencies associated with a trainee's relationship with that sergeant can be activated by new leaders who are similar to that sergeant. The effects of a parent or a favorite (or hated) teacher also can generalize to new settings when the new individual is similar to prior significant others. Through such mechanisms, parent–child behavioral relations can generalize to spouse–spouse relations or to superior–subordinate relations (see Keller, 1999, for an empirical example of such processes).

Applying this idea to organizations implies that organizations may need to pay as much attention to leadership systems as they do to the leadership qualities of specific individuals. When selection–attraction–attrition processes (Schneider, 1987) create homogeneity among leaders in a particular culture, then relational leadership qualities are likely to generalize from one leader to another, producing consistency in the activated WSCs and associated skills of subordinates. This process may have both desirable and undesirable consequences. When turnover among leaders is high for whatever reason (e.g., among leaders in military combat or among team leaders at McDonalds), transference processes may produce continuity in the WSC that is evoked by leader–member relations and the self-regulatory processes that it elicits in subordinates. On the other hand, dissimilarities with prior leaders, particularly those associated with memberships in salient social categories (e.g., race, and gender), may make it harder for new leaders to inspire or motivate individuals because they do not automatically activate the appropriate WSC. Female leaders in traditionally male organizational hierarchies may experience such problems.

In short, we suggest that both individuals and leader–member relations can travel through time, relying on the WSC as a vehicle that transports skills, affective reactions, self-guides, and self-regulatory tendencies to new possible selves or new social relations. This process needs to be effectively managed in many types of organizations, from businesses to government to education to the military. Analyzing this process in terms of the WSC and the level at which it is defined, as did in this book, provides a framework for thinking about how organizations should manage such leader transference processes.

Interestingly, leadership prototypes, which prior research has shown to be constrained by contexts like business, education, military, or religion (Lord, Brown, Harvey, & Hall, 2001; Lord & Maher, 1991), may thus function not only to help perceivers recognize leaders but also to activate the skills and self-regulatory capacities associated with prior leaders in these specific contexts. Thus, the recognition of leadership by observers (which may be an implicit as well as explicit process) may be the first step in the transference of prior, context-dependent relational identities to new leadership relations. When transference works well, effective leadership and effective self-regulation by organization members should be much easier. However, it is also possible that inappropriate self-regulatory strategies (e.g., reactance, feared selves, and low self-efficacy) will also be activated by transference processes. In such circumstances, the effectiveness of current leaders may be diminished by the negative effects of prior leaders. For example, the carryover of a bad teacher's negative effects on a student's attitudes toward learning may be one such problem that must be addressed by new teachers who have superficial similarities with the prior teacher.

FUTURE RESEARCH NEEDS

Need for Empirical Assessment

In this book we proposed a new way to think of leadership based on so-cial–cognitive and self-regulatory theories. The theory that was developed was based on extensive social science research; nevertheless, it reflects our interpretation and our inferences from this research. Hence, it needs to be empirically tested, particularly before it is applied. Our discussion of ap-plied relevance was mainly to show how the theory could be useful, but our suggestions should be carefully assessed with validation studies as part of their application.

Critical Research Issues and Propositions

As a convenient way to summarize the main ideas, we developed several key propositions in each chapter. These propositions are summarized in Table 8.1 and provide specific guides to further research. However, be-cause there are many propositions, 31 in all, it may be useful to discuss fu-ture research needs in broader terms, which we do in the following brief sections.

Self-Regulation with Respect to the Self.   Based on many per-suasive treatments of the self and self-regulatory processes (e.g., Carver & Scheier, 1998; Cropanzano et al., 1993; Higgins, 1998; Markus & Wurf, 1987), we explained self-regulation in terms of hierarchies that extend from abstract principles, to individual identities, to specific task objectives. We also proposed a framework shown in Fig. 2.1, that used pairs of WSC components—self-views and goals, possible selves and goals, and possible selves and self-views—to create three different types of self-regulatory systems associated with proximal motivation, distal motivation, and self-development motivation, respectively. This framework is consistent with extensive motivational and social cogni-tive research, yet it has not been tested in precisely these terms. Future research needs to determine whether differentiating between self-views and possible selves has the many effects on motivation that we sug-gested in Propositions 2.1 through 2.4, and it also needs to demonstrate the value of focusing on the three types of self-regulatory systems that we depict on the sides of the triangle in Fig. 2.1.

TABLE 8.1

Summary of Propositions by Topic and Chapter

Topics and Propositions

Motivation, self-views, possible selves, and goals

2.1. Linking goals to self-views will accentuate self-enhancement motivations and affective reactions to task feedback, whereas linking goals to possible selves will promote self-verification motivation and cognitive reactions to task feedback.

2.2. The relation of current goal–performance discrepancies to task satisfaction will be highest when task goals are strongly linked to self-views and proximal motivational processes are salient.

2.3. The relation of rate of change in goal–performance discrepancies (i.e., velocity) to task satisfaction will be highest when task goals are strongly linked to possible selves and distal motivational processes are salient.

2.4. The resiliency of task motivation when discrepancies are encountered will be higher when task goals are strongly linked to possible selves and lower when task goals are linked to self-views.

Identities as communicated by leaders and as boundaries to leadership processes

3.1. A leader's reflected appraisal will have a powerful impact on a subordinate's self-view. The appraisal will be communicated through both cognitive and affective channels and by both explicit and implicit processes.

3.2. Reflected appraisals will be an important medium for signaling the potential benefits of a social exchange to both leaders and subordinates. These signals will be assimilated into affective evaluations of the other party and into evaluations of the value of the dyadic exchange.

3.3. The relationship between a leader's self-fulfilling prophecies and a subordinate's expectancies is mediated by changes in subordinates' self-views, a subordinate's affective evaluations of the leader, and the subordinate's satisfaction with the dyadic exchange.

3.4. Leadership activities will be more effective when they are matched to appropriate identity levels of subordinates.

3.5. Identity level is a critical boundary variable for leadership theory, with the importance of many social and leadership processes varying with identity level.

   3.5a. When the self is defined at the individual level, leader expectancy effects, effects of performance feedback, effects of contingent rewards, and procedures related to distributive justice will have greater effects on subordinates' behaviors and attitudes.

   3.5b. When the self is defined at the relational level, perceived and actual leader–subordinate congruence in attitudes and values, leader affective behaviors, and interactional justice will have greater effects on subordinate behavior and attitudes.

continued on next page

3.5c. When the self is defined at the group (or organizational) level, structural aspects of procedural justice, organizational identities, and team-based or collective leadership will have greater effects on the behavior and attitudes of group member.

Temporary and enduring effects of leaders on subordinates' identities

4.1. Effective leadership will be directly proportional to the degree to which leaders are able to prime relevant aspects of a subordinate's self-concept.

4.2. Leaders can prime subordinate identities through multiple means, with the effectiveness of priming processes varying with (a) the strength and coherence of primes, (b) the salience of leaders, (c) subordinate sensitivity to leadership, and (d) follower differences in the ease with which different aspects of the self can be activated.

4.3. Leaders can become chronic, indirect primes when work environments activate the values and social identities repeatedly emphasized by leaders.

4.4. Leaders can produce permanent changes in subordinate identities by (a) making peripheral aspects of self-identities chronically accessible; and (b) by creating new chronically accessible identities through subordinates' observation, experimentation, and evaluation of provisional selves.

4.5. The development of new, chronically accessible identities is most likely during (a) employee transitions and (b) dramatic organization change.

Meaning, values, and WSC activation

5.1. Subordinate cognitions and affective reactions are the internal structures that mediate between leader behavior and subordinate responses.

5.2. The cognitive and affective meaning of leader behaviors constructed by a perceiver depends on the simultaneous consideration of multiple contextual constraints.

5.3. Patterns of values activated by leader behaviors can be organized along an individual–collective dimension.

5.4. Patterns of values mediate between leader behavior and WSC activation.

5.5. Leader behavior has its greatest effect when it activates coherent patterns of values.

5.6. Behavior, thoughts, and feelings are regulated by the joint effects of identities (self-views or possible selves) and goals.

Leadership as an affective event (see Table 6.1)

6.1. Affective events are proximal determinants of affective reactions toward leaders.

6.2. Microlevel assessment is required because affective reactions change over time in response to leadership events.

6.3. Primary and secondary affective appraisals are mediational processes linking leadership events and reactions to leaders.

6.4. Biologically based individual differences moderate affective reactions to events.

6.5. The structure of behavior and perceptions reflects the structure of basic emotions.

6.6. Behavior or attitudes toward leaders may be affectively or cognitively (attitudinally) driven.

Social justice, leadership, and the WSC

7.1. Identity will influence the dimension of justice that is salient, with individual level identity priming distributive justice, relational-level identity priming interactional justice, and collective-level identity priming procedural justice.

7.2. Evaluation of organizational justice will involve sequential evaluation of justice dimensions, beginning with that dimension most closely associated with the current level of the WSC, and terminating when a dimension indicates that fairness has occurred.

7.3. There will be interactions among justice dimensions such that negative reactions to organizational justice will be most extreme when all dimensions that are considered indicate a lack of fairness.

7.4. The level of justice standards will depend on evaluations of self-worth, and evaluations of self-worth will depend on the level of the WSC that is activated.

7.5. Fairness judgments will show an upward bias with an individual-level identity yielding greater-than-average expected outcomes, a relational-level identity yielding greater-than-average expected consideration and interaction with one's leader, and a collective-level identity yielding expectations of greater-than-average conformity to group prototypes.

Are There Really Three Distinct Identity Levels? There is overwhelming empirical support for differentiating between individual- and collective-level identities, but despite the persuasive arguments (Brewer & Gardner, 1996; Sedikides & Brewer, 2001) and other support that was discussed in this book (S. M. Andersen & Chen, 2002; Gabriel & Gardner, 1999; Gardner et al., 1999; Selenta & Lord, 2002), the three-level identity system we based our theory on has not been conclusively established. This issue needs further research, particularly with respect to leadership.

Specifically, we need to establish whether the activation of a WSC involving relational identities precludes the simultaneous activation of a WSC at individual and collective levels, as we suggested, or whether relational identities are more complementary, adding to rather than supplanting a WSC defined at the other two levels. Our expectation is that at all three levels, the WSCs (which are systems of self-relevant information, not unitary wholes) tend to show lateral inhibition in that when one type of WSC is activated, competing WSCs are inhibited. Lateral inhibition has been demonstrated with respect to goals and intentions, so it makes sense to apply it to WSCs as well. As Marsh, Hicks, and Bryan (1999) explained, this lateral inhibition of competing intentions can also be understood by assuming that there is simply a fixed amount of activation in working memory, and if it is allocated to one intention, less activation is available for other possible intentions. We expect that the same principle applies at the WSC level.

Critical types of evidence related to these issues would be research that determines whether priming contrasting levels (e.g., collective or individual) makes WSCs associated with relational identities less accessible. The differential accessibility of WSCs at these three levels of self should also be related to the ability to functionally organize tasks that may exist at competing identity levels. Research showing that these three identity levels moderate processes in specific substantive areas, as we showed for social justice in chapter 7 (see also Johnson et al., 2003), would also be quite helpful. We make one more methodological note: It is critical for such research to control for gender-related effects because initial research (Johnson et al., 2003; Selenta & Lord, 2002), as well as that of others (Gabriel & Gardner, 1999; Gardner et al., 1999), shows that relational identities tend to be more important for women, whereas collective identities are more important to men.

It is worth taking time to elaborate the functional reasoning behind expecting lateral inhibition among all three levels of the self-identity. Namely, we argued that the WSC manages self-regulation by integrating self-knowledge, current goals, and knowledge of potential threats or benefits into the environment. For such a system to function effectively, the WSC must be a source of organization, simplification, and selection of this information in forming intentions. Although people certainly have the capacity to process some types of information in parallel, the human physical implementation system is generally constrained to operate in a serial fashion (e.g., we cannot be in two different places at the same time). Thus, as we move from thought systems to action systems, parallel capacities must be seriated, and this may occur, in part, by keeping the WSCs associated with alternative identity levels separate. Because the collective, relational, and individual identities map onto different types of entities—collectives, dyads, or individuals—it also seems logical that actions related to such entities will be relatively distinct. Thus, we expect that the coherence and independence of WSCs at different levels may be related to the ability to maintain a functional organization of thoughts and actions.

One danger with the intermixing of information, affect, and intention associated with different WSCs is that the activation from the self would be spread among so many competing constructs that needed actions would never be implemented.

We argued that leaders need to be coherent in activating a specific WSC level. Such coherence would complement the capacity of lateral inhibition processes to keep various WSCs separate while engaged in self-relevant action. This capacity of followers may be important to understanding both individual differences in self-regulatory effectiveness and the dynamics guiding behavior within an individual over time.

Intraindividual Variability. An additional issue warranting research concerns the extent to which the WSC changes over time. A particularly interesting question is whether variability tends to occur within a particular identity level (e.g., shifting from proximal to distal motivational concerns at the individual level) or whether changes tend to occur across levels (e.g., changing from individual to relational identities). We assumed that people are malleable, but degree of malleability may be an important individual difference. We also assumed that primes from connectionist networks, particularly value networks, were important sources of variability. This assumption needs to be empirically investigated using available priming methodology (see Martin, Strack, & Stapel, 2001). One point Martin et al. (2001) noted is that blatant primes often produce contrast effects, whereas more subtle primes produce assimilation of constructs with primes. Research using priming to influence the WSC (as well as practicing leaders) should use less blatant approaches.

Leadership and WSC Change. We argued that leaders can operate through connectionist networks to alter the WSC of subordinates in Propositions 4.1 through 4.5. These propositions also need to be tested. Martin et al.'s (2001) review on priming implies that leader-priming processes may work better if they are subtle rather than blatant. Because behavior implicitly activates a value rather than activating it explicitly, the symbolic value of a leader's behavior may be particularly important in priming a subordinate's WSC, as we suggested previously. Our assertion that activating values is the main medium by which leaders prime various WSCs (Propositions 5.2 through 5.6) also needs to be tested, as do our distinctions between short-run (Propositions 4.1 and 4.2) and more enduring changes (Propositions 4.3 through 4.5).

Emotions and Leadership Events. In chapter 6, we developed a perspective on emotions and leadership processes based on AET. This has several implications for understanding leadership and the self-related processes that are detailed in Propositions 6.1 through 6.6. Several ideas in this chapter suggest exciting areas of future research. One is that emotions are triggered by primary appraisals that involve threats or benefits to the self and operate as mediational processes linking leadership events and reactions to a leader (Proposition 6.3). We would expect that this process would be moderated by the level of one's WSC. For example, events that produced threats to an individual-level identity would produce less extreme emotional responses when collective- rather than individual-level WSCs were active. Another important idea is that affective events have a microlevel structure that is important for understanding leadership and may not be well represented in typical leadership questionnaires (Proposition 6.2). This perspective requires careful experimental research.

We also think the proposal that the structure of behavior and leadership perceptions reflects the underlying structure of emotions (Proposition 6.5) should be carefully evaluated. Consistent with this idea, L. A. James and L. R. James (1989) showed that hedonic relevance was important to the hierarchical structure of leadership measures, and Naidoo and Lord (2002a) also found a hierarchical factor underlying leadership scales that was based on emotions. Specifically, Naidoo and Lord's research found that negative affectivity was more central to leadership measures than positive affectivity, which is consistent with other research that suggests leadership perceptions are affected by crisis, but this idea also needs to be tested more extensively.

Leadership, Justice, and the WSC. We noted that social justice in organizations is often an event that produces emotional reactions and, thus, is affected by the level of the currently active WSC. We suggested several propositions with respect to this idea in chapter 7 that need to be empirically examined (Propositions 7.1 through 7.5). Such research should keep in mind that our theory implies that there is a dual role of leaders in justice events. Leaders can be central factors because they allocate rewards, interact directly with subordinates, and often determine organizational procedures. Through such behaviors leaders can thereby directly affect all three justice dimensions that were discussed. Leaders also play a second role in that they can activate various WSCs, which moderate justice reactions according to our theory. Researchers attempting to understand leadership and social justice need to consider this indirect effect as well as the more direct effects of leaders.

CONCLUDING THOUGHTS

In this chapter we have considered several issues relevant to the value of the leadership framework developed in this book. We believe that the case for the value added by our framework is compelling. Further, we think that the practical implications are also substantial, although application should await further scientific research. Though the issues we covered were complex and research is continually evolving, we think three general conclusions are warranted. First, there is a great deal to be gained from a scientifically-based, follower-centered approach to understanding leadership processes. Second, this approach can be structured by thinking in terms of follower self-concepts that can exist at individual, relational or collective levels. Third, many process-related dynamics can be clarified by recognizing that the currently active self, the working self-concept, changes across time and circumstances. Leaders have much to do with such changes.

Having said this, we will close by simply restating our definition from Chapter 1 of what we believe is the most fundamental aspect of leadership processes: *Leadership is a process through which one individual, the leader, changes the way followers envision themselves.* Through this process leaders and followers jointly create meaning for many organizational behaviors and events. This is a critical processes because subordinates' responses to organizational events are guided by the meaning they help to create.

References

Adams, J. S. (1965). Inequity in social exchange. In L. Berkowitz (Ed.), *Advances in experimental social psychology* (Vol. 2, pp. 267–299). New York: Academic Press.

Adelmann, P. K., & Zajonc, R. B. (1989). Facial efference and the experience of emotion. *Annual Review of Psychology, 40,* 249–280.

Ajzen, I. (1991). The theory of planned behavior *Organizational Behavior and Human Decision Processes, 50,* 179–211.

Allen, P. A., Kaut, K., Lord, R. G., Hall, R. J., Bowie, T., Grabbe, J., & Kopera-Frye, K. (2002). *An emotional mediation theory of differential age effects in episodic and semantic memory.* Manuscript submitted for publication.

Andersen, S. M., & Chen, S. (2002). The relational self: An interpersonal social–cognitive theory. *Psychological Review, 109,* 619–645.

Anderson, J. R. (1983). *The architecture of cognition.* Cambridge, MA: Harvard University Press.

Anderson, J. R. (1987). Skill acquisition: Compilation of weak-method problem solutions. *Psychological Review, 94,* 192–210.

Aron, A., & McLaughlin-Volpe, T. (2001). Including others in the self: Extensions to own and partner's group memberships. In C. Sedikides & M. B. Brewer (Eds.), *Individual self, relational self, collective self* (pp. 89–108). Philadelphia: Psychology Press.

Ashforth, B. E., & Saks, A. M. (2002). Feeling your way: Emotions and organizational entry. In R. G. Lord, R. J. Klimoski, & R. Kanfer (Eds.), *Emotions in the workplace: Understanding the structure and role of emotions in organizational behavior* (pp. 331–369). San Francisco: Jossey-Bass.

Atwater, L., Roush, P., & Fischthal, A. (1995). The influence of upward feedback on self- and follower ratings of leadership. *Personnel Psychology, 48,* 35–59.

Awamleh, R., & Gardner, W. L. (1999). Perceptions of leader charisma and effectiveness: The effects of vision content, delivery, and organizational performance. *Leadership Quarterly, 10,* 345–373.

Baker, S. (1998). *Salience of outcome, treatment, and structural neutrality standards.* Unpublished manuscript.

Baldwin, M. W. (1992). Relational schemas and the processing of social information. *Psychological Bulletin, 112,* 461–484.

Baldwin, M. W. (1994). Primed relational schemas as a source of self-evaluative reactions. *Journal of Social and Clinical Psychology, 13,* 380–403.

Baldwin, M. W. (1997). Relational schemas as a source of if–then self inference procedures. *Review of General Psychology, 1,* 326–335.

Baldwin, M. W., Carrell, S. E., & Lopez, D. F. (1990). Priming relationship schemas: My advisor and the Pope are watching me from the back of my mind. *Journal of Experimental Social Psychology, 26,* 435–454.

Baldwin, M. W., & Holmes, J. G. (1987). Salient private audiences and awareness of the self. *Journal of Personality and Social Psychology, 52,* 1087–1098.

Baldwin, M. W., Keelan, J. P. R., Fehr, B., Enns, V., & Koh-Rangarajoo, E. (1997). Social cognitive conceptualization of attachment working models: Availability and accessibility effects. *Journal of Personality and Social Psychology, 71,* 94–109.

Baldwin. M. W.. & Sinclair. L. (1996). Self-esteem and "If … Then" contingencies of interpersonal acceptance. *Journal of Personality and Social Psychology. 71.* 1130–1141.

Banaji. M. R.. & Prentice. D. A. (1994). The self in social contexts. *Annual Review of Psychology. 45.* 297–332.

Bandura. A. (1977). *Social learning theory.* Englewood Cliffs. NJ.: Prentice Hall.

Bandura. A. (1986). *Social foundation of though and action: A social cognitive theory.* Englewood Cliffs. NJ: Prentice Hall.

Bandura. A.. & Cervone. D. (1986). Differential engagement of self-reactive influences in cognitive motivation. *Organizational Behavior and Human Decision Processes. 38.* 92–113.

Bargh. J. A.. Chen. M.. & Burrows. L. (1996). Automaticity of social behavior: Direct effects of trait construct and stereotype activation on action. *Journal of Personality and Social Psychology. 71.* 230–244.

Barling. J.. Weber. T.. & Kelloway. E. T. (1996). Effects of tranformational leadership training on attitudinal and financial outcomes: A field experiment. *Journal of Applied Psychology. 81.* 827–832.

Barsade. S. G.. Ward. A. J.. Turner. J. D. F.. & Sonnenfeld. J. A. (2000). To your heart's content: A model of affective diversity in top management teams. *Administrative Science Quarterly. 45.* 802–836.

Barsalou. L. W. (1987). The instability of graded structure: Implications for the nature of the concepts. In U. Neisser (Ed.). *Concepts and conceptual development: Ecological and intellectual factors in categorization* (pp. 101–140). New York: Cambridge University Press.

Bass. B. M. (1985). *Leadership and performance beyond expectations.* New York: Free Press.

Bass. B. M. (1999). Two decades of research and development in transformational leadership. *European Journal of Work and Organizational Psychology. 8.* 9–32.

Bass. B. M.. & Avolio. B. J. (1990). *Manual for the Multifactor Leadership Questionnaire.* Palo Alto. CA: Consulting Psychologists Press.

Bauer. T. N.. & Green. S. G. (1998). Testing the combined effects of newcomer information seeking and manager behavior on socialization. *Journal of Applied Psychology. 83.* 72–83.

Baumeister. R. F.. & Leary. M. R. (1995). The need to belong: Desire for interpersonal attachment as a fundamental human motivation. *Psychological Bulletin. 117.* 497–529.

Baumgardner. T. L.. Lord. R. G.. & Forti. J. C. (1990). *A prescription for aspiring leadership: Implications of expert–novice schema differences and alternative leadership categorization models.* Unpublished manuscript. University of Akron. Akron. OH.

Beach. L. R. (1990). *Image theory: Decision making in personal and organizational contexts.* Chichester. England: Wiley.

Bernstein. A. (1997. March 24). A blast from Neutron Jack. *Business Week.* Issue 3519. 178.

Bies. R. J.. & Moag. J. S. (1986). Interactional justice: Communication criteria of fairness. In R. J. Lewicki. B. H. Sheppard. & M. H. Bazerman (Eds.). *Research on negotiation in organizations* (pp. 43–55). Greenwich. CT: JAI.

Bies. R. J. (2001). Interactional (in)justice: The sacred and the profane. In J. Greenberg & R. Cropanzano (Eds.). *Advances in organizational justice* (pp. 89–118). Stanford. CA: Stanford University Press.

Birnbaum. M. H. (1999). How to show that 9 > 221: Collect judgments in a between-subjects design. *Psychological Methods. 4.* 243–249.

Bower. G. H. (1981). Emotional mood and memory. *American Psychologist. 36.* 129–148.

Bretz. R. D.. & Judge. T. A. (1994). Person–organization fit and the theory of work adjustment: Implications for satisfaction. tenure. and career success. *Journal of Vocational Behavior. 44*(1). 32–54.

Brewer. M. B.. & Gardner. W. (1996). Who is this "we"? Levels of collective identity and self representations. *Journal of Personality and Social Psychology. 71.* 83–93.

Brief. A. P.. & Weiss. H. M. (2002). Organizational behavior: Affect in the workplace. *Annual Review of Psychology. 53.* 279–307.

Brockner, J., Chen, Y., Mannix, E. A., Leung, K., & Skarlicki, D. P. (2000). Cross-cultural variation in the interactive relationship between procedural fairness and outcome favorability: The cause of self-construal. *Administrative Science Quarterly, 45,* 138–159.

Brockner, J., & Greenberg, J. (1990). The impact of layoffs on survivors: An organizational justice perspective. In J. S. Carroll (Ed.), *Applied social psychology in organizational settings* (pp. 45–75). Hillsdale, NJ: Lawrence Erlbaum Associates.

Brockner, J. & Wiesenfeld, B. M. (1996). An integrative framework for explaining reactions to decisions: Interactive effects of outcomes and procedures. *Psychological Bulletin, 120,* 189–208.

Brower, H. H., Schoorman, F. D., & Tan, H. H. (2000). A model of relational leadership: The integration of trust and leader–member exchange. *Leadership Quarterly, 11,* 227–250.

Brown, D. J. (2000). *The implied presence of a supervisor and its effect on a subordinate's self-concept.* Unpublished doctoral dissertation, University of Akron, Akron, OH.

Brown, D. J., & Lord, R. G. (2001). Leadership and perceiver cognition: Moving beyond first order constructs. In M. London (Ed.), *How people evaluate others in organizations* (pp. 181–202). Mahwah, NJ: Lawrence Erlbaum Associates.

Brown, D. J., Scott, K., & Mattison, C. (2002). Unpublished raw data. Spontaneous trait inferences and gender bias in leaderhsip.

Brunstein, J. C. (1993). Personal goals and subjective well-being: A longitudinal study. *Journal of Personality and Social Psychology, 71,* 1006–1019.

Burns, J. M. (1978). *Leadership.* New York: Harper & Row.

Cable, D. M., & Judge, T. A. (1996). Person-organization fit, job choice decisions, and organizational entry. *Organizational Behavior and Human Decision Processes, 67,* 294–311.

Calder, B. J. (1977). An attribution theory of leadership. In B. M. Staw & G. R. Salancik (Eds.), *New directions in organizational behavior* (pp. 179–204). Chicago: St. Clair Press.

Campion, M. E., & Lord, R. G. (1982). A control systems conceptualization of the goal-setting and changing process. *Organizational Behavior and Human Performance, 30,* 265–287.

Canli, T., Zhao, Z., Kang, E., Gross, J., Desmond, J. E., & Gabrieli, J. D. E. (2001). An fMRI study of personality influences on brain reactivity to emotional stimuli. *Behavioral Neuroscience, 1,* 33–42.

Cantor, N., Kemmelmeier, M., Basten, J., & Prentice, D. A. (2002). Life task pursuit in social groups: Balancing self-exploration and social integration. *Self and Identity, 1,* 177–184.

Cantor, N., & Kihlstrom, J. (1986). *Personality and social intelligence.* Englewood Cliffs, NJ: Prentice-Hall.

Carver, C. S. (2001). Affect and the functional basis of behavior: On the dimensional structure of affective experience. *Personality and Social Psychology Bulletin, 5,* 345–356.

Carver, C. S., Lawrence, J. W., & Scheier, M. F. (1999). Self-discrepancies and affect: Incorporating the role of feared selves. *Personality and Social Psychology Bulletin, 25,* 783–792.

Carver, C. S., & Scheier, M. F. (1981). *Attention and self-regulation: A control-theory approach to human behavior.* New York: Springer-Verlag.

Carver, S. C., & Scheier, M. F. (1990). Origins and functions of positive and negative affect: A control-process view. *Psychological Review, 97,* 19–36.

Carver, C. S., & Scheier, M. F. (1998). *On the self-regulation of behavior.* Cambridge, England: Cambridge University Press.

Casimir, G. (2001). Combinative aspects of leadership style: The ordering and temporal spacing of leadership behaviors. *Leadership Quarterly, 12,* 245–278.

Catrambone, R., Beike, D., & Niedenthal, P. (1996). Is the self-concept a habitual referent in judgments of similarity? *Psychological Science, 7,* 158–163.

Catrambone, R., & Markus, H. (1987). The role of self-schemas in going beyond the information given. *Social Cognition, 5,* 349–368.

Cawley, B. D., Keeping, L., & Levy, P. E. (1998). Participation in the performance appraisal process and employee reactions: A meta-analytic review of field investigations. *Journal of Applied Psychology, 83,* 615–633.

Chartrand, T. L., & Bargh, J. A. (1996). Automatic activation of impression formation and memorization goals: Nonconscious goal priming reproduces effects of explicit task instructions. *Journal of Personality and Social Psychology, 71,* 464–478.

Chemers, M. M. (1997). *An integrative theory of leadership.* Mahwah, NJ: Lawrence Erlbaum Associates.

Chemers, M. M. (2001). *An integrative theory of leadership.* Mahwah, NJ: Lawrence Erlbaum Associates.

Chemers, M. M., Watson, C. B., & May, S. T. (2000). Dispositional affect and leadership effectiveness: A comparison of self-esteem, optimism, and efficacy. *Personality and Social Psychology Bulletin, 26,* 267–277.

Chen, M., & Bargh, J. A. (1997). Nonconscious behavioral confirmation processes: The self-fulfilling consequences of automatic stereotype activation. *Journal of Experimental Social Psychology, 33,* 541–560.

Cherulnik, P. D., Donley, D. A., Wiewel, T. S. R., & Miller, S. R. (2001). Charisma is contagious: The effects of leader's charisma on observers' affect. *Journal of Applied Social Psychology, 31,* 2149–2159.

Cohen-Carasch, Y., & Spector, P. E. (2001). The role of justice in organizations: A meta-analysis. *Organizational Behavior and Human Decision Processes, 86,* 278–321.

Colquitt, J. A. (2001). On the dimensionality of organizational justice: A construct validation of a measure. *Journal of Applied Psychology, 86,* 386–400.

Conger, J. A. (1991). Inspiring others: The language of leadership. *Academy of Management Executive, 5*(1), 31–45.

Conger, J. A., & Kanungo, R. N. (1998). *Charismatic leadership in organizations.* Thousand Oaks, CA: Sage.

Conger, J. A., Kanungo, R. N., & Menon, S. T. (2000). Charismatic leadership and follower effects. *Journal of Organizational Behavior, 21,* 747–767.

Cooley, C. H. (1902). *Human nature and the social order.* New York: Scribners.

Cosmides, L., & Tooby, J. (2000). Evolutionary psychology and the emotions. In M. Lewis & J. M. Haviland-Jones (Eds.), *Handbook of emotions* (2nd ed., pp. 91–115). New York: Guilford.

Cropanzano, R., & Greenberg, J. (1997). Progress in organizational justice: Tunneling through the maze. *International Review of Industrial and Organizational Psychology, 12.* 317–372.

Cropanzano, R., James, K., & Citera, M. (1993). A goal hierarchy model of personality, motivation, and leadership. *Research in Organizational Behavior, 15,* 267–322.

Cropanzano, R., Weiss, H. M., Suckow, K. J., & Grandey, A. A. (2000). Doing justice to workplace emotions. In N. M. Ashkanasy, C. E. J. Hartel, & W. J. Zerbe (Eds.), *Emotions in the workplace: Research, theory, and practice* (pp. 49–62). Westport, CT: Quorum Books.

Cross, S. E., & Madson, L. (1997). Models of the self: Self-construals and gender. *Psychological Bulletin, 122,* 5–37.

Csikszentmihalyi, M. (1990). *Flow: The psychology of optimal experience.* New York: Harper & Row.

Damasio, A. (1994). *Decarte's error: Emotion, reason, and the human brain.* New York: Putnam.

Damasio, A. (1999). *The feeling of what happens* London: Harcourt.

Dansereau, F. (Ed.). (1995). Leadership: The multiple-level approaches (Part 1). [Special issue]. *The Leadership Quarterly, 6.*

Dansereau, F., Alutto, J. A., & Yammarino, F. J. (1984). *Theory testing in organizational behavior: The variant approach.* Englewood Cliffs, NJ: Prentice–Hall.

Dansereau, F., & Yammarino, F. J. (Eds.). (1998). *Leadership: The multiple-level approaches: Contemporary and alternative.* Stamford, CT: JAI.

Davidson, R. J. (1992). Prolegomenon to the structure of emotion: Gleanings from neuropsychology. *Cognition and Emotion, 6,* 245–268.

Day, D. V. (2001). Leadership development: A review in context. *Leadership Quarterly, 11,* 581–613.

Day, D. V., & Lord, R. G. (1988). Executive leadership and organizational performance: Suggestions for a new theory and methodology. *Journal of Management, 14,* 111–122.

Day, D. V., Schleicher, D. J., Unckless, A. L., & Hiller, N. J. (2002). Self-monitoring personality at work: A meta-analytic investigation of construct validity. *Journal of Applied Psychology, 87,* 390–401.

Deckers, L. (2001). *Motivation: Biological, psychological and environmental.* Boston: Allyn & Bacon.

De Cremer, D. (2002). Charismatic leadership and cooperation in social dilemmas: A matter of transforming motives? *Journal of Applied Social Psychology, 32,* 997–1016.

De Cremer, D., & van Knippenberg, D. (2002). How do leaders promote cooperation? The effects of charisma and procedural fairness. *Journal of Applied Psychology, 87,* 858–866.

Den Hartog, D. N., House, R. J., Hanges, P. J., Ruiz-Quintanilla, S. A., Dorfman, P. W., & GLOBE Coordinating Team. (1999). Culture specific and cross-culturally generalizable implicit leadership theories: Are attributes of charismatic/transformational leadership universally endorsed? *Leadership Quarterly, 10,* 219–256.

Dickson, M. W., Smith, D. B., Grojean, M. W., & Ehrhart, M. (2001). An organizational climate regarding ethics: The outcome of leader values and the practices that reflect them. *Leadership Quarterly, 12,* 197–217.

Diener, E. (1999). Introduction to the special section on the structure of emotion. *Journal of Personality and Social Psychology, 76,* 803–804.

Dijksterhuis, A., & van Knippenberg, A. (1998). The relation between perception and behavior, or how to win a game of Trivial Pursuit. *Journal of Personality and Social Psychology, 74,* 865–877.

Dirk, K. T. (2000). Trust in leadership and team performance: Evidence from NCAA basketball. *Journal of Applied Psychology, 85,* 1004–1012.

Dunning, D., & Hayes, A. F. (1996). Evidence for egocentric comparison in social judgment. *Journal of Personality and Social Psychology, 71,* 213–229.

Durso, F. T., & Gronlund, S. D. (1999). Situational awareness. In F. T. Durso (Ed.), *Handbook of applied cognition* (pp. 283–314). Chichester, England: Wiley.

Dvir, T., Eden, D., Avolio, B. J., & Shamir, B. (2002). Impact of transformational leadership on follower development and performance: A field experiment. *Academy of Management Journal, 45,* 735–744.

Eagly, A. H. (1987). *Sex differences in social behavior: A social-role interpretation.* Hillsdale, NJ: Lawrence Erlbaum Associates.

Eagly, A. H., & Johnson, B. T. (1990). Gender and leadership style: A meta-analysis. *Psychological Bulletin, 108,* 233–256.

Eagly, A. H., Makhijani, M. G., & Klonsky, B. G. (1992). Gender and the evaluation of leader: A meta-analysis. *Psychological Bulletin, 111,* 3–22.

Eden, D. (1992). Leadership and expectations: Pygmalion effects and other self-fulfilling prophecies in organizations. *Leadership Quarterly, 3,* 271–305.

Eden, D., Geller, D., Gewirtz, A., Gordon-Terner, R., Inbar, I., Liberman, M., Pass, Y., Salomon-Segev, I., & Shalit, M. (2000). Implanting Pygmanion leadership style through workshop training: Seven field experiments. *Leadership Quarterly, 11,* 171–210.

Eden, D., & Shani, A. B. (1982). Pygmalion goes to boot camp: Expectancy, leadership, and trainee performance. *Journal of Applied Psychology, 72,* 387–392.

Emrich, C. G. (1999). Context effects in leadership perception. *Personality and Social Psychology Bulletin, 25,* 991–1006.

Emrich, C. G., Brower, H. H., Feldman, J. M., & Garland, H. (2001). Images in words: Presidential rhetoric, charisma, and greatness. *Administrative Science Quarterly, 46,* 527–557.

Engle, E. M., & Lord, R. G. (1997). Implicit theories, self-schemas, and leader–member exchange. *Academy of Management Journal, 40,* 988–1010.

Fabes, R. A., & Eisenberg, N. (1997). Regulatory control and adults' stress-related responses to daily life events. *Journal of Personality and Social Psychology, 73,* 1107–1117.

Fabrigar, L. R., & Petty, R. E. (1999). Role of affect and cognitive bases of attitudes in suscepti-bility of affectively and cognitively based persuasion. *Personality and Social Psychology Bulletin, 25,* 363–381.

Fazio, R. H., Sanbonmatsu, D. M., Powell, M. C., & Kardes, F. R. (1986). On the automatic acti-vation of attitudes. *Journal of Personality and Social Psychology, 50,* 229–238.

Feldman, J. M., & Lynch, J. G. (1988). Self-generated validity and other effects of measurement on belief, attitude, intention, and behavior. *Journal of Applied Psychology, 73*(3), 421–435.

Fenigstein, A., Scheier, M. F., & Buss, A. H. (1975). Public and private self-consciousness: As-sessment and theory. *Journal of Consulting and Clinical Psychology, 43,* 522–527.

Festinger, L. (1954). A theory of social comparison processes. *Human Relations, 7,* 117–140.

Fiedler, F. E. (1964). A contingency model of leadership effectiveness. In L. Berkowitz (Ed.), *Advances in experimental social psychology* (Vol. 1, pp. 149–190). New York: Academic Press.

Fiedler, F. E. (1971). Validation and extension of the contingency model of leadership effective-ness: A review of empirical findings. *Psychological Bulletin, 76,* 128–148.

Fiedler, F. E., Chemers, M. M., & Mahar, L. (1976). *Improving leadership effectiveness: The leader match concept.* New York: Wiley.

Fiedler, K., & Schenck, W. (2001). Spontaneous inferences from pictorially presented behav-iors. *Personality and Social Psychological Bulletin, 27,* 1533–1546.

Fiol, C. M., Harris, D., & House, R. J. (1999). Charismatic leadership: Strategies for effecting social change. *Leadership Quarterly, 10,* 449–482.

Fiske, A. P. (2002). Socio-moral emotions motivate action to sustain relationships. *Self and Identity, 1,* 169–175.

Fitness, J. (2000). Anger in the workplace: An emotion script approach to anger episodes be-tween workers and their superiors, co-workers, and subordinates. *Journal of Organizational Behavior, 21,* 147–162.

Fredrickson, B. L. (1998). What good are positive emotions? *Review of General Psychology, 2,* 300–319.

Gabriel, G., & Gardner, W. L. (1999). Are there "his" and "hers" types of interdependence? The implications of gender differences in collective versus relational interdependence for affect, behavior, and cognition. *Journal of Personality and Social Psychology, 77,* 642–655.

Gardner, W. L., & Avolio, B. J. (1998). The charismatic relationship: A dramaturgical perspec-tive. *Academy of Management Review, 23,* 32–58.

Gardner, W. L., Gabriel, S., & Lee, A. Y. (1999). "I" value freedom, but "we" value relation-ships: Self-construal priming mirrors cultural differences in judgment. *Psychological Sci-ence, 10,* 321–326.

Gehani, R. R., & Lord, R. G. (2003). *Leadership and role reversal in leader–member exchange for technology-driven organizations in rapidly-changing environments.* Manuscript in preparation.

Gerstner, C. R., & Day, D. V. (1994). Cross-cultural comparison of leadership prototypes. *The Leadership Quarterly, 5,* 121–134.

Gerstner, C. R., & Day, D. V. (1997). Meta-analytic review of leader–member exchange theory: Correlates and construct issues. *Journal of Applied Psychology, 82,* 827–844.

Gilbert, D. T. (1989). Thinking lightly about others: Automatic components of the social infer-ence process. In J. A. Bargh & J. S. Uleman (Eds.), *Unintended thought* (pp. 189–211). New York: Guilford.

Glomb, T. M., & Hulin, C. L. (1997). Anger and gender effects in observed supervisor-subordi-nate dyadic interactions. *Organizational Behavior and Human Decision Processes, 72,* 281–307.

Glynn, M. A. (1994). Effects of work task cues and play cues on information processing, judg-ment, and motivation. *Journal of Applied Psychology, 79,* 34–45.

Goleman, D., Boyatzis, R., & McKee, A. (2002). *Primal leadership: Realizing the power of emotional intelligence.* Boston: Harvard Business School Press.

Graen, G. B., & Scandura, T. A. (1987). Toward a psychology of dyadic organizing. *Research in Organizational Behavior, 9,* 175–208.

Gray, J. A. (1990). Brain systems that mediate both emotion and cognition. *Cognition and Emotion, 4,* 269–288.

Greenberg, J. (1994). Using socially fair treatment to promote acceptance of a work site smoking ban. *Journal of Applied Psychology, 79*(2), 288–297.

Hains, S. C., Hogg, M. A., & Duck, J. M. (1997). Self-categorization and leadership: Effects of group prototypicality and leader stereotypicality. *Personality and Social Psychology Bulletin, 23,* 1087–1099.

Hall, R. J., & Lord, R. G. (1995). Multi-level information-processing explanations of followers' leadership perceptions. *Leadership Quarterly, 6,* 265–287.

Hall, R. J., Workman, J. W., & Marchioro, C. A. (1998). Sex, task, and behavioral flexibility effects on leadership perceptions. *Organizational Behavior and Human Decision Processes, 74,* 1–32.

Hanges, P. J., Lord, R. G., & Dickson, M. W. (2000). An information processing perspective on leadership and culture: A case for connectionist architecture. *Applied Psychology: An International Review, 49,* 133–161.

Hanges, P. J., Lord, R. G., Godfrey, E. G., & Raver, J. L. (2002). Modeling nonlinear relationships: Neural networks and catastrophe analysis. In S. G. Rogelberg (Ed.), *Handbook of research methods in industrial and organizational psychology* (pp. 431–455). Oxford, England: Blackwell.

Harvey, J. L., & Lord, R. G. (1999). *The effects of perceived velocity on job satisfaction: An expansion of current theory.* Unpublished manuscript.

Hatfield, E., Cacioppo, J. T., & Rapson, R. L. (1994). *Emotional contagion.* Cambridge, England: Cambridge University Press.

Higgins, E. T. (1989). Self-discrepancy theory: What patterns of self-beliefs cause people to suffer? *Advances in Experimental Social Psychology, 22,* 93–136.

Higgins, E. T. (1996). The "self digest": Self-knowledge serving self-regulatory functions. *Journal of Personality and Social Psychology, 71,* 1062–1083.

Higgins, E. T. (1998). The aboutness principle: A pervasive influence on human inference. *Social Cognition, 16,* 173–198.

Higgins, E. T., & Brendl, C. M. (1995). Accessibility and applicability: Some "activation rules" influencing judgment. *Journal of Experimental Social Psychology, 31,* 218–243.

Higgins, E. T., & May, D. (2001). Individual self-regulatory functions: It's not "we" regulation, but it's still social. In C. Sedikides & M. B. Brewer (Eds.), *Individual self, relational self, collective self* (pp. 47–67). Philadelphia: Psychology Press.

Hilton, J. L., Klein, J. G., & von Hippel, W. (1991). Attention allocation and impression formation. *Personality and Social Psychology Bulletin, 17,* 548–559.

Hofstede, G. (1980). *Culture's consequences: International differences in work related beliefs.* Beverly Hills, CA: Sage.

Hogan, R., Curphy, G. J., & Hogan, J. (1994). What we know about leadership: Effectiveness and personality. *American Psychologist, 49,* 493–504.

Hogg, M. A. (2001). A social identity theory of leadership. *Personality and Social Psychology Review, 5,* 184–200.

Hogg, M. A., Hains, S. C., & Mason, I. (1998). Identification and leadership in small groups: Salience, frame of reference, and leader stereotypicality effects on leader evaluations. *Journal of Personality and Social Psychology, 75,* 1248–1263.

Hogg, M. A., & Terry, D. J. (2000). Social identity and self-categorization processes in organizational contexts. *Academy of Management Review, 25,* 121–140.

Holladay, S. J., & Coombs, W. T. (1993). Communicating visions: An exploration of the role of delivery in the creation of leader charisma. *Management Communication Quarterly, 6,* 405–427.

Hollander, E. P. (1992). Leadership, followership, self, and others. *Leadership Quarterly, 3,* 43–54.

Hollander, E. P. (1964). Leadership, groups, and influence. New York: Oxford University Press.

Hollander, E. P., & Offerman, L. R. (1990). Power and leadership in organizations: Relationships in transition. *American Psychologist, 45*, 179–189.

Holman, E. A., & Silver, R. C. (1998). Getting stuck in the past: Temporal orientation and coping with trauma. *Journal of Personality and Social Psychology, 74*, 1146–1163.

House, R. J. (1971). A path–goal theory of leader effectiveness. *Administrative Science Quarterly, 16*, 321–338.

House, R. J. (1996). Path-goal theory of leadership: Lessons, legacy, and a reformulated theory. *Leadership Quarterly, 7*, 323–352.

Howell, J. M., & Hall-Merenda, K. E. (1999). The ties that bind: The impact of leader–member exchange, transformational and transactional leadership, and distance on predicting follower performance. *Journal of Applied Psychology, 84*, 680–694.

Hsee, C. K., & Abelson, R. P. (1991). Velocity relation: Satisfaction as a function of the first derivative of outcome over time. *Journal of Personality and Social Psychology, 60*, 341–347.

Hunt, J. G., Boal, K. B., & Dodge, G. E. (1999). The effects of visionary and crisis-responsive charisma on followers: An experimental examination of two kinds of charismatic leadership. *Leadership Quarterly, 10*, 423–448.

Hyland, M. E. (1988). Motivational control theory: An integrative framework. *Journal of Personality and Social Psychology, 55*, 642–651.

Iaffaldano, M. T., & Muchinsky, P. M. (1985). Job satisfaction and job performance: A meta-analysis. *Psychological Bulletin, 97*, 251–273.

Ibarra, H. (1999). Provisional selves: Experimenting with image and identity in professional adaptation. *Administrative Science Quarterly, 44*, 764–791.

Illingworth, A. (2001). *Predicting organizational citizenship behavior from manipulation of the self-concept in the theory of planned behavior.* Unpublished manuscript, The University of Akron, Akron, OH.

Ireland, R. D., & Hitt, M. A. (1999). Achieving and maintaining strategic competitiveness in the 21st century: The role of strategic leadership. *Academy of Management Executive, 13*, 43–57.

Iyengar, S. S., & Lepper, M. R. (1999). Rethinking the value of choice: A cultural perspective on intrinsic motivation. *Journal of Personality and Social Psychology, 76*, 349–366.

Jack Welch. (2001, September 17). *Business Week*, Issue 3749, p. 130.

Jackson, S. E., & Dutton, J. E. (1988). Discerning threats and opportunities. *Administrative Science Quarterly, 33*(3), 370–387.

James, L. A., & James, L. R. (1989). Integrating work environment perceptions: Explorations into the measurement of meaning. *Journal of Applied Psychology, 74*, 739–751.

James, W. (1890). *The principles of psychology.* New York: Holt.

Johnson, R. E., Selenta, C., & Lord, R. G. (2003). *The impact of organizational justice: Self-concept matters.* Manuscript submitted for publication.

Johnson-Laird, P. N. (1989). Mental models. In M. E. Posner (Ed.), *Foundations of cognitive science* (pp. 469–499). Cambridge, MA: MIT Press.

Judge, T. A., & Bono, J. E. (2000). Five-factor model of personality and transformational leadership. *Journal of Applied Psychology, 85*, 751–765.

Jung, D. I., & Avolio, B. J. (1999). Effects of leadership style and followers' cultural orientation on performance in group and individual task conditions. *Academy of Management Journal, 42*, 208–218.

Kahneman, D., & Tversky, A. (1979). Prospect theory: An analysis of decisions under risk. *Econometrica, 47*, 263–291.

Kanfer, R. (1990). Motivation theory and industrial and organizational psychology. In M. D. Dunnette & L. M. Hough (Eds.), *Handbook of industrial & organizational psychology* (Vol. 1, pp. 147–198). Palo Alto, CA: Consulting Psychologists Press.

Kanfer, R., & Klimoski, R. J. (2002). Affect and work: Looking back to the future. In R. G. Lord, R. J. Klimoski, & R. Kanfer (Eds.), *Emotions in the workplace: Understanding the structure and role of emotions in organizational behavior* (pp.473–490.). San Francisco, CA.: Jossey-Bass.

Karniol, R., & Ross, M. (1996). The motivational impact of temporal focus: Thinking about the future and the past. *Annual Review of Psychology, 47,* 593–620.

Karoly, P. (1993). Mechanisms of self-regulation: A systems view. *Annual Review of Psychology, 44,* 23–52.

Kashima, Y., Woolcock, J., & Kashima, E. S. (2000). Group impressions as dynamic configurations: The tensor product model of group impression formation and change. *Psychological Review, 107*(4), 914–942.

Kass, D. S., & Lord, R. G. (2002). *A new model of motivation: The impact of goal framing on regulator, focus, motivation, and performance.* Manuscript submitted for publication.

Keller, T. (1999). Images of the familiar: Individual differences and implicit leadership theories. *The Leadership Quarterly, 10,* 589–607.

Keltner, D., & Ekman, P. (2000). Facial expression of emotion. In M. Lewis & J. M. Haviland-Jones (Eds.), *Handbook of emotions* (2nd ed., pp.236–249). New York: Guilford.

Keltner, D., & Kring, A. M. (1998). Emotion, social function, and psychopathology. *Review of General Psychology, 2,* 320–342.

Kendzierski, D., & Whitaker, D. J. (1997). The role of self-schema in linking intentions to behavior. *Personality and Social Psychology Bulletin, 23,* 139–147.

Kennedy, John Fitzgerald (1999). *Microsoft Encarta® Encyclopedia.* Seattle, WA: Microsoft Corp.

Kernan, M. C., & Lord, R. G. (1991). An application of control theory to understanding the relationship between performance and satisfaction. *Human Performance, 4,* 173–185.

Kerr, S., & Jerimier, J. M. (1978). Substitutes for leadership: Their meaning and measurement. *Organizational Behavior and Human Performance, 22,* 375–403.

Kerr, S., & Schriesheim, K. (1974). Consideration, initiating structure, and organizational criteria: An update of Korman's 1966 review. *Personnel Psychology, 27,* 555–568.

Kerwin, G. (2002, July–August.). IBEW local 332—the "photovotaic local." *Solar Today, 16,* 32–35.

Kihlstrom, J. F., & Klein, S. B. (1994). The self as a knowledge structure. In R. S. Wyer, Jr. & T. K. Srull (Eds.), *Handbook of social cognition* (2nd ed., pp.153–208). Hillsdale, NJ: Lawrence Erlbaum Associates.

Klein, K. J., Dansereau, F., & Hall, R. J. (1994). Levels issues in theory development, data collection and analysis. *Academy of Management Review, 19,* 195–229.

Klein, S. B. (2001). A self to remember: A cognitive neuropsychological perspective on how self creates memory and memory creates self. In C. Sedikides & M. B. Brewer (Eds.), *Individual self, relational self, collective self* (pp. 25–46). Philadelphia: Psychology Press.

Kluger, A. N., & DeNisi, A. (1996). Effects of feedback intervention on performance: A historical review, a meta-analysis, and a preliminary feedback intervention theory. *Psychological Bulletin, 119,* 254–284.

Koene, B. A. S., Vogelaar, A. L. W., & Soeters, J. L. (2002). Leadership effects on organizational climate and financial performance: Local leadership effect in chain organizations. *Leadership Quarterly, 13,* 193–215.

Komaki, J. L. (1986). Toward effective supervision: An operant analysis and comparison of managers at work. *Journal of Applied Psychology, 71,* 270–279.

Komar, S., & Brown, D. J. (2002). [Do transformational leaders activate self-transcendent values? A preliminary test of Lord and Brown's value priming hypothesis.] Unpublished raw data.

Korsgaard, M. A., Brodt, S. E., & Whitener, E. M. (2002). Trust in the face of conflict: The role of managerial trustworthy behavior and organizational context. *Journal of Applied Psychology, 87,* 312–319.

Korsgaard, M. A., Meglino, B. M., & Lester, S. W. (1996). The effect of other-oriented values on decision making: A test of propositions of a theory of concern for others in organizations. *Organizational Behavior and Human Decision Processes, 68*(3), 234–245.

Korsgaard, M. A., Meglino, B. M., & Lester, S. W. (1997). Beyond helping: Do other-oriented values have broader implications in organizations? *Journal of Applied Psychology, 82*(1), 160–177.

Kozlowski, S. W., & Doherty, M. L. (1989). Integration of climate and leadership: Examination of a neglected issue. *Journal of Applied Psychology, 74,* 546–553.

Kram, K. E. (1985). *Mentoring at work: Developmental relationships in organizational life.* Glenview, IL: Scott, Foresman.

Kristof, A. L. (1996). Person–organization fit: An integrative review of its conceptualizations, measurement, and implications. *Personnel Psychology, 49,* 1–49.

Kristof-Brown, A. L. (2000). Perceived applicant fit: Distinguishing between recruiters' perceptions of person–job and person–organization fit. *Personnel Psychology, 53,* 643–671.

Kruger, J., & Dunning, D. (1999). Unskilled and unaware of it: How difficulties in recognizing one's own incompetence lead to inflated self-assessments. *Journal of Personality and Social Psychology, 77,* 1121–1134.

Kuhl, J. (1994). A theory of action and state orientations. In J. Kuhl & J. Beckmann (Eds.), *Volition and personality.* Seattle, WA: Hogrefe & Huber.

Kuhn, T. S. (1970). *The structure of scientific revolutions.* (2nd ed.). Chicago: University of Chicago Press.

Kuhnen, U., Hannover, B., & Schubert, B. (2001). The semantic-procedural interface model of the self: The role of self-knowledge for context-dependent versus context-independent modes of thinking. *Journal of Personality and Social Psychology, 80,* 397–409.

Kunda, Z. (1999). *Social cognition.* Cambridge, MA: MIT Press.

Kwong, J. Y. Y., & Leung, K. (2002). A moderator of the interaction effect of procedural justice and outcome favorability: Importance of the relationship. *Organizational Behavior and Human Decision Processes, 87,* 278–299.

Larson, J. R., & Callahan, C. (1990). Performance monitoring: How it affects work productivity. *Journal of Applied Psychology, 75,* 530–538.

Lawrence, J. W., Carver, C. S., & Scheier, M. F. (1997). Velocity toward goal attainment in immediate experience as a determinant of affect. *Journal of Applied Social Psychology, 32,* 665–683.

Lazarus, R. S. (1991). *Emotion and adaptation.* New York: Oxford University Press.

Leary, R. M., & Baumeister, R. F. (2000). The nature and function of self-esteem: Sociometer theory. In M. Zanna (Ed.), *Advances in experimental social psychology* (Vol. 32, pp. 1–62). San Diego, CA: Academic Press.

Levenson, R. (1994). Human emotion: A functional view. In P. Ekman & R. J. Davidson (Eds.), *The nature of emotion* (pp. 123–126). New York. Oxford University Press.

Levy, B. (1996). Improving memory in old age through implicit self-stereotyping. *Journal of Personality and Social Psychology, 71*(6), 1092–1107.

Lewicki, P. (1985). Nonconscious biasing effects of single instances on subsequent judgments. *Journal of Personality and Social Psychology, 48,* 563–574.

Lewis, K. M. (2000). When leaders display emotion: How followers respond to negative emotional expression of male and female leaders. *Journal of Organizational Behavior, 21,* 221–234.

Liden, R. C., Wayne, S. J., Judge, T. A., Sparrowe, R. T., Kraimer, M. L., & Franz, T. M. (1999). Management of poor performance: A comparison of manager, group member, and group disciplinary decisions. *Journal of Applied Psychology, 84,* 835–850.

Liden, R. C., Wayne, S. A., & Stilwell, D. (1993). A longitudinal study on the early development of leader–member exchanges. *Journal of Applied Psychology, 78,* 662–674.

Likert, R. (1967). *The human organization: Its management and value.* New York: McGraw-Hill.

Lind, E. A. (2001). Fairness heuristic theory: Justice judgements as pivotal cognitions in organizational relations. In J. Greenberg & R. Cropanzano (Eds.), *Advances in organizational justice* (pp. 56–88). Stanford, CA: Stanford University Press.

Lind, E. A., Kray, L., & Thompson, L. (1998). The social construction of injustice: Fairness judgments in response to own and others' unfair treatment by authorities. *Organizational Behavior and Human Decision Processes, 75,* 1–22.

Lind, E. A., & Tyler, T. R. (1988). *The social psychology of procedural justice.* New York: Plenum.

Linville, P. W. (1987). Self-complexity as a cognitive buffer against stress related disease and illness. *Journal of Personality and Social Psychology, 52,* 663–676.

Litwin, G. H., & Stringer, R. A. (1968). *Motivation and organizational climate.* Boston: Division of Research, Graduate School of Business Administrations. Harvard University.

Locke, E. P., & Latham, G. P. (1990). *A theory of goal setting & task performance.* Englewood Cliffs, NJ: Prentice-Hall.

Lockwood, P., & Kunda, Z. (1997). Superstars and me: Predicting the impact of role models on the self. *Journal of Personality and Social Psychology, 73,* 91–103.

Lord, R. G. (1985). An information processing approach to social perceptions, leadership perceptions and behavioral measurement on organizational settings. In B. M. Staw & L. Cummings (Eds.), *Research in organizational behavior* (pp. 87–128). Greenwich, CT: JAI.

Lord, R. G., Binning, J. F., Rush, M. C., & Thomas, J. C. (1978). The effect of performance cues and leader behavior on questionnaire ratings of leadership behavior. *Organizational Behavior and Human Decision Processes, 21,* 27–39.

Lord, R. G., & Brown, D. J. (2001). Leadership, values, and subordinate self-concepts. *Leadership Quarterly, 12,* 133–152.

Lord, R. G., Brown, D. J., & Freiberg, S. J. (1999). Understanding the dynamics of leadership: The role of follower self-concepts in the leader/follower relationship. *Organizational Behavior and Human Decision Processes, 78,* 167–203.

Lord, R. G., Brown, D. J., & Harvey, J. L. (2001). System constraints on leadership perceptions, behavior, and influence: An example of connectionist level processes. In M. A. Hogg & R. S. Tindale (Eds.), *Blackwell handbook of social psychology: Group processes* (pp. 283–310). Oxford, England: Blackwell.

Lord, R. G., Brown, D. J., Harvey, J. L., & Hall, R. J. (2001). Contextual constraints on prototype generation and their multilevel consequences for leadership perceptions. *Leadership Quarterly, 12,* 311–338.

Lord, R. G., De Vader, C., & Alliger, G. (1986). A meta-analysis of the relation between personality traits and leadership perceptions: An application of validity generalization procedures. *Journal of Applied Psychology, 71,* 402–410.

Lord, R. G., & Emrich, C. G. (2000). Thinking outside the box by looking inside the box: Extending the cognitive revolution in leadership research. *Leadership Quarterly, 11,* 551–580.

Lord, R. G., Foti, R. J., & De Vader, C. L. (1984). A test of leadership categorization theory: Internal structure, information processing, and leadership perceptions. *Organizational Behavior and Human Performance, 34,* 343–378.

Lord, R. G., & Hanges, P. J. (1987). A control systems model of organizational motivation: Theoretical development and applied implications. *Behavioral Science, 32,* 161–178.

Lord, R. G., Hanges, P. J., & Godfrey, E. G. (2002, April). *Integrating neural networks into theories of motivation and decision making.* Paper presented at the 17th annual conference of the Society for Industrial and Organizational Psychology, Toronto, Ontario, Canada.

Lord, R. G., & Harvey, J. L. (2002). An information processing framework for emotional regulation. In R. G. Lord, R. J. Klimoski, & R. Kanfer (Eds.), *Emotions in the workplace: Understanding the structure and role of emotions in organizational behavior* (pp. 115–146). San Francisco: Jossey-Bass.

Lord, R. G., & Kernan, M. C. (1987). Scripts as determinants of purposeful behavior in organizations. *Academy of Management Review, 12,* 265–277.

Lord, R. G., & Levy, P. J. (1994). Moving from cognition to action: A control theory perspective. *Applied Psychology: An International Review, 43,* 335–398.

Lord, R. G., & Maher, K. J. (1991). *Leadership and information processing.* Boston: Routledge.

Lord, R. G., & Smith, W. G. (1999). Leadership and the changing nature of work performance. In D. R. Ilgen & E. D. Palacos (Eds.). *The changing nature of work performance: Implications for staffing, personnel decisions, and development* (pp. 192–239). San Francisco: Jossey-Bass.

Lowe, K. B., Kroeck, K. G., & Sivasubramaniam, N. (1996). Effectiveness of correlates of transformational and transactional leadership: A meta-analytic review of the MLQ literature. *Leadership Quarterly, 7*, 385–425.

MacDonald, M. C., & Christiansen, M. H. (2002). Reassessing working memory: Comment on Just and Carpenter (1992) and Waters and Caplan (1996). *Psychological Review, 109*(1), 35–54.

Macrae, C. N., Milne, A. B., & Bodenhausen, G. V. (1994). Stereotypes as energy-saving devices: A peek inside the cognitive toolbox. *Journal of Personality and Social Psychology, 66*, 37–47.

Maio, G. R., & Olson, J. M. (1998). Values as truisms: Evidence and implications. *Journal of Personality and Social Psychology, 74*, 294–311.

Malt, B. C., Ross, B. H., & Murphy, G. L. (1995). Predicting features for members of natural categories when categorization is uncertain. *Journal of Experimental Psychology: Learning, Memory, and Cognition, 21*, 646–661.

Mann, R. D. (1959). A review of the relationship between personality and performance in small groups. *Psychological Bulletin, 56*, 241–270.

Markus, H. (1977). Self-schemata and processing information about the self. *Journal of Personality and Social Psychology, 35*, 63–78.

Markus, H., & Kitayama, S. (1991). Culture and the self: Implications for cognitions, emotion, and motivation. *Psychological Review, 98*, 224–353.

Markus, H., & Nurius, P. (1986). Possible selves. *American Psychologist, 41*, 954–969.

Markus, H., Smith, J., & Moreland, R. L. (1985). Role of the self-concept in the perception of others. *Journal of Personality and Social Psychology, 49*, 1494–1512.

Markus, H., & Wurf, E. (1987). The dynamic self-concept: A social psychological perspective. *Annual Review of Psychology, 38*, 299–337.

Marques, J. M., Abrams, D., Paez, D., & Hogg, M. A. (2001). Social categorization, social identification, and rejection of deviant group members. In M. A. Hogg & S. Tindale (Eds.), *Blackwell handbook of social psychology: Group processes* (pp. 400–424). Malden, MA: Blackwell.

Marsh, R. L., Hicks, J. L., & Bryan, E. (1999). The activation of unrelated and canceled intentions. *Memory & Cognition, 27*, 320–327.

Martin, L. L., Strack, F., & Stapel, D. A. (2001). How the mind moves: Knowledge accessibility and the fine-tuning of the cognitive system. In A. Tesser & N. Schwartz (Eds.), *Blackwell handbook of social psychology: Intraindividual processes* (pp. 236–256). Oxford, England: Blackwell.

Martindale, C. C. (1980). Subselves: The internal representation of situational and personal dispositions. In L. Wheeler (Ed.), *Review of personality and social psychology*. Beverly Hills, CA: Sage.

Martinko, M. J., & Gardner, W. L. (1987). The leader/member attribution process. *Academy of Management Review, 12*, 235–249.

Masters, I. G. (2000, September 28). Sony co-founder faced opposition on walkman. *The Toronto Star*, p. 2, H.

Masterson, S. S., Lewis, K., Goldman, B. M., & Taylor, M. S. (2000). Integrating justice and social exchange: The differing effects of fair procedures and treatment on work relationships. *Academy of Management Journal, 43*, 738–748.

McClelland, J. L., & Rumelhart, D. E. (Eds.). (1986). *Parallel distributed processing: Explorations in the microstructure of cognition: Vol. 2. Psychological and biological models*. London: MIT Press.

McGregor, D. (1960). *The human side of enterprise*. New York: McGraw-Hill.

McGuire, W. J., & Padawer-Singer, A. (1976). Trait salience in the spontaneous self-concept. *Journal of Personality and Social Psychology, 33,* 743–754.

McNulty, S. E., & Swann, W. B. (1994). Identity negotiations in roommate relationships: The self as architect and consequence of social reality. *Journal of Personality and Social Psychology, 130,* 385–396.

Mead, G. H. (1934). *Mind, self and society.* Chicago: University of Chicago Press.

Meindl, J. R. (1995). The romance of leadership as a follower-centric theory: A social constructionist approach. *Leadership Quarterly, 6,* 329–341.

Meindl, J. R., & Erlich, S. B. (1987). The romance of leadership and the evaluation of organizational performance. *Academy of Management Journal, 30,* 91–109.

Meindl, J. R., Ehrlich, S. B., & Dukerich, J. M. (1985). The romance of leadership. *Administrative Science Quarterly, 30,* 78–102.

Miller, D. T., & Prentice, D. A (1994). Collective errors and errors about the collective. *Personality and Social Psychology Bulletin, 20,* 541–550.

Miller, D. W., & Marks, L. J. (1997). The effects of imagery-evoking radio advertising strategies on affective responses. *Psychology and Marketing, 14,* 337–360.

Mischel, W., & Shoda, Y. (1995). A cognitive-affective system theory of personality: Reconceptualizing situations, dispositions, dynamics and invariance in personality structure. *Psychological Review, 102,* 246–268.

Mitchell, T. R., & Beach, L. R. (1990). "... Do I love thee? Let me count ..." Towards an understanding of intuitive and automatic decision making. *Organizational Behavior and Human Decision Processes, 47,* 1–20.

Moorman, R. H., Blakely, G. L., & Niehoff, B. P. (1998). Does perceived organizational support mediate the relationship between procedural justice and organizational citizenship behavior? *Academy of Management Journal, 41,* 351–357.

Morris, M. W., & Peng, K. (1994). Culture and cause: American and Chinese attributions for social and physical events. *Journal of Personality and Social Psychology, 67,* 949–971.

Mortensen, C. (2001, Sept. 26). Retrieved from http:www.espn.go.com/chrismortensen

Murphy, M. R., & Jones, A. P. (1993). The influences of performance cues and observational focus on performance rating accuracy. *Journal of Applied Social Psychology, 23,* 1523–1545.

Murphy, S. T., & Zajonc, R. B. (1993). Affect, cognition, and awareness: Affective priming with optimal and suboptimal stimulus exposures. *Journal of Personality and Social Psychology, 64,* 723–739.

Murray, S. L., Holmes, J. G., & Griffin, D. W. (1996). The self-fulfilling nature of positive illusions in romantic relationships: Love is not blind, but prescient. *Journal of Personality and Social Psychology, 71,* 1155–1180.

Naidoo, L. J., & Lord, R. G. (2002a). *Affect in leadership measurement: A new approach to gathering questionnaire data.* Manuscript submitted for publication.

Naidoo, L. J., & Lord, R. G. (2002b). *Emotions and perceptions of charismatic leadership: The effects of speech imagery and subliminal facial expression.* Manuscript submitted for publication.

Neck, C. P., Stewart, G. L., & Manz, C. C. (1996). Self-leaders within self-leading teams: Toward an optimal equilibrium. In M. M. Beyerlein, D. A. Johnson, & S. T. Beyerlein (Eds.), *Advances in interdisciplinary studies of work teams: Team leadership* (Vol. 3, pp. 43–65). Stamford, CT: JAI.

Neuberg, S. L. (1988). Behavioral implications of information presented outside of conscious awareness: The effect of subliminal presentation of trait information on behavior in the Prisoner's Dilemma game. *Social Cognition, 6,* 207–230.

Newman, L. S. (1993). How individualists interpret behavior: Idiocentrism and spontaneous trait inference. *Social Cognition, 9,* 221–253.

Norrell, R. J. (1998). Martin Luther King, Jr. *Microsoft Encarta Encyclopedia 99* [Computer software]. Seattle, WA: Microsoft.

Norris-Watts, C., & Lord, R. G. (2002). *Women and leadership: A motivational explanation of stereotype threat.* Manuscript submitted for publication.

Offermann, L. R., Kennedy, J. K., Jr., & Wirtz, P. W. (1994). Implicit leadership theories: Content, structure and generalizability. *Leadership Quarterly, 5*, 43–58.

Ohlsson, S. (1996). Learning from performance errors. *Psychological Review, 103*, 241–262.

Oishi, S., Schmmack, U., Diener, E., & Suh, E. M. (1998). The measurement of values and individualism–collectivism. *Personality and Social Psychology Bulletin, 24*, 1177–1189.

Paivio, A. (1986). Mental representations: A dual coding approach. New York: Oxford University Press.

Panksepp, J. (2000). Emotions as natural kinds within the mammalian brain. In M. Lewis & J. M. Haviland-Jones (Eds.), *Handbook of emotions* (2nd ed., pp. 137–156). New York: Guilford.

Paul, J., Costley, D. L., Howell, J. P., Dorfman, P. W., & Trafimow, D. (2001). The effects of charismatic leadership on followers' self-concept accessibility. *Journal of Applied Social Psychology, 31*, 1821–1844.

Pavlov, I. P. (1927). *Conditioned reflexes.* London: Oxford University Press.

Pelham, W. B., & Swann, W. B. (1989). From self-conceptions to self-worth: On the sources and structure of global self-esteem. *Journal of Personality and Social Psychology, 57*, 672–680.

Peterson, R. S. (1999). Can you have too much of a good thing? The limits of voice for improving satisfaction with leaders. *Personality and Social Psychology Bulletin, 25*(3), 313–324.

Petty, M. M., McGee, G. W., & Cavender, J. W. (1984). A meta-analysis of the relationships between individual job satisfaction and individual performance. *Academy of Management Review, 9*, 712–721.

Phillips, J. S., & Lord, R. G. (1981). Causal attributions and perceptions of leadership. *Organizational Behavior and Human Decision Processes, 28*, 143–163.

Pillai, R. (1996). Crisis and the emergence of charismatic leadership in groups: An experimental investigation. *Journal of Applied Social Psychology, 26*, 543–562.

Pillai, R., & Meindl, J. R. (1998). Contex and charisma: A "meso" level examination of the relationship of organic structure, collectivism, and crisis to charismatic leadership. *Journal of Management, 24*, 643–671.

Pillai, R., Schriesheim, C. A., & Williams, E. S. (1999). Fairness perceptions and trust as mediators for transformational and transactional leadership: A two-sample study. *Journal of Management, 25*, 897–933.

Ployhart, R. E., & Ryan, A. M. (1997). Toward an explanation of applicant reactions: An examination of organizational justice and attribution frameworks. *Organizational Behavior and Human Decision Processes, 72*, 308–335.

Ployhart, R. E., Ryan, A. M., & Bennett, M. (1999). Examinations for selection decisions: Applicants' reactions to informational and sensitivity features of explanations. *Journal of Applied Psychology, 84*, 87–106.

Podsakoff, P. M., Mackenzie, S. B., Moorman, R. H., & Fetter, R. (1990). Transformational leader behaviors and their effects on followers' trust in leader, satisfaction, and organizational citizenship behavior. *Leadership Quarterly, 1*, 107–142.

Podsakoff, P. M., Todor, W. D., & Skov, R. (1982). Effects of leader contingent and noncontingent reward and punishment behaviors on subordinate performance and satisfaction. *Academy of Management Journal, 25*, 810–821.

Porac, J., Thomas, H., & Baden-Fuller, C. (1989). Competitive groups as cognitive communities: The case of Scottish knitwear manufacturers. *Journal of Management Studies, 26*, 397–416.

Powers, W. T. (1973). Feedback: Beyond behaviorism. *Science, 179*, 351–362.

Pugh, S. D. (2001). Service with a smile: Emotional contagion in the service encounter. *Academy of Management Journal, 44*, 1018–1027.

Queller, S., & Smith, E. R. (2002). Subtyping versus bookkeeping in stereotype learning and change: Connectionist simulations and empirical findings. *Journal of Personality and Social Psychology, 82*(3), 300–313.

Read, S. J., & Miller, L. C. (1998). On the dynamic construction of meaning: An interactive activation and competition model of social perception. In S. J. Read & L. C. Miller (Eds.), *Connectionist models of social reasoning and social behavior* (pp. 27–68). Mahwah, NJ: Lawrence Erlbaum Associates.

Read, S. J., Vaneman, E. J., & Miller, L. C. (1997). Connectionism, parallel constraint satisfaction processes, and gestalt principles: (Re) Introducing cognitive dynamics to social psychology. *Personality and Social Psychology Review, 1,* 26–53.

Reicher, S. (2002, June). *On the science of the art of leadership.* Paper presented at the 13th general meeting of the European Association of Experimental Social Psychology, San Sebastian, Spain.

Reicher, S., & Hopkins, N. (in press). Entrepreneurs of identity: On the psychological craft of leadership. In D. van Knippenberg & M. A. Hogg (Eds.), *Identity, leadership, and power.* Beverly Hills, CA: Sage.

Roberts, W. A. (2002). Are animals stuck in time? *Psychological Bulletin, 128,* 473–489.

Rohan, M. J. (2000). A rose by any name? The values constuct. *Personality and Social Psychology Review, 4,* 255–277.

Rosch, E. (1978). Principles of categorization. In E. Rosch & B. B. Lloyd (Eds.), *Cognition and categorization* (pp. 28–48). Hillsdale, NJ: Lawrence Erlbaum Associates.

Ross, L. (1977). The intuitive psychologist and his shortcomings. In L. Berkowitz (Ed.), *Advances in experimental social psychology* (Vol. 10, pp. 173–220). San Diego: Academic Press.

Rumelhart, D. E., & McClelland, J. L. (1986). *Parallel distributed processing: Explorations in the microstructure of cognition: Vol. 1. Foundations.* London: MIT Press.

Rush, M. C., Phillips, J. S., & Lord, R. G. (1981). Effects of a temporal delay in rating on leader behavior descriptions: A laboratory investigation. *Journal of Applied Psychology, 66,* 442–450.

Russell, J. A., & Feldman Barrett, L. (1999). Core affect, prototypical emotional episodes, and other things called *emotion:* Discussing the elephant. *Journal of Personality and Social Psychology, 76,* 805–819.

Rusting, C. L., & Larsen, R. J. (1998). Personality and cognitive processing of affective information. *Personality and Social Psychology Bulletin, 24,* 200–213.

Ryan, R. M., & Deci, E. L. (2000). Self-determinantion theory and the facilitation of intrinsic motivation, social development, and well-being. *American Psychologist, 55,* 68–78.

Scandura, T. A. (1999). Rethinking leader–member exchange: An organizational justice perspective. *Leadership Quarterly, 10,* 25–40.

Schein, E. H. (1992). *Organizational culture and leadership* (2nd ed.). San Francisco: Jossey-Bass.

Scherer, K. R. (1994). Emotion serves to decouple stimulus and response. In P. Ekman & R. J. Davidson (Eds.), *The nature of emotion: Fundamental questions* (pp. 127–130) New York: Oxford University Press.

Schneider, B. (1987). The people make the place. *Personnel Psychology, 40,* 437–453.

Schriesheim, C. A., & Stogdill, R. M. (1975). Differences in factor structure across three versions of the Ohio State Leadership Scales. *Personnel Psychology, 28,* 189–206.

Schroth, H. A., & Pradhan, S. P. (2000). Procedures: Do we really want to know them? An examination of the effects of procedural justice on self-esteem. *Journal of Applied Psychology, 85,* 462–471.

Schwartz, S. H. (1992). Universals in the content and structure of values: Theoretical advances and empirical tests in 20 countries. In M. P. Zanna (Ed.), *Advances in experimental social psychology* (Vol. 25, pp. 1–65). San Diego: Academic Press.

Schwartz, S. H. (1999). A theory of cultural values and some implications for work. *Applied Psychology: An International Review, 48,* 23–47.

Schwartz, S. H. & Bilsky, W. (1987). Toward a universal psychological structure of human values. *Journal of Personality and Social Psychology, 53,* 550–562.

Schwartz, S. H. & Bilsky, W. (1990). Toward a theory of universal content and structure of values: Extensions and cross-cultural replications. *Journal of Personality and Social Psychology, 58,* 878–891.

Sedikides, C., & Brewer, M. B. (Eds.). (2001). *Individual self, relational self, collective self.* Philadelphia: Psychology Press.

Selenta, C., & Lord, R. G. (2002). *The individual, relational, and collective levels: Construct refinement and development of a measure of the self-concept levels.* Manuscript submitted for publication.

Shamir, B., Arthur, M. B., & House, R. J. (1994). The rhetoric of charismatic leadership: A theoretical extension, a case study, and implications for research. *Leadership Quarterly, 5,* 25–42.

Shamir, B., House, R. J., & Arthur, M. B. (1993). The motivational effects of charismatic leadership: A self-concept based theory. *Organization Science, 4,* 577–594.

Shamir, B., Zakay, E., Breinin, E., & Popper, M. (1998). Correlates of charismatic leader behavior in military units: Subordinates' attitudes, unit characteristics, and superiors' appraisals of leader performance. *Academy of Management Journal, 41,* 387–409.

Shaw, J. B. (1990). A cognitive categorization model for the study of intercultural management. *Academy of Management Review, 10,* 435–454.

Shipper, F., & Manz, C. C. (1992). Employee self-management without formally designated teams: An alternative road to empowerment. *Organizational Dynamics, 20,* 48–61.

Shoda, Y., Mischel, W., & Wright, J. C. (1994). Intraindividual stability in the organization and patterning of behavior: Incoporating psychological situations into the idiographic analysis of personality. *Journal of Personality and Social Psychology, 67,* 674–687.

Shrauger, J. S., & Schoneman, T. J. (1979). Symbolic interactionist view of self-concept: Through the looking glass darkly. *Psychological Bulletin, 86,* 549–573.

Skarlicki, D. P., & Folger, R. (1997). Retaliation in the workplace: The roles of distributive, procedural, and interactional justice. *Journal of Applied Psychology, 82,* 434–443.

Skarlicki, D. P., Folger, R., & Tesluk, P. (1999). Personality as a moderator in the relationship between fairness and retaliation. *Academy of Management Journal, 42,* 100–108.

Skarlicki, D. P., & Latham, G. P. (1996). Increasing citizenship behavior within a labor union: A test of organizational justice theory. *Journal of Applied Psychology, 81,* 161–169.

Smith, E. R. (1996). What do connectionism and social psychology offer each other? *Journal of Personality and Social Psychology, 70,* 893–912.

Smith, P. B., & Schwartz, S. H. (1997). Values. In J. W. Berry, M. H. Segall, & C. Kagitcibasi (Eds.), *Handbook of cross-cultural psychology* (Vol. 3, 2nd ed., pp. 77–118). Boston: Allyn & Bacon.

Smith, W., Brown, D. J., Lord, R. G., & Engle, E. M. (1999). *Leadership self-schema, leadership perceptions and leadership activities. Unpublished manuscript..*

Snyder, M. (1979). Self-monitoring processes. In L. Berkowitz (Ed.), *Advances in experimental social psychology* (Vol. 12, pp.86–128). New York: Academic Press.

Spence, J. T., & Helmreich, R. L. (1978). *Masculinity & femininity: Their psychological dimensions, correlates, and antecedents.* Austin: University of Texas Press.

Srull, T. K., & Wyer, R. S. (1989). Person memory and judgment. *Psychological Review, 96,* 58–83.

Steele, C. M., Spencer, S. J., & Aronson, J. (2002). Contending with group image: The psychology of stereotype and social identity threat. *Advances in Experimental Social Psychology, 34,* 379–440.

Stephanopoulos, G. (1999). *All too human: A political education.* Boston: Little, Brown.

Stogdill, R. G. (1948). Personal factors associated with leadership: A survey of the literature. *Journal of Psychology, 25,* 35–71.

Stogdill, R. G. (1963). *Manual for the Leader Behavior Description Questionnaire—Form XII.* Columbus, OH: Bureau of Business Research, The Ohio State University.

Strock, J. M. (1998). *Reagan on leadership: Executive lessons from the great communicator.* Roseville, CA: Prima Publishing.

Tepper, B. J. (2000). Consequences of abusive supervision. *Academy of Management Journal, 43,* 178–190.

Thagard. P.. & Kunda. Z. (1998). Making sense of people: Coherence mechanisms. In S. J. Read & L. C. Miller (Eds.). *Connectionist models of social reasoning and social behavior.* (pp. 3–26). Mahwah, NJ: Lawrence Erlbaum Associates.

Thomas, J. L.. Dickson, M. W.. & Bliese, P. D. (2001). Values predicting leader performance in the U.S. Army Reserve Officer Training Corps Assessment Center: Evidence for a personality-mediated model. *Leadership Quarterly, 12,* 181–196.

Thomas. K. M.. & Mathieu, J. E. (1994). Role of causal attributions in dynamic self-regulation and goal processes. *Journal of Applied Psychology, 79,* 812–818.

Tice. D. M.. & Baumeister, R. F. (2001). The primacy of the interpersonal self. In C. Sedikides & M. B. Brewer (Eds.). *Individual self, relational self, collective self* (pp. 71–88). Philadelphia, PA.: Psychology Press.

Tiedens. L. Z. (2000). Powerful emotions: The vicious cycle of social status positions and emotions. In N. M. Ashkanasy, C. E. J. Hartel, & W. J. Zerbe (Eds.). *Emotions in the workplace: Research, theory, and practice* (pp. 71–81). Westport, CT: Quorum Books.

Tindale, R. S., Meisenhleder, H. M.. Dykema-Engblade, A. A.. & Hogg, M. (2001). Shared cognition in small groups. In M. A. Hogg & R. S. Tindale (Eds.). *Blackwell handbook of social psychology: Vol. 3. Group processes* (pp. 1–30). Oxford, England: Blackwell.

Triandis, H. C. (1989). The self and social behavior in differing cultural contexts. *Psychological Bulletin, 96,* 506–520.

Triandis, H. C. (1994). Cross-cultural industrial and organizational psychology. In H. C. Traindis, M. D. Dunnette. & L. M. Hough (Eds.). *Handbook of industrial and organizational psychology* (2nd Ed.. Vol. 4, pp. 103–172). Palo Alto, CA: Consulting Psychologists Press.

Tulving. E. (2002). Episodic memory: From mind to brain. *Annual Review of Psychology, 53,* 1–25.

Turner, J. C.. Oakes, P. J., Haslam, S. A.. & McGarty. C. (1994). Self and collective: Cognition and social context. *Personality and Social Psychology Bulletin, 20,* 454–463.

Tushman, M. L.. & Anderson, P. (1986). Technological discontinuities and organizational environments. *Administrative Science Quarterly, 31,* 439–465.

Tushman, M. L.. & Romanelli, E. (1985). Organizational evolution: A metamorphosis model of convergence and reorientation. *Research in Organizational Behavior, 7,* 171–222.

Tyler. T. R. (1997). The psychology of legitimacy: A relational perspective on voluntary deference to authorities. *Personality and Social Psychological Review, 1,* 323–345.

Tyler. T. R.. & Caine. A. (1981). The influence of outcomes and procedures on satisfaction with formal leaders. *Journal of Personality and Social Psychology, 41,* 642–655.

Tyler. T. R.. Degoey, P.. & Smith. H. (1996). Understanding why the justice of groups procedures matters: A test of the psychological dynamics of the group-value model. *Journal of Personality and Social Psychology, 70,* 913–930.

Tyler. T. R.. & Lind. E. A. (1992). A relational model of authority in groups. *Advances in Experimental Social Psychology, 25,* 115–191.

Uleman. J. S.. & Moskowitz, G. B. (1994). Unintended effects of goals on unintended inferences. *Journal of Personality and Social Psychology, 66,* 490–501.

Van den Bos, K.. & Lind, E. A. (2002). Uncertainty management by means of fairness judgment. *Advances in Experimental Social Psychology, 34,* 1–60.

Van Knippenberg, D.. & Hogg, M. A. (Eds.). (2003). *Identity, leadership, and power.* Beverly Hills, CA: Sage.

Van Overwalle, F., Drenth, T.. & Marsman, G. (1999). Spontaneous trait interferences: Are they linked to the actor or the action? *Personality and Social Psychology Bulletin, 25,* 450–462.

Van Overwalle, F.. & Van Rooy, D. (2001). How one cause discounts or augments another: A connectionist account of causal competition. *Personality and Social Psychology Bulletin, 27*(12), 1613–1626.

Venkatesh, V.. Morris, M. G.. & Ackerman, P. L. (2000). A longitudinal field investigation of gender differences in individual technology adoption decision-making processes. *Organizational Behavior and Human Decision Processes, 83,* 33–60.

Verplanken, B., & Holland, R. W. (2002). Motivative decision making: Effects of activation and self-centrality of values on choices and behavior. *Journal of Personality and Social Psychology, 82,* 434–447.

Vygotsky, L. S. (1978). *Mind in society.* Cambridge, MA: Harvard University Press.

Watson, D., Clark, L. A., & Tellegen, A. (1988). Development and validation of brief measures of positive and negative affect: The PANAS scale. *Journal of Personality and Social Psychology, 54,* 1063–1070.

Wegner, D. M. (1994). Ironic processes of mental control. *Psychological Review, 101,* 34–52.

Weick, K. E. (1995). *Sensemaking in organizations.* London: Sage.

Weick, K. E. (1979). *The social psychology of organizing* (2nd ed.). Reading, MA.: Addison-Wesley.

Weiss, H. M. (2002). Conceptual and empirical foundations for the study of affect at work. In R. G. Lord, R. J. Klimoski, & R. Kanfer (Eds.), *Emotions in the workplace: Understanding the structure and role of emotions in organizational behavior* (pp. 20–63). San Francisco: Jossey-Bass.

Weiss, H. M., & Cropanzano, R. (1996). Affective events theory: A theoretical discussion of the structure, causes, and consequences of affective experiences at work. In B. M. Staw & L. L. Cummings (Eds.), *Research in organizational behavior: An annual series of analytical essays and critical reviews* (Vol. 18, pp. 1–74). Stamford, CT: JAI.

Wenzlaff, R. M., & Bates, D. E. (2000). The relative efficacy of concentration and suppression strategies of mental control. *Personality and Social Psychology Bulletin, 26,* 1200–1212.

Wheeler, M. A., Stuss, D. T., & Tulving, E. (1997). Towards a theory of episodic memory: The frontal lobes and autonoetic consciousness. *Psychological Review, 121,* 331–354.

Wilson, T. D., & Hodges, S. D. (1992). Attitudes as temporary constructions. In L. L. Martin & A. Tesser (Eds.), *The construction of social judgments* (pp. 37–65). Hillsdale, NJ: Lawrence Erlbaum Associates.

Wofford, J. C., & Goodwin, V. L. (1994). A cognitive interpretation of transactional and transformational leadership theories. *Leadership Quarterly, 5,* 161–186.

Wofford, J. C., Goodwin, V. L., & Whittington, J. L. (1998). A field study of a cognitive approach to understanding transformational and transactional leadership. *Leadership Quarterly, 9,* 55–84.

Wofford, J. C., Joplin, J. R., & Comforth, B. (1996). Use of simultaneous verbal protocols in analysis of group leaders' cognitions. *Psychological Reports, 79,* 847–858.

Worline, M. C., Wrzesniewski, A., & Rafaeli, A. (2002). Courage and work: Breaking routines to improve performance. In R. G. Lord, R. J. Klimoski, & R. Kanfer (Eds.), *Emotions in the workplace: Understanding the structure and role of emotions in organizational behavior* (pp. 295–330). San Francisco: Jossey-Bass.

Yammarino, F. J., & Dubinsky, A. J. (1994). Transformational leadership theory: Using levels of analysis to determine boundary conditions. *Personnel Psychology, 47,* 787–811.

Ybarra, O., & Trafimow, D. (1998). How priming of the private or collective self affects the relative weights of attitudes and subjective norms. *Personality and Social Psychology Bulletin, 24,* 362–370.

Yorges, S., Weiss, H. M., & Strickland, O. J. (1999). The effects of leader outcomes on influence, attributions, and perceptions of charisma. *Journal of Applied Psychology, 84,* 428–436.

Yukl, G. A. (2002). *Leadership in organizations* (5th ed.). Upper Saddle River, NJ: Prentice Hall.

Yukl, G. A., & Van Fleet, D. D. (1992). Theory and research on leadership in organizations. In M. D. Dunnette & L. M. Hough (Eds.), *Handbook of industrial and organizational psychology* (Vol. 1, pp. 147–198). Palo Alto, CA: Consulting Psychologists Press.

Zaccaro, S. J., & Banks, D. J. (2001). Leadership, vision, and organizational effectiveness. In S. J. Zaccaro & R. Klimoski (Eds.), *The nature of organizational leadership.* (pp. 181–218). San Francisco: Jossey-Bass.

Zaccaro, S. J., Foti, R. J., & Kenny, D. A. (1991). Self-monitoring and trait-based variance in leadership: An investigation of leader flexibility across multiple group situations. *Journal of Applied Psychology, 76,* 308–315.

Zaccaro, S. J., & Klimoski, R. J. (Eds.). (2001). *The nature of organizational leadership: Understanding the performance imperatives confronting today's leaders.* San Francisco: Jossey-Bass.

Zarate, M. A., Uleman, J. S., & Voils, C. I. (2001). Effects of culture and processing goals on the activation and binding of trait concepts. *Social Cognition, 19,* 295–323.

Author Index

Note: *f* indicates figure

A

Abelson, R. P., 22
Abrams, D., 117
Ackerman, P. L., 197
Adams, J. S., 178
Adelman, P. K., 131
Ajzen, I., 197
Allen, P. A., 9, 130, 146
Alliger, G., 3, 53
Alutto, J. A., 203
Andersen, S. M., 190, 194, 207, 208, 213
Anderson, J. R., 178, 194
Anderson, P., 98
Aron, A., 46, 58
Aronson, J., 70
Arthur, M. B., 2, 26, 75, 84, 102, 126, 147
Ashforth, B. E., 130
Atwater, L., 202
Avolio, B. J., 4, 5, 83, 84, 101, 102, 112, 191, 202
Awamleh, R., 112, 125, 130

B

Baden-Fuller, C., 145
Baker, S., 75
Baldwin, M. W., 10, 72, 76, 86
Banaji, M. R., 10, 20, 26, 27, 33, 196

Bandura, A., 56, 93, 108
Banks, D. J., 109
Bargh, J. A., 8, 25, 72, 73, 94
Barling, J., 101
Barsade, S. G., 58, 138
Barsalou, L. W., 16
Bass, B. M., 3, 47, 75, 101, 102, 153
Basten, J., 131
Bates, D. E., 142
Bauer, T. N., 96
Baumeister, R. F., 42, 131, 132, 147, 151
Baumgardner, T. L., 16
Beach, L. R., 20, 22
Beike, D., 21
Bennett, M., 156
Bernstein, A., 96
Bies, R. J., 43, 59, 127, 156, 161
Bilsky, W., 51
Binning, J. F., 104
Birnbaum, M. H., 111
Blakely, G. L., 156, 165
Bliese, P. D., 118
Boal, K. B., 53, 82, 112
Bodenhausen, G. V., 70, 71
Bono, J. E., 3, 102
Bower, G. H., 94
Bowie, T., 9, 130, 146
Boyatzis, R., 148
Breinin, E., 2

237

242   AUTHOR INDEX

Miller, L. C., 111, 118
Miller, S. R., 58, 131, 143
Milne, A. B., 70, 71
Mischel, W., 15, 72, 193
Mitchell, T. R., 20, 22
Moag, J. S., 156, 161
Moorman, R. H., 156, 165, 191
Moreland, R. L., 19
Morris, M. G., 197
Morris, M. W., 199
Mortensen, C., 109
Moskowitz, G. B., 110
Muchinsky, P. M., 25
Murphy, G. L., 48
Murphy, M. R., 136
Murphy, S. T., 94, 151
Murray, S. L., 10

N

Naidoo, L. J., 103, 112, 136, 138, 139,
    140, 143, 146, 151, 152, 216
Neck, C. P., 61
Neuberg, S. L., 72, 83
Newman, L. S., 199
Niedenthal, P., 21
Niehoff, B. P., 156, 165
Norrell, R. J., 24
Norris-Watts, C., 141
Nurius, P., 22, 25, 30, 157

O

Oakes, P. J., 17, 33
Offerman, L. R., 3, 105, 110, 155
Ohlsson, S., 58
Oishi, S., 115, 116
Olson, J. M., 58, 115

P

Padawer-Singer, A., 76
Paez, D., 117
Paivio, A., 81
Panksepp, J., 132
Pass, Y., 5, 44, 101
Paul, J., 78, 130, 191
Pavlov, I. P., 86
Pelham, W. B., 21

Peng, K., 199, 200
Peterson, R. S., 155
Petty, M. M., 25
Petty, R. E., 151
Phillips, J. S., 2, 112, 136, 143
Pillai, R., 53, 82, 138, 152, 155, 165
Ployhart, R. E., 156
Podsakoff, P. M., 188, 191
Popper, M., 2
Porac, J., 145
Powell, M. C., 8
Powers, W. T., 173, 186
Pradhan, S. P., 199
Prentice, D. A., 10, 20, 26, 27, 33, 34,
    131, 196
Pugh, S. D., 58

Q

Queller, S., 107

R

Rafaeli, A., 91, 128, 145, 146, 152
Rapson, R. L., 131
Raver, J. L., 106, 108, 118
Read, S. J., 111, 118
Reicher, S., 24, 126
Roberts, W. A., 9, 10, 13, 20, 131, 207
Rohan, M. J., 115, 116, 117, 118, 119f
Romanelli, E., 98, 145
Rosch, E., 16
Ross, B. H., 48
Ross, L., 199
Ross, M., 29, 30
Roush, P., 202
Ruiz-Quintanilla, S. A., 16
Rumelhart, D. E., 17, 106
Rush, M. C., 104, 112
Russell, J. A., 132, 141
Rusting, C. L., 26
Ryan, A. M., 156
Ryan, R. M., 36, 198

S

Saks, A. M., 130
Salomon-Segev, I., 5, 44
Sanbonmatsu, D. M., 8

Subject Index

Note: *f* indicates figure, *t* indicates table

A

Accessible knowledge, 8
Adaptive Control of Thought (ACT), 194
Affective events theory (AET), 128
  and levels of self-identity, 147–148
  and the emotional aspects of leadership,
    132–134
  approach to leadership, 134
  crisis and, 152
  feedback, 148–149
  meaning and, 149–152
  model of emotional leadership, 133*f*
  principles of, 134*t*
Anger, 127
Autonoetic consciousness, 9

B

Business leaders, 16

C

Cognitive changes, 35
Collective-level leadership theories,
    190–191
Connectionism, 107–108
Connectionist networks, 107, 151–152
Control systems, 20
Current goals, 18–19

Cybernetic processes, 19

D

Distal motivational systems, 39

E

Emotions
  and interpersonal processes, 130–132
  and leadership events, 216
  and self-structures, 127
  and social status, 127
  as social cues, 42
  circumplex model of, 140*f*–141
  cognitive assessments of, 143–144
  evolutionary view of, 129–130
  integrating, 192–193
Episodic memory, 9, 13

F

Feedback
  and AET, 148
  affective, 42–43
  behavioral, 35
  negative, 37, 96
  performance, 25, 27–28
  sensed, 35
First-order constructs, 3–4

Thagard, P., & Kunda, Z. (1998). Making sense of people: Coherence mechanisms. In S. J. Read & L. C. Miller (Eds.), *Connectionist models of social reasoning and social behavior.* (pp. 3–26). Mahwah, NJ: Lawrence Erlbaum Associates.

Thomas, J. L., Dickson, M. W., & Bliese, P. D. (2001). Values predicting leader performance in the U.S. Army Reserve Officer Training Corps Assessment Center: Evidence for a personality-mediated model. *Leadership Quarterly, 12,* 181–196.

Thomas, K. M., & Mathieu, J. E. (1994). Role of causal attributions in dynamic self-regulation and goal processes. *Journal of Applied Psychology, 79,* 812–818.

Tice, D. M., & Baumeister, R. F. (2001). The primacy of the interpersonal self. In C. Sedikides & M. B. Brewer (Eds.), *Individual self, relational self, collective self* (pp. 71–88). Philadelphia, PA.: Psychology Press.

Tiedens, L. Z. (2000). Powerful emotions: The vicious cycle of social status positions and emotions. In N. M. Ashkanasy, C. E. J. Hartel, & W. J. Zerbe (Eds.), *Emotions in the workplace: Research, theory, and practice* (pp. 71–81). Westport, CT: Quorum Books.

Tindale, R. S., Meisenhleder, H. M., Dykema-Engblade, A. A., & Hogg, M. (2001). Shared cognition in small groups. In M. A. Hogg & R. S. Tindale (Eds.), *Blackwell handbook of social psychology: Vol. 3. Group processes* (pp. 1–30). Oxford, England: Blackwell.

Triandis, H. C. (1989). The self and social behavior in differing cultural contexts. *Psychological Bulletin, 96,* 506–520.

Triandis, H. C. (1994). Cross-cultural industrial and organizational psychology. In H. C. Traindis, M. D. Dunnette, & L. M. Hough (Eds.), *Handbook of industrial and organizational psychology* (2nd Ed., Vol. 4. pp. 103–172). Palo Alto, CA: Consulting Psychologists Press.

Tulving, E. (2002). Episodic memory: From mind to brain. *Annual Review of Psychology, 53,* 1–25.

Turner, J. C., Oakes, P. J., Haslam, S. A., & McGarty, C. (1994). Self and collective: Cognition and social context. *Personality and Social Psychology Bulletin, 20,* 454–463.

Tushman, M. L., & Anderson, P. (1986). Technological discontinuities and organizational environments. *Administrative Science Quarterly, 31,* 439–465.

Tushman, M. L., & Romanelli, E. (1985). Organizational evolution: A metamorphosis model of convergence and reorientation. *Research in Organizational Behavior, 7,* 171–222.

Tyler, T. R. (1997). The psychology of legitimacy: A relational perspective on voluntary deference to authorities. *Personality and Social Psychological Review, 1,* 323–345.

Tyler, T. R., & Caine, A. (1981). The influence of outcomes and procedures on satisfaction with formal leaders. *Journal of Personality and Social Psychology, 41,* 642–655.

Tyler, T. R., Degoey, P., & Smith, H. (1996). Understanding why the justice of groups procedures matters: A test of the psychological dynamics of the group-value model. *Journal of Personality and Social Psychology, 70,* 913–930.

Tyler, T. R., & Lind, E. A. (1992). A relational model of authority in groups. *Advances in Experimental Social Psychology, 25,* 115–191.

Uleman, J. S., & Moskowitz, G. B. (1994). Unintended effects of goals on unintended inferences. *Journal of Personality and Social Psychology, 66,* 490–501.

Van den Bos, K., & Lind, E. A. (2002). Uncertainty management by means of fairness judgment. *Advances in Experimental Social Psychology, 34,* 1–60.

Van Knippenberg, D., & Hogg, M. A. (Eds.). (2003). *Identity, leadership, and power.* Beverly Hills, CA: Sage.

Van Overwalle, F., Drenth, T., & Marsman, G. (1999). Spontaneous trait interferences: Are they linked to the actor or the action? *Personality and Social Psychology Bulletin, 25,* 450–462.

Van Overwalle, F., & Van Rooy, D. (2001). How one cause discounts or augments another: A connectionist account of causal competition. *Personality and Social Psychology Bulletin, 27*(12), 1613–1626.

Venkatesh, V., Morris, M. G., & Ackerman, P. L. (2000). A longitudinal field investigation of gender differences in individual technology adoption decision-making processes. *Organizational Behavior and Human Decision Processes, 83,* 33–60.

Verplanken, B., & Holland, R. W. (2002). Motivative decision making: Effects of activation and self-centrality of values on choices and behavior. *Journal of Personality and Social Psychology, 82,* 434–447.

Vygotsky, L. S. (1978). *Mind in society.* Cambridge, MA: Harvard University Press.

Watson, D., Clark, L. A., & Tellegen, A. (1988). Development and validation of brief measures of positive and negative affect: The PANAS scale. *Journal of Personality and Social Psychology, 54,* 1063–1070.

Wegner, D. M. (1994). Ironic processes of mental control. *Psychological Review, 101,* 34–52.

Weick, K. E. (1995). *Sensemaking in organizations.* London: Sage.

Weick, K. E. (1979). *The social psychology of organizing* (2nd ed.). Reading, MA.: Addison-Wesley.

Weiss, H. M. (2002). Conceptual and empirical foundations for the study of affect at work. In R. G. Lord, R. J. Klimoski, & R. Kanfer (Eds.), *Emotions in the workplace: Understanding the structure and role of emotions in organizational behavior* (pp. 20–63). San Francisco: Jossey-Bass.

Weiss, H. M., & Cropanzano, R. (1996). Affective events theory: A theoretical discussion of the structure, causes, and consequences of affective experiences at work. In B. M. Staw & L. L. Cummings (Eds.), *Research in organizational behavior: An annual series of analytical essays and critical reviews* (Vol. 18, pp. 1–74). Stamford, CT: JAI.

Wenzlaff, R. M., & Bates, D. E. (2000). The relative efficacy of concentration and suppression strategies of mental control. *Personality and Social Psychology Bulletin, 26,* 1200–1212.

Wheeler, M. A., Stuss, D. T., & Tulving, E. (1997). Towards a theory of episodic memory: The frontal lobes and autonoetic consciousness. *Psychological Review, 121,* 331-354.

Wilson, T. D., & Hodges, S. D. (1992). Attitudes as temporary constructions. In L. L. Martin & A. Tesser (Eds.), *The construction of social judgments* (pp. 37–65). Hillsdale, NJ: Lawrence Erlbaum Associates.

Wofford, J. C., & Goodwin, V. L. (1994). A cognitive interpretation of transactional and transformational leadership theories. *Leadership Quarterly, 5,* 161-186.

Wofford, J. C., Goodwin, V. L., & Whittington, J. L. (1998). A field study of a cognitive approach to understanding transformational and transactional leadership. *Leadership Quarterly, 9,* 55–84.

Wofford, J. C., Joplin, J. R., & Comforth, B. (1996). Use of simultaneous verbal protocols in analysis of group leaders' cognitions. *Psychological Reports, 79,* 847–858.

Worline, M. C., Wrzesniewski, A., & Rafaeli, A. (2002). Courage and work: Breaking routines to improve performance. In R. G. Lord, R. J. Klimoski, & R. Kanfer (Eds.), *Emotions in the workplace: Understanding the structure and role of emotions in organizational behavior* (pp. 295–330). San Francisco: Jossey-Bass.

Yammarino, F. J., & Dubinsky, A. J. (1994). Transformational leadership theory: Using levels of analysis to determine boundary conditions. *Personnel Psychology, 47,* 787–811.

Ybarra, O., & Trafimow, D. (1998). How priming of the private or collective self affects the relative weights of attitudes and subjective norms. *Personality and Social Psychology Bulletin, 24,* 362–370.

Yorges, S., Weiss, H. M., & Strickland, O. J. (1999). The effects of leader outcomes on influence, attributions, and perceptions of charisma. *Journal of Applied Psychology, 84,* 428–436.

Yukl, G. A. (2002). *Leadership in organizations* (5th ed.). Upper Saddle River, NJ: Prentice Hall.

Yukl, G. A., & Van Fleet, D. D. (1992). Theory and research on leadership in organizations. In M. D. Dunnette & L. M. Hough (Eds.), *Handbook of industrial and organizational psychology* (Vol. 1, pp. 147–198). Palo Alto, CA: Consulting Psychologists Press.

Zaccaro, S. J., & Banks, D. J. (2001). Leadership, vision, and organizational effectiveness. In S. J. Zaccaro & R. Klimoski (Eds.), *The nature of organizational leadership.* (pp. 181–218). San Francisco: Jossey-Bass.

Zaccaro, S. J., Foti, R. J., & Kenny, D. A. (1991). Self-monitoring and trait-based variance in leadership: An investigation of leader flexibility across multiple group situations. *Journal of Applied Psychology, 76*, 308–315.

Zaccaro, S. J., & Klimoski, R. J. (Eds.). (2001). *The nature of organizational leadership: Understanding the performance imperatives confronting today's leaders.* San Francisco: Jossey-Bass.

Zarate, M. A., Uleman, J. S., & Voils, C. I. (2001). Effects of culture and processing goals on the activation and binding of trait concepts. *Social Cognition, 19*, 295–323.

Author Index

Note: *f* indicates figure

A

Abelson, R. P., 22
Abrams, D., 117
Ackerman, P. L., 197
Adams, J. S., 178
Adelman, P. K., 131
Ajzen, I., 197
Allen, P. A., 9, 130, 146
Alliger, G., 3, 53
Alutto, J. A., 203
Andersen, S. M., 190, 194, 207, 208, 213
Anderson, J. R., 178, 194
Anderson, P., 98
Aron, A., 46, 58
Aronson, J., 70
Arthur, M. B., 2, 26, 75, 84, 102, 126, 147
Ashforth, B. E., 130
Atwater, L., 202
Avolio, B. J., 4, 5, 83, 84, 101, 102, 112, 191, 202
Awamleh, R., 112, 125, 130

B

Baden-Fuller, C., 145
Baker, S., 75
Baldwin, M. W., 10, 72, 76, 86
Banaji, M. R., 10, 20, 26, 27, 33, 196

Bandura, A., 56, 93, 108
Banks, D. J., 109
Bargh, J. A., 8, 25, 72, 73, 94
Barling, J., 101
Barsade, S. G., 58, 138
Barsalou, L. W., 16
Bass, B. M., 3, 47, 75, 101, 102, 153
Basten, J., 131
Bates, D. E., 142
Bauer, T. N., 96
Baumeister, R. F., 42, 131, 132, 147, 151
Baumgardner, T. L., 16
Beach, L. R., 20, 22
Beike, D., 21
Bennett, M., 156
Bernstein, A., 96
Bies, R. J., 43, 59, 127, 156, 161
Bilsky, W., 51
Binning, J. F., 104
Birnbaum, M. H., 111
Blakely, G. L., 156, 165
Bliese, P. D., 118
Boal, K. B., 53, 82, 112
Bodenhausen, G. V., 70, 71
Bono, J. E., 3, 102
Bower, G. H., 94
Bowie, T., 9, 130, 146
Boyatzis, R., 148
Breinin, E., 2

237

Subject Index

Note: *f* indicates figure, *t* indicates table